JAMESTOWN EDUCATION

Literature

An Adapted Reader

Grade 7

Glencoe

New York, New York   Columbus, Ohio   Chicago, Illinois   Peoria, Illinois   Woodland Hills, California

JAMESTOWN  EDUCATION

 Glencoe

The McGraw·Hill Companies

ACKNOWLEDGMENTS

Grateful acknowledgment is given authors, publishers, photographers, museums, and agents for permission to reprint the following copyrighted material. Every effort has been made to determine copyright owners. In case of any omissions, the Publisher will be pleased to make suitable acknowledgments in future editions.
Acknowledgments continued on p. 268.

Send all inquiries to:
Glencoe/McGraw-Hill
8787 Orion Place
Columbus, OH 43240-4027

ISBN-13: 978-0-07-874314-6 (Student Edition)
ISBN-10: 0-07-874314-1 (Student Edition)

ISBN-13: 978-0-07-874327-6 (Annotated Teacher Edition)
ISBN-10: 0-07-874327-3 (Annotated Teacher Edition)

Printed in the United States of America
2 3 4 5 6 7 8 9 10 079 11 10 09 08 07

Contents

UNIT ① Short Story 1

UNIT ② Short Story 84

UNIT ③ Drama 140

Why Use This Book?

Read a Variety of Texts

The notes and features of *Jamestown Literature* guide you through the process of reading and understanding each literature selection. As you use these notes and features, you practice the skills and strategies that good readers use whenever they read.

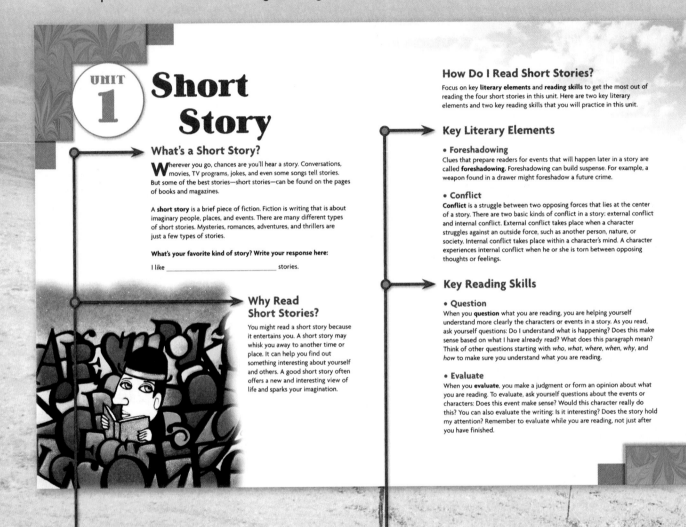

UNIT 1 — Short Story

What's a Short Story?

Wherever you go, chances are you'll hear a story. Conversations, movies, TV programs, jokes, and even some songs tell stories. But some of the best stories—short stories—can be found on the pages of books and magazines.

A **short story** is a brief piece of fiction. Fiction is writing that is about imaginary people, places, and events. There are many different types of short stories. Mysteries, romances, adventures, and thrillers are just a few types of stories.

What's your favorite kind of story? Write your response here:

I like _____ stories.

Why Read Short Stories?

You might read a short story because it entertains you. A short story may whisk you away to another time or place. It can help you find out something interesting about yourself and others. A good short story often offers a new and interesting view of life and sparks your imagination.

How Do I Read Short Stories?

Focus on key **literary elements** and **reading skills** to get the most out of reading the four short stories in this unit. Here are two key literary elements and two key reading skills that you will practice in this unit.

Key Literary Elements

• Foreshadowing

Clues that prepare readers for events that will happen later in a story are called **foreshadowing**. Foreshadowing can build suspense. For example, a weapon found in a drawer might foreshadow a future crime.

• Conflict

Conflict is a struggle between two opposing forces that lies at the center of a story. There are two basic kinds of conflict in a story: external conflict and internal conflict. External conflict takes place when a character struggles against an outside force, such as another person, nature, or society. Internal conflict takes place within a character's mind. A character experiences internal conflict when he or she is torn between opposing thoughts or feelings.

Key Reading Skills

• Question

When you **question** what you are reading, you are helping yourself understand more clearly the characters or events in a story. As you read, ask yourself questions: Do I understand what is happening? Does this make sense based on what I have already read? What does this paragraph mean? Think of other questions starting with *who, what, where, when, why,* and *how* to make sure you understand what you are reading.

• Evaluate

When you **evaluate**, you make a judgment or form an opinion about what you are reading. To evaluate, ask yourself questions about the events or characters: Does this event make sense? Would this character really do this? You can also evaluate the writing: Is it interesting? Does the story hold my attention? Remember to evaluate while you are reading, not just after you have finished.

What Is It? Why Read?

The genre, or type of writing, is defined for you at the beginning of the unit. Learn why reading a particular genre could be important to you.

Literary Elements and Reading Skills

New literary elements and reading skills are introduced in each unit opener. Use these elements and skills to get the most out of your reading.

UNIT 2 — Short Story

How Is a Short Story Organized?

Now that you have read a few short stories, let's take a closer look at how a short story is put to Understanding the parts of a story can help you be

A short story always has a **beginning**, a **middle**, and

Most stories also include a conflict. As discussed be a struggle between a character and his or her own feelings. It can also be a struggle between a char else, nature, or another outside force.

What's the Plan?

Within the three parts of a story,

Exposition: The story is set up. C
introduced.
Rising Action: Conflicts or prob
Climax: This is the turning poi
of greatest interest or suspens
Falling Action: These are the
Resolution: This is the final

As you read the next fou
in each story. In the tex
stage occurs.

64

UNIT 3 — Drama

What's Drama?

If you've ever seen a drama, you know that it can grab you whether it is a play, a movie, or a TV show, brings literat

A **drama** is a story that is performed by actors for an aud printed form of a drama is called a script. When you read can use your imagination to see the stage, the scenery, a A script has different parts that help you imagine what y

- The **cast of characters** tells you who is in the Sometimes a brief description is given for ea

- **Dialogue** is the conversation between the ch name of the character speaking appears bef of dialogue.

- **Stage directions** describe the setting and t They also tell actors how to move or speak are often in *italics*.

- Longer dramas are divided into sections may be divided into smaller sections call

What kinds of drama do you like to wat favorite movie, play, or TV series? What

Why Read Drama?

Dramas amuse, teach, and inspire us. V or read their words in a play, we can l other people, and sometimes even le ourselves. Drama, like other literatur worlds or give us a new view of our

140

UNIT 4 — Myth and Folktale

What's a Myth? What's a Folktale?

Before written language, there were stories called folklore. Different cultures used different types of folklore to tell stories of heroes, humor, and tragedy. These stories usually have a message about life. Myths and folktales are two kinds of folklore.

A **myth** is a traditional story about gods and goddesses or how things came to be. Myths usually reflect a culture's religious or other deeply held beliefs.

A **folktale** is a story that has been passed down through generations by word of mouth. Folktales often reflect what is important to the people who tell them. Folktale characters can be animals or people who have unusual powers or experiences.

Hercules is a character from a myth. Paul Bunyan is a folktale hero. What other characters and creatures from myths and folktales can you think of? Write your responses below.

Why Read Myths and Folktales?

People today read these kinds of tales to enjoy a good story! But these stories can also tell you about the cultures they came from. You can learn how the people in a culture viewed the world and what was important to them. Reading these stories and sharing them makes the oldest stories in the world feel new.

162

Explore Literature

Your book features several of the most popular types of writing. Find out what makes each genre unique. Discover new and exciting types of writing.

UNIT 5 — Nonfiction

What's Nonfiction?

Pick up a newspaper or magazine, or check out many Web sites, and you will find writing that is nonfiction.

Nonfiction is the name for writing that is about real people and real events. This kind of writing concentrates on facts. There are many kinds of nonfiction. Biography, autobiography, memoir, and essay are popular types of this kind of writing.

A **biography** is the story of a person's life written by someone other than that person. An **autobiography** is the story of a person's life written by that person. A **memoir** is a story of the narrator's personal experience. An **essay** is a short piece of nonfiction about a single topic.

Nonfiction can deal with many topics. What nonfiction subjects would you like to read about? It can be a biography of someone you admire, or maybe an essay about a different country or a famous historical event. Write your responses below.

Why Read Nonfiction?

Read nonfiction to learn about new places, new people, and new ideas. By reading nonfiction and learning so many new things, you can better understand the world around you. Nonfiction can even help you understand yourself better.

Get Set!

The first page of each lesson helps you get ready to read. It sets the stage for your reading. The more you know about the reading up front, the more meaning it will have for you.

Get Ready to Read!

Home

Meet Gwendolyn Brooks

Gwendolyn Brooks was born in Kansas in 1917. Her family moved to Chicago after her birth. Her stories are usually set in cities. Her characters are ordinary people trying to make it from day to day. In 1950 Brooks became the first African American author to win the Pulitzer Prize for Poetry. The story "Home" is taken from Gwendolyn Brooks's novel *Maud Martha*, which was first published in 1953. Brooks died in 2000.

What You Know

When you hear the word *home*, what do you think about? What are some things that make a home important to the people who live there?

Reason to Read

As you read this story, look for what makes home important to the characters.

Background Info

The story "Home" is set on Chicago's South Side, where Gwendolyn Brooks grew up. By the 1920s, most of Chicago's African American population lived on the South Side. Since African Americans were usually prevented from moving into other neighborhoods, South Side residents set up their own churches, businesses, and entertainment centers. In time, the South Side of Chicago became one of the most active African American communities in the United States.

What You Know

Think about your own experience and share your knowledge and opinions. Then, build on what you know as you read the lesson.

Reason to Read

Set a purpose for reading. Having a reason to read helps you get involved in what you read.

Background Info

Get a deeper insight into the reading. Knowing some background information helps you gain a greater appreciation and understanding of what you read.

Meet the Author

Meet the authors to get to know where they come from, what or who inspires them, and why they write.

Build Vocabulary

Each lesson introduces you to words that help build your vocabulary. You'll find these words in the reading. Understanding these words before you read makes reading easier.

Word Power

In an after-reading activity, you practice the vocabulary words you learned in the lesson.

Word Power

decisively (di si´ siv lē) *adv.* in a way that brings a clear decision; p. 26
The coach blew the whistle *decisively* when practice was done.

dutifully (dōō´ ti fal ē) *adv.* doing something you are supposed to do; p. 28
He *dutifully* returned home at dinnertime.

resolutions (rez´ a lōō´ shanz) *n.* things that have been decided or determined; p. 28
Every New Year's Day, we make fresh *resolutions.*

accompanied (a kum´ pa nēd) *v.* went along with; p. 28
Her dog always *accompanied* her on visits to the lake.

objection (ab jek´ shan) *n.* a feeling of dislike; a protest; p. 29
At the meeting, a parent offered an *objection* to the new plan.

assured (a shoord´) *v.* promised; made a person sure of something; p. 29
The doctor *assured* us that Mom would be fine.

strictly (strikt´ lē) *adv.* following a rule in an exact way; p. 35
Eating in the classroom is *strictly* forbidden.

Answer the following questions that contain the new words above. Write your answers in the spaces provided.

1. If your team's victory is *assured,* would you expect to win or lose?

2. If you *decisively* made a choice, are you sure or not sure about the choice?

3. If you were *accompanied* on a trip, did you go with someone or go alone?

4. Are *resolutions* actions that you definitely plan to take or actions that you might not take?

5. If you *strictly* follow a recipe, do you do exactly what it says or follow only some of the directions?

6. If your father has an *objection* to your plan, is he for your plan or against it?

7. If you do something *dutifully,* do you do it as you are supposed to or any way you want?

My Workspace

"He's staying at the Fisherman's Arms—I mean his owner is."
"Then he must go back there."
"I wonder how he found his way here," Mrs. Pengelly said.
"Fisherman's Arms is right round the other side of the harbor."

Lob's owner scolded him and thanked Mr. Pengelly for bringing him back. Jean Pengelly warned the children that they had better not encourage Lob any more if they met him on the beach. So they **dutifully** took no notice of him the next day until their good **resolutions** by dashing up to them with joyful
They had a happy day, playing on the sand.

The next day was Saturday. Sandy had found out that Mr. Dodsworth was to catch the 9:30 train. She went o down to the station. She saw Mr. Dodsworth get on th **accompanied** by an unhappy-looking Lob with dro and tail.

A week passed. Then, one evening, Mrs. Pengelly younger children were in the front room playing ladders. Suddenly, history repeating itself, there w the kitchen. Jean Pengelly leaped up, crying. "My But Sandy was ahead of her mother. With flu eyes like stars she had darted into the kitchen were hugging one another joyfully.

"Good heavens!" exclaimed Jean. "How in get here?"

"He must have walked," said Sandy. "Loo They were worn, dusty, and tarry. One "What'll we do about him, Mother?" s

Word Power
dutifully (dōō´ ti fal ē) *adv.* doing som
resolutions (rez´ a lōō´ shanz) *n.* thin determined
accompanied (a kum´ pa nēd) *v.* we

28

Connect to the Text

Reread the boxed text. Has anyone you were close to ever gone far away? How did that make you feel? How do you think the person who was leaving felt?

English Coach

Here, *eyes like stars* means that Sandy's eyes are bright when she sees Lob. This means Sandy is happy. If a character has "eyes like saucers," what do you think that character is feeling?

Respond to Literature

C Word Power

Complete each sentence below, using one of the words in the box.

| decisively | dutifully | resolutions |
| accompanied | objection | assured | strictly |

1. It is _____ against the rules to stay out after dark.

2. The children kept their _____ about eating their vegetables and doing their chores every day.

3. The players _____ the coach that they would do their best.

4. After much discussion, Judge Santos said firmly and _____ that the man was guilty of the crime.

5. When the rules were changed to make sure the game was fair to everyone, there was no _____.

6. Mrs. Johnson _____ her daughter on her first trip to the dentist.

7. When its owner whistled, the dog _____ trotted over.

38

Word Power

Before you read, you learn key vocabulary words and their definitions. The definitions and sample sentences help you complete the questions that follow.

Word Power Footnotes

Look for pronunciations and definitions of vocabulary words at the bottom of pages throughout the reading. Vocabulary words appear in dark type in the text.

My Personal Dictionary

My Personal Dictionary

As you read, jot down words in your personal dictionary that you want to learn more about. Later, ask a classmate or your teacher what they mean, or look them up in a dictionary.

Read, Respond, Interact

Notes in "My Workspace" support and guide you through the reading process. Interact with and respond to the text by answering the questions or following the directions in the workspace notes.

English Coach notes explain difficult or unusual words and cultural references. Whenever you read text that is highlighted in red, look for an English Coach note in your workspace.

Reading Skill notes let you practice active reading strategies that help good readers think as they read. Whenever you read text that is highlighted in green, look for a Reading Skill note in your workspace.

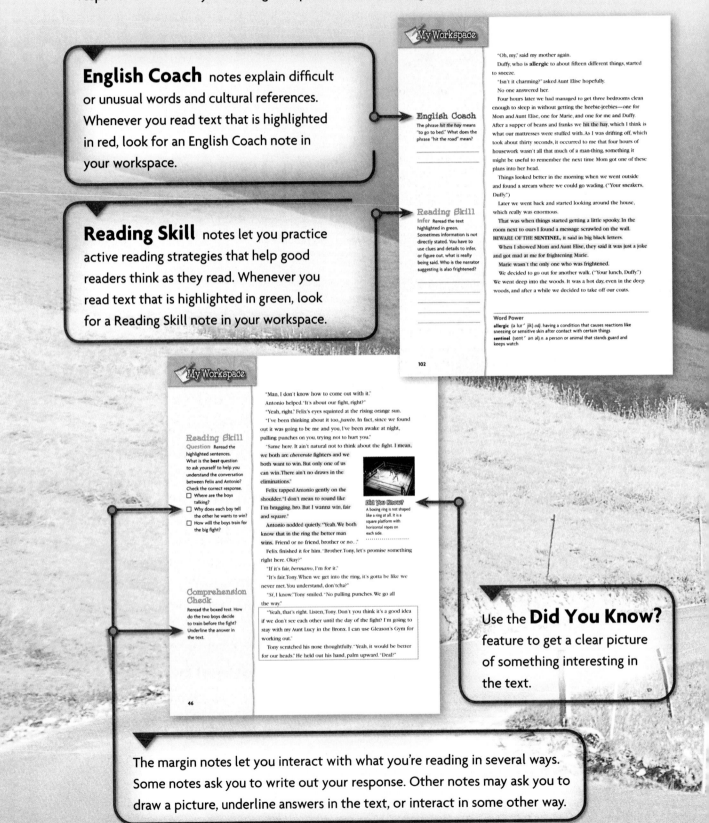

My Workspace

English Coach
The phrase *hit the hay* means "to go to bed." What does the phrase "hit the road" mean?

_____

Reading Skill
Infer Reread the text highlighted in green. Sometimes information is not directly stated. You have to use clues and details to infer, or figure out, what is really being said. Who is the narrator suggesting is also frightened?

_____
_____
_____

"Oh, my," said my mother again.

Duffy, who is **allergic** to about fifteen different things, started to sneeze.

"Isn't it charming?" asked Aunt Elise hopefully.

No one answered her.

Four hours later we had managed to get three bedrooms clean enough to sleep in without getting the heebie-jeebies—one for Mom and Aunt Elise, one for Marie, and one for me and Duffy. After a supper of beans and franks we hit the hay, which I think is what our mattresses were stuffed with. As I was drifting off, which took about thirty seconds, it occurred to me that four hours of housework wasn't all that much of a man-thing, something it might be useful to remember the next time Mom got one of these plans into her head.

Things looked better in the morning when we went outside and found a stream where we could go wading. ("Your sneakers, Duffy.")

Later we went back and started looking around the house, which really was enormous.

That was when things started getting a little spooky. In the room next to ours I found a message scrawled on the wall. BEWARE OF THE **SENTINEL**, it said in big black letters.

When I showed Mom and Aunt Elise, they said it was just a joke and got mad at me for frightening Marie.

Marie wasn't the only one who was frightened.

We decided to go out for another walk. ("Your lunch, Duffy.") We went deep into the woods. It was a hot day, even in the deep woods, and after a while we decided to take off our coats.

Word Power
allergic (a lur´ jik) *adj.* having a condition that causes reactions like sneezing or sensitive skin after contact with certain things
sentinel (sent´ an al) *n.* a person or animal that stands guard and keeps watch

102

My Workspace

Reading Skill
Question Reread the highlighted sentences. What is the **best** question to ask yourself to help you understand the conversation between Felix and Antonio? Check the correct response.
☐ Where are the boys talking?
☐ Why does each boy tell the other he wants to win?
☐ How will the boys train for the big fight?

Comprehension Check
Reread the boxed text. How do the two boys decide to train before the fight? Underline the answer in the text.

"Man, I don't know how to come out with it."

Antonio helped. "It's about our fight, right?"

"Yeah, right." Felix's eyes squinted at the rising orange sun.

"I've been thinking about it too, *panín*. In fact, since we found out it was going to be me and you, I've been awake at night, pulling punches on you, trying not to hurt you."

"Same here. It ain't natural not to think about the fight. I mean, we both are *cheverote* fighters and we both want to win. But only one of us can win. There ain't no draws in the eliminations."

Felix tapped Antonio gently on the shoulder. "I don't mean to sound like I'm bragging, bro. But I wanna win, fair and square."

Antonio nodded quietly. "Yeah. We both know that in the ring the better man wins. Friend or no friend, brother or no..."

Felix finished it for him. "Brother. Tony, let's promise something right here. Okay?"

"If it's fair, *bermano*, I'm for it."

"It's fair, Tony. When we get into the ring, it's gotta be like we never met. You understand, don'tcha?"

"*Sí*, I know." Tony smiled. "No pulling punches. We go all the way."

"Yeah, that's right. Listen, Tony. Don't you think it's a good idea if we don't see each other until the day of the fight? I'm going to stay with my Aunt Lucy in the Bronx. I can use Gleason's Gym for working out."

Tony scratched his nose thoughtfully. "Yeah, it would be better for our heads." He held out his hand, palm upward. "Deal?"

Did You Know?
A boxing ring is not shaped like a ring at all. It is a square platform with horizontal ropes on each side.

46

Use the **Did You Know?** feature to get a clear picture of something interesting in the text.

The margin notes let you interact with what you're reading in several ways. Some notes ask you to write out your response. Other notes may ask you to draw a picture, underline answers in the text, or interact in some other way.

By the time I was in high school, I was a popular kid. It showed in my name. Friends called me *Jules* or *Hey Jude*. Once a group of troublemaking friends my mother wouldn't let me hang out with called me Alcatraz. I was *Hoo-lee-tah* only to Mami and Papi and uncles and aunts who came over to eat a meat stew called *sancocho* on Sunday afternoons. They were old-fashioned people. I would just as soon have had them go back to where they came from and leave me to pursue whatever mischief I wanted to in America. *JUDY ALCATRAZ*: the name on the Wanted Poster would read. Who would ever trace her to me?

My older sister had the hardest time getting an American name for herself because Mauricia did not translate into English. Although she had the most **foreign**-sounding name, she and I were the Americans in the family. We had been born in New York City when our parents had first tried immigration. Then they went back "home," too homesick to stay. My mother often told the story of how she had almost changed my sister's name in the hospital.

After the delivery, Mami and some other new mothers were fussing over their new baby sons and daughters and exchanging names and weights and delivery stories. My mother was embarrassed among the Sallys and Janes and Georges and Johns to reveal the rich, noisy name of *Mauricia*. When her turn came to brag, she gave her baby's name as *Maureen*.

"Why'd ya give her an Irish name with so many pretty Spanish names to choose from?" one of the women asked her.

My mother blushed and admitted her baby's real name to the group. She apologized by saying that her mother-in-law had recently died and her husband had insisted that the first daughter b...

Alcatraz is an island in San Francisco Bay. It once was the home of a prison for the worst criminals.

Literary Element

Point of View Reread the highlighted text. This event happens before the narrator is born. In first-person point of view, the narrator can only tell about what she sees, hears, or knows. How is she able to tell this story about her older sister's birth? How can she know how her mother feels at this event?

Background Info notes give information about a particular event, time, person, or place mentioned in the text. Whenever you read text that is boxed in orange, look for a Background Info note in your workspace.

Literary Element notes help you understand important features of literature. Whenever you read text that is highlighted in blue, look for a Literary Element note in your workspace.

The fight had created great interest in the neighborhood. Antonio and Felix were well-liked and respected. Each had his own loyal following.

The fight was scheduled to take place in Tompkins Square Park. It had been decided that the gymnasium of the Boys Club was not large enough to hold all the people who were sure to attend. In Tompkins Square Park, everyone who wanted could view the fight from ringside or window fire escapes or apartment building rooftops.

The junior high school across from Tompkins Square Park served as the dressing room for all the fighters. Each was given a separate classroom with desktops, covered with mats, serving as resting tables.

The fighters changed from their street clothes into fighting gear. Antonio wore white trunks, black socks, and black shoes. Felix wore sky blue trunks, red socks, and white boxing shoes. Each had dressing gowns to match their fighting trunks with their names neatly stitched on the back.

The loudspeakers blared into the open windows of the school. There were speeches by honored guests, community leaders, and great boxers of yesteryear. Mixed with the speeches were the sounds of other boxing events. After the sixth bout, Felix was much relieved when his trainer Charlie said, "Time change. Quick knockout. This is it. We're on."

Waiting time was over. Felix was **escorted** from the classroom by a dozen fans in white T-shirts with the word FELIX across their fronts. Antonio was escorted down a different stairwell and guided through a roped-off path.

Word Power

escorted (es kor´ tid) v. traveled with someone to show support or to honor

Comprehension Check

Reread the paragraph boxed in green. Where will the fight be held? Why is it being held at this location?

Connect to the Text

Reread the text boxed in purple. Have you ever waited and waited for something you were looking forward to? How did you feel as you waited?

Comprehension Check notes help you understand what you're reading. Whenever you read text that is boxed in green, look for a Comprehension Check note in your workspace.

Connect to the Text notes help you connect what you're reading to something in your own life. Whenever you read text that is boxed in purple, look for a Connect to the Text note in your workspace.

Wrap It Up!

The Break Time, Respond to Literature, and Compare and Contrast pages help you focus your understanding of the text. You apply the skills and strategies you've practiced during reading.

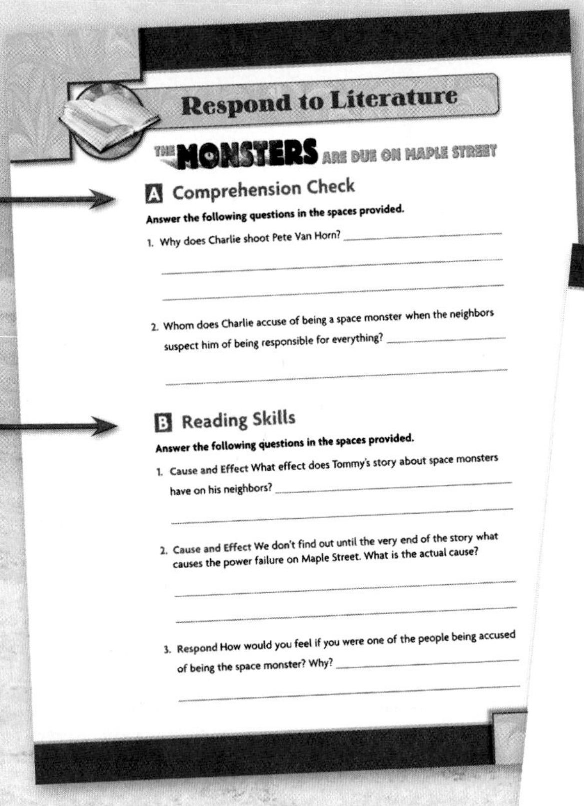

Respond to Literature

THE MONSTERS ARE DUE ON MAPLE STREET

A Comprehension Check

Answer the following questions in the spaces provided.

1. Why does Charlie shoot Pete Van Horn? ______

2. Whom does Charlie accuse of being a space monster when the neighbors suspect him of being responsible for everything? ______

B Reading Skills

Answer the following questions in the spaces provided.

1. Cause and Effect What effect does Tommy's story about space monsters have on his neighbors? ______

2. Cause and Effect We don't find out until the very end of the story what causes the power failure on Maple Street. What is the actual cause? ______

3. Respond How would you feel if you were one of the people being accused of being the space monster? Why? ______

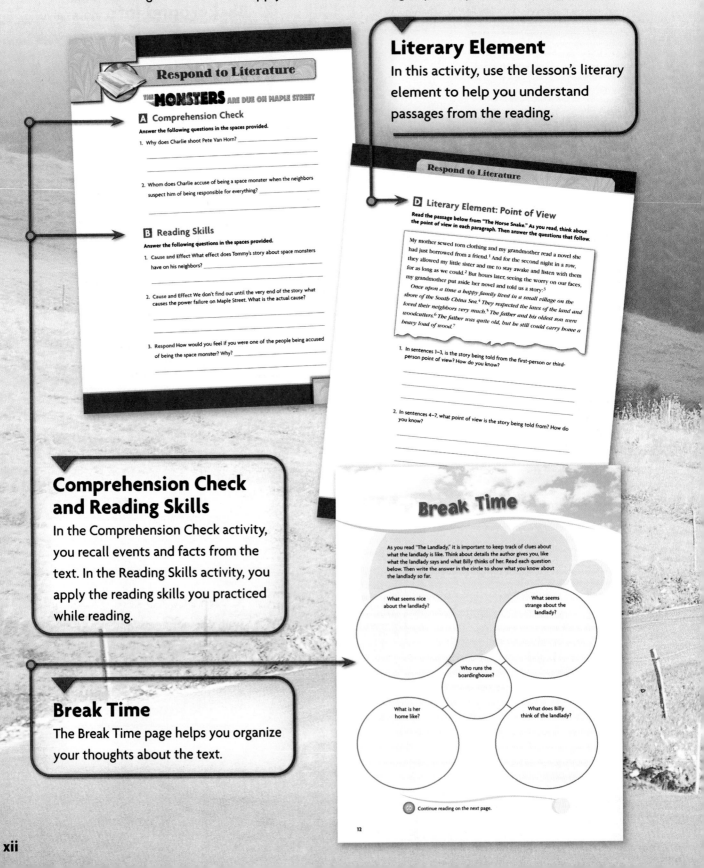

Literary Element

In this activity, use the lesson's literary element to help you understand passages from the reading.

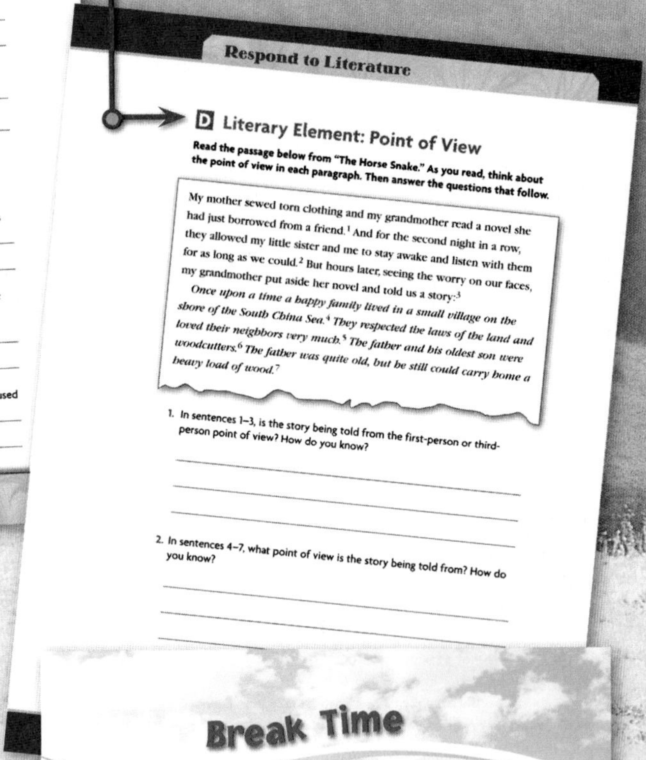

Respond to Literature

D Literary Element: Point of View

Read the passage below from "The Horse Snake." As you read, think about the point of view in each paragraph. Then answer the questions that follow.

My mother sewed torn clothing and my grandmother read a novel she had just borrowed from a friend.[1] And for the second night in a row, they allowed my little sister and me to stay awake and listen with them for as long as we could.[2] But hours later, seeing the worry on our faces, my grandmother put aside her novel and told us a story:[3]

Once upon a time a happy family lived in a small village on the shore of the South China Sea.[4] They respected the laws of the land and loved their neighbors very much.[5] The father and his oldest son were woodcutters.[6] The father was quite old, but he still could carry home a heavy load of wood.[7]

1. In sentences 1–3, is the story being told from the first-person or third-person point of view? How do you know? ______

2. In sentences 4–7, what point of view is the story being told from? How do you know? ______

Comprehension Check and Reading Skills

In the Comprehension Check activity, you recall events and facts from the text. In the Reading Skills activity, you apply the reading skills you practiced while reading.

Break Time

The Break Time page helps you organize your thoughts about the text.

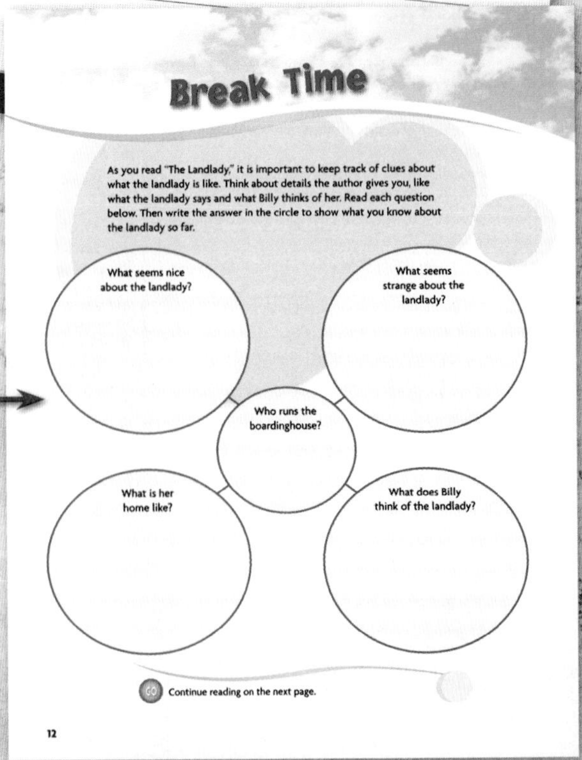

Break Time

As you read "The Landlady," it is important to keep track of clues about what the landlady is like. Think about details the author gives you, like what the landlady says and what Billy thinks of her. Read each question below. Then write the answer in the circle to show what you know about the landlady so far.

What seems nice about the landlady?
What seems strange about the landlady?
Who runs the boardinghouse?
What is her home like?
What does Billy think of the landlady?

Continue reading on the next page.

12

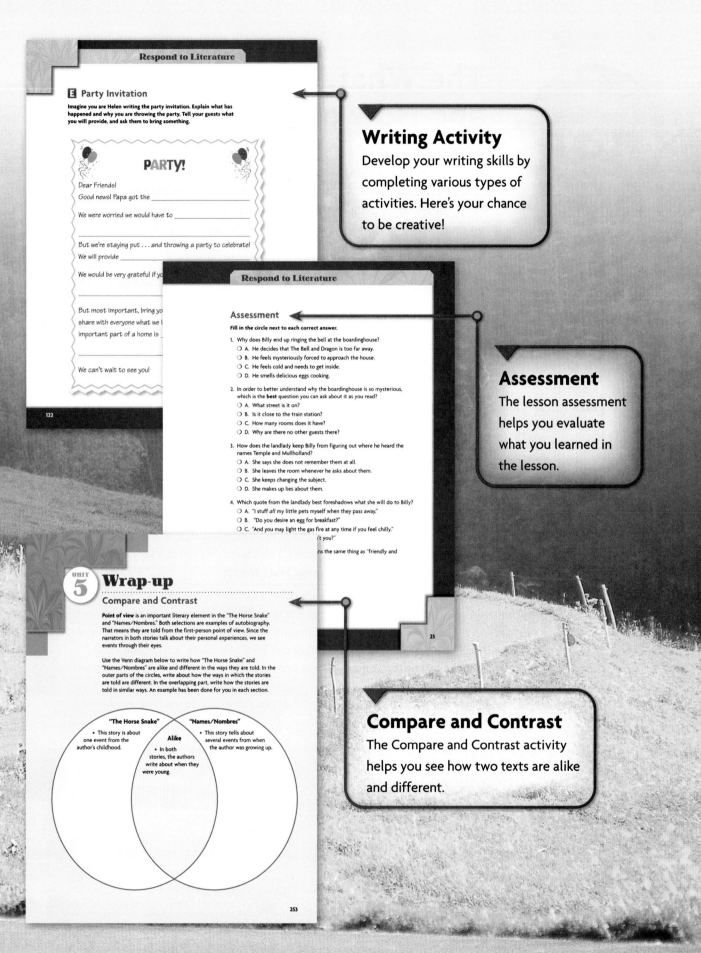

Respond to Literature

E Party Invitation

Imagine you are Helen writing the party invitation. Explain what has happened and why you are throwing the party. Tell your guests what you will provide, and ask them to bring something.

PARTY!

Dear Friends!

Good news! Papa got the _____

We were worried we would have to _____

But we're staying put . . . and throwing a party to celebrate!
We will provide _____

We would be very grateful if y_____

But most important, bring yo_____
share with everyone what we_____
important part of a home is _____

_____

We can't wait to see you!

122

Writing Activity
Develop your writing skills by completing various types of activities. Here's your chance to be creative!

Respond to Literature

Assessment

Fill in the circle next to each correct answer.

1. Why does Billy end up ringing the bell at the boardinghouse?
   ○ A. He decides that The Bell and Dragon is too far away.
   ○ B. He feels mysteriously forced to approach the house.
   ○ C. He feels cold and needs to get inside.
   ○ D. He smells delicious eggs cooking.

2. In order to better understand why the boardinghouse is so mysterious, which is the **best** question you can ask about it as you read?
   ○ A. What street is it on?
   ○ B. Is it close to the train station?
   ○ C. How many rooms does it have?
   ○ D. Why are there no other guests there?

3. How does the landlady keep Billy from figuring out where he heard the names Temple and Mullholland?
   ○ A. She says she does not remember them at all.
   ○ B. She leaves the room whenever he asks about them.
   ○ C. She keeps changing the subject.
   ○ D. She makes up lies about them.

4. Which quote from the landlady best foreshadows what she will do to Billy?
   ○ A. "I stuff *all* my little pets myself when they pass away."
   ○ B. "Do you desire an egg for breakfast?"
   ○ C. "And you may light the gas fire at any time if you feel chilly."
   ○ D. "_____'t you?"
   _____s the same thing as "friendly and

23

Assessment
The lesson assessment helps you evaluate what you learned in the lesson.

UNIT 5 Wrap-up

Compare and Contrast

Point of view is an important literary element in the "The Horse Snake" and "Names/Nombres." Both selections are examples of autobiography. That means they are told from the first-person point of view. Since the narrators in both stories talk about their personal experiences, we see events through their eyes.

Use the Venn diagram below to write how "The Horse Snake" and "Names/Nombres" are alike and different in the ways they are told. In the outer parts of the circles, write about how the ways in which the stories are told are different. In the overlapping part, write how the stories are told in similar ways. An example has been done for you in each section.

"The Horse Snake"
• This story is about one event from the author's childhood.

Alike
• In both stories, the authors write about when they were young.

"Names/Nombres"
• This story tells about several events from when the author was growing up.

253

Compare and Contrast
The Compare and Contrast activity helps you see how two texts are alike and different.

The What, Why, and How of Reading

LITERARY ELEMENTS

Each lesson focuses on one literary element. Before you begin a lesson, read carefully the explanations of the literary elements found at the beginning of the unit. You can refer to this chart for an overview. The more familiar you become with these important features, the more you will understand and appreciate each reading.

	What Is It?	Example
Unit 1	**Foreshadowing** Clues that prepare you for events that will happen later in a story are called foreshadowing. Foreshadowing can build suspense.	In "The Landlady," details of the landlady's behavior and how she acts toward Billy hint that she is going to do something bad to him.
	Conflict Conflict is a struggle between two opposing forces. External conflict involves the struggle between a character and an outside force. Internal conflict is a struggle that takes place within a character's mind.	In "Amigo Brothers," the friends Antonio and Felix must box each other. (This shows external conflict.) Each boy struggles with how he feels about fighting his best friend. (This shows internal conflict.)
Unit 2	**Character** A character is an actor in a story. Characters can be people, animals, robots, or whatever the writer chooses. You can learn about characters by looking at how they act, think, talk, and feel.	In "Thank You, M'am," after the boy tries to steal the lady's purse, the lady takes him home to feed him, and then she gives him money. This shows that she is a very kind and generous character.
	Theme A theme is the message you can take from the story. A story may have more than one theme, but one message will probably be the strongest. Sometimes a theme is suggested by the words, thoughts, and actions of the characters.	In "Home," Mama tells her children that Papa doesn't want the house unless he has his family with him. This reflects the theme that the most important part of a home is the family that lives in it.

Unit 3	What Is It?	Example
	Science Fiction Science fiction is a kind of fiction that uses ideas from science. Sometimes it is about imaginary worlds and may include creatures from a different planet. Often science fiction explores our own world as it might be in the future.	In "The Monsters Are Due on Maple Street," people on a small suburban street believe that monsters from outer space have invaded their town.
Unit 4	**Tone** The tone of a piece of writing expresses the author's feelings toward his or her subject, ideas, theme, or characters. The writing may express seriousness, humor, sadness, excitement, or any number of other feelings.	In "Prometheus," the tone is serious when the author writes about the disagreement between Zeus and Prometheus.
	Fantasy Fantasy explores unreal worlds. It can also explore the real world with unreal elements, like ghosts, magic, or people who have superhuman qualities.	In "Aunty Misery," an old woman meets a traveling stranger who magically grants her a wish.
Unit 5	**Description** Description is writing that includes many details about a person, animal, object, place, or event. Good description helps you picture what you are reading about.	In "We Will Remain at Peace with Your People Forever," the author's description of the Spanish soldiers and their weapons helps you picture how powerful the soldiers are.
	Point of View Point of view is the viewpoint from which a piece of writing is told. When the narrator is a character in the story, that story is told from the *first-person point of view*. When a story is told by a narrator who is outside the story, that story is told from the *third-person point of view*.	In "Names/Nombres," the narrator tells of her experience of moving to a different country. Her use of the words *I* and *me* tells you that this is first-person point of view.

READING SKILLS

You will use reading skills to respond to questions in the lessons. Before you begin a lesson, read carefully the explanations of the reading skills found at the beginning of the unit. You can refer to this chart for an overview. The more you practice the skills in the chart, the more these active reading strategies will become a natural part of the way you read.

Unit 1	What Is It?	Why It's Important	How To Do It
	Question Questioning is asking questions to make sense of information in the text. Questioning is also asking yourself whether you understand what you've read.	When you question what you are reading, you are helping yourself understand more clearly the characters or events in a story.	As you read, ask yourself questions starting with *who, what, where, when, why,* and *how* to make sure you understand what you are reading.
	Evaluate Evaluating is making judgments or forming opinions about what you are reading and how it is presented.	When you evaluate what happens in a story or how a text is written, you are helping yourself understand what you are reading.	Think about your reaction to what happens in the story, and to the way the writer presents information. Ask yourself: What do I think about what I just read?
Unit 2	**Predict** Predicting is guessing what will happen next in the story.	Predicting helps you get involved in the story. Predicting also encourages you to read on so you can find out if your predictions are right.	Use story clues and what you already know to guess what will happen next. As you read, you can check your predictions by finding out what really happens.
	Infer Inferring is making reasonable guesses based on clues and details that the author gives.	Authors do not always directly state information. Inferring helps you figure out what the author wants you to know.	Look for clues the author provides. Notice descriptions, dialogue, events, and relationships that might tell you something the author is trying to express to you.

Unit 3	What Is It?	Why It's Important	How To Do It
	Respond Responding is stopping to consider your thoughts and feelings about something you've read.	When you react in a personal way to what you are reading, you enjoy the text more and understand it better.	Think about what you like or don't like, what surprises you, what scares you, or what makes you laugh. You can also respond by putting yourself in a character's place.
	Cause and Effect A cause is a condition or event that makes something happen. What happens as a result of a cause is an effect. A cause can have more than one effect.	Understanding cause and effect helps you make connections between the events in the story. It helps you understand why certain events take place.	As you read, ask yourself: Did what just happened occur because of something that happened earlier? Look for clue words such as *because*, *therefore*, *since*, and so.
Unit 4	**Visualize** Visualizing is picturing in your mind what you are reading.	Visualizing helps bring the text alive. Visualizing is a great way to understand and remember places, characters, and other details in what you are reading.	As you read, use details in the text to help you create mental pictures. Also use your own experiences to help you imagine the scene.
	Sequence Sequence is the order in which thoughts or actions are arranged in a story. Many stories tell events in the order in which the events happen.	Following the sequence of events helps you see how a story is organized. It will be easier to remember what happens when you understand the order of events.	As you read, look for words like *first*, *then*, *meanwhile*, *eventually*, and *later*. These words can help you figure out when things happen.
Unit 5	**Author's Purpose** The author's purpose is the goal that the author tries to achieve in the text. The author may want to entertain, describe, inform, explain, or persuade.	Knowing the author's purpose helps you understand why the author is writing the text. It can also help you decide which ideas are most important.	As you read, ask yourself: What is the author trying to do here? Why is the author telling this story? Look for clues that the author may give about his or her purpose.
	Main Idea and Details The main idea is the most important thought of a passage or paragraph. The sentences that support the main idea contain the details.	Knowing the main idea of a text helps you figure out the important information. Finding details helps you see how the author supports the main idea.	The main idea can often be found in the first or last sentence of a paragraph. Ask yourself: What is this paragraph about? What details help show its meaning?

UNIT 1

Short Story

What's a Short Story?

Wherever you go, chances are you'll hear a story. Conversations, movies, TV programs, jokes, and even some songs tell stories. But some of the best stories—short stories—can be found on the pages of books and magazines.

A **short story** is a brief piece of fiction. Fiction is writing that is about imaginary people, places, and events. There are many different types of short stories. Mysteries, romances, adventures, and thrillers are just a few types of stories.

What's your favorite kind of story? Write your response here:

I like _____ stories.

Why Read Short Stories?

You might read a short story because it entertains you. A short story may whisk you away to another time or place. It can help you find out something interesting about yourself and others. A good short story often offers a new and interesting view of life and sparks your imagination.

How Do I Read Short Stories?

Focus on key **literary elements** and **reading skills** to get the most out of reading the four short stories in this unit. Here are two key literary elements and two key reading skills that you will practice in this unit.

Key Literary Elements

• Foreshadowing

Clues that prepare readers for events that will happen later in a story are called **foreshadowing.** Foreshadowing can build suspense. For example, a weapon found in a drawer might foreshadow a future crime.

• Conflict

Conflict is a struggle between two opposing forces that lies at the center of a story. There are two basic kinds of conflict in a story: external conflict and internal conflict. External conflict takes place when a character struggles against an outside force, such as another person, nature, or society. Internal conflict takes place within a character's mind. A character experiences internal conflict when he or she is torn between opposing thoughts or feelings.

Key Reading Skills

• Question

When you **question** what you are reading, you are helping yourself understand more clearly the characters or events in a story. As you read, ask yourself questions: Do I understand what is happening? Does this make sense based on what I have already read? What does this paragraph mean? Think of other questions starting with *who, what, where, when, why,* and *how* to make sure you understand what you are reading.

• Evaluate

When you **evaluate**, you make a judgment or form an opinion about what you are reading. To evaluate, ask yourself questions about the events or characters: Does this event make sense? Would this character really do this? You can also evaluate the writing: Is it interesting? Does the story hold my attention? Remember to evaluate while you are reading, not just after you have finished.

The Landlady

Meet Roald Dahl

Roald Dahl was born in Wales in 1916. After serving in the Royal Air Force in 1939, he wrote a story about his flying experiences. Dahl went on to write many famous stories and novels for adults and children, including *Charlie and the Chocolate Factory*. Dahl died in 1990. "The Landlady" was first published in 1959.

What You Know

Think of a time when you met someone who seemed nice, but also a little bit unusual. What about this person seemed different to you? Did you try to find out more about the person? Did you change your mind when you got to know the person better?

Reason to Read

Read this short story to find out what happens when a man goes to a new town and meets a mysterious stranger.

Background Info

This story takes place in a boardinghouse in England. A boardinghouse is a family home with extra bedrooms for people to rent. People staying in a boardinghouse usually share the other rooms, such as the bathroom, living room, and dining room. In England, boardinghouses are often run by a landlady (the owner of the house). Because the rent usually includes breakfast as well as the room, a boardinghouse may be cheaper than staying at a hotel or an apartment.

Word Power

characteristic (kar´ ik tə ris´ tik) *n.* a special quality of a person or thing; p. 5
The actor's best *characteristic* is his confidence.

congenial (kən jēn´ yəl) *adj.* pleasant; friendly and agreeable; p. 6
When I went to my neighbor's house for dinner, everyone was very *congenial*.

compelling (kəm pel´ ing) *v.* forcing; urging; p. 6
My hunger was *compelling* me to raid the refrigerator.

tantalizing (tant´ əl īz´ ing) *adj.* teasingly out of reach; p. 15
While standing in the cold rain, the woman had *tantalizing* thoughts of a warm bath.

blemish (blem´ ish) *n.* a mark or stain that causes something to be less pleasing than it could be; p. 17
Bob considered the scar on his lip to be a *blemish* to his face.

lapsed (lapsd) *v.* gradually fell or slipped into a different condition; p. 17
After a few polite remarks, the conversation *lapsed* into uncomfortable silence.

inclining (in klīn´ ing) *v.* bending or slanting; leaning; p. 18
The old man was *inclining* his head forward to get a closer look at his newspaper.

**Answer the following questions, using one of the new words above.
Write your answers in the spaces provided.**

1. Which word goes with "a scar"? _____

2. Which word goes with "something you want but can't get"? _____

3. Which word goes with "leaning in a particular direction"? _____

4. Which word goes with "friendly"?_____

5. Which word goes with "a part of someone's personality"? _____

6. Which word goes with "forcing a person to do something"? _____

7. Which word goes with "slipped or sank into"? _____

The *Landlady*

Roald Dahl

The Lunch (Le Dejeuner), 1932. Pierre Bonnard. Musée du Petit Palais, Paris.

Background Info

London is the capital city of the United Kingdom. Reading is a town outside London. Bath is an English city famous for its hot springs.

English Coach

The root of the word *porter*, *port*, comes from the Latin *portare*, meaning "to carry." The suffix *-er* means "someone who does." So a *porter* is someone who carries things. Write two other jobs you know of that end with *-er*.

_____

_____

Billy Weaver had traveled down from London on the slow afternoon train, with a change at Reading on the way, and by the time he got to Bath, it was about nine o'clock in the evening, and the moon was coming up out of a clear starry sky over the houses opposite the station entrance. But the air was deadly cold, and the wind was like a flat blade of ice on his cheeks.

"Excuse me," he said, "but is there a fairly cheap hotel not too far away from here?"

"Try The Bell and Dragon," the porter answered, pointing down the road. "They might take you in. It's about a quarter of a mile along on the other side."

Billy thanked him and picked up his suitcase and set out to walk the quarter-mile to The Bell and Dragon. He had never been to Bath before. He didn't know anyone who lived there. But Mr. Greenslade at the head office in London had told him it was a splendid town. "Find your own lodgings," he had said, "and then go along and report to the branch manager as soon as you've got yourself settled."

Billy was seventeen years old. He was wearing a new navy-blue overcoat, a new brown trilby hat, and a new brown suit, and he was feeling fine. He walked briskly down the street. He was trying to do everything briskly these days. Briskness, he had decided, was *the* one common **characteristic** of all successful businessmen. The big shots up at the head office were absolutely fantastically brisk all the time. They were amazing.

There were no shops on this wide street that he was walking along, only a line of tall houses on each side, all of them identical. They had porches and pillars and four or five steps going up to their front doors, and it was obvious that once upon a time they had been very swanky residences. But now, even in the darkness, he could see that the paint was peeling from the woodwork on their doors and windows and that the handsome white facades were cracked and blotchy from neglect.

Suddenly, in a downstairs window that was brilliantly illuminated by a street lamp not six yards away, Billy caught sight of a printed notice propped up against the glass in one of the upper panes. It said BED AND BREAKFAST. There was a vase of yellow chrysanthemums, tall and beautiful, standing just underneath the notice.

He stopped walking. He moved a bit closer. Green curtains (some sort of velvety material) were hanging down on either side of the window. The chrysanthemums looked wonderful beside them. He went right up and peered through the glass into the room, and the first thing he saw was a bright fire burning in the hearth. On the carpet in front of the fire, a pretty little dachshund was curled up asleep with its nose tucked into its belly.

Did You Know?

A dachshund (däks´ hoond´) is a dog with short legs and a long body. Because of their body shape, dachshunds are sometimes called "wiener dogs" or "sausage dogs."

Connect to the Text

Reread the boxed text. Think about a quality you admire in another person. What is that quality? Why do you admire it? Have you tried to copy it yourself?

_____

_____

_____

_____

_____

_____

Word Power

characteristic (kar´ ik tə ris´ tik) *n.* a special quality of a person or thing

The room itself, so far as he could see in the half darkness, was filled with pleasant furniture. There was a baby grand piano and a big sofa and several plump armchairs, and in one corner he spotted a large parrot in a cage. Animals were usually a good sign in a place like this, Billy told himself; and all in all, it looked to him as though it would be a pretty decent house to stay in. Certainly it would be more comfortable than The Bell and Dragon.

On the other hand, a pub would be more **congenial** than a boardinghouse. There would be beer and darts in the evenings, and lots of people to talk to, and it would probably be a good bit cheaper, too. He had stayed a couple of nights in a pub once before and he had liked it. He had never stayed in any boardinghouses, and, to be perfectly honest, he was a tiny bit frightened of them. The name itself conjured up images of watery cabbage, rapacious landladies, and a powerful smell of kippers in the living room.

After dithering about like this in the cold for two or three minutes, Billy decided that he would walk on and take a look at The Bell and Dragon before making up his mind. He turned to go.

And now a queer thing happened to him. He was in the act of stepping back and turning away from the window when all at once his eye was caught and held in the most peculiar manner by the small notice that was there. BED AND BREAKFAST, it said. BED AND BREAKFAST, BED AND BREAKFAST, BED AND BREAKFAST. Each word was like a large black eye staring at him through the glass, holding him, **compelling** him, forcing him to stay where he was and not to walk away from that house, and the next thing he knew, he was actually moving across from the window to the front door of the house, climbing the steps that led up to it, and reaching for the bell.

Word Power

congenial (kən jēn´ yəl) *adj.* pleasant; friendly and agreeable
compelling (kəm pel´ ing) *v.* forcing; urging

He pressed the bell. Far away in a back room he heard it ringing, and then *at once*—it must have been at once because he hadn't even had time to take his finger from the bell button—the door swung open and a woman was standing there.

Normally you ring the bell and you have at least a half-minute's wait before the door opens. But this dame was like a jack-in-the-box. He pressed the bell—and out she popped! It made him jump.

She was about forty-five or fifty years old, and the moment she saw him, she gave him a warm, welcoming smile.

"*Please* come in," she said pleasantly. She stepped aside, holding the door wide open, and Billy found himself automatically starting forward. The compulsion or, more accurately, the desire to follow after her into that house was extraordinarily strong.

"I saw the notice in the window," he said, holding himself back.

"Yes, I know."

"I was wondering about a room."

"It's *all* ready for you, my dear," she said. She had a round pink face and very gentle blue eyes.

"I was on my way to The Bell and Dragon," Billy told her. "But the notice in your window just happened to catch my eye."

"My dear boy," she said, "why don't you come in out of the cold?"

"How much do you charge?"

"Five and sixpence a night, including breakfast."

It was fantastically cheap. It was less than half of what he had been willing to pay.

Reading Skill

Evaluate Reread the highlighted text. Do you think the author makes the landlady sound like a nice person? Why or why not?

_____

_____

_____

_____

_____

_____

Connect to the Text

Think about the way the author has been describing the boardinghouse. Then look at the picture. Do you think the boardinghouse in the story and the boardinghouse in the picture sound and look inviting? Is there a special place you like to go to that makes you feel welcome and cozy?

_____

_____

_____

_____

_____

Room for Tourists, 1945. Edward Hopper. Oil on canvas, 30¼ x 42⅛ in. Yale University Art Gallery, New Haven, CT.

"If that is too much," she added, "then perhaps I can reduce it just a tiny bit. Do you desire an egg for breakfast? Eggs are expensive at the moment. It would be sixpence less without the egg."

"Five and sixpence is fine," he answered. "I should like very much to stay here."

"I knew you would. Do come in."

She seemed terribly nice. She looked exactly like the mother of one's best school friend welcoming one into the house to stay for the Christmas holidays. Billy took off his hat and stepped over the threshold.

"Just hang it there," she said, "and let me help you with your coat."

There were no other hats or coats in the hall. There were no umbrellas, no walking sticks—nothing.

"We have it *all* to ourselves," she said, smiling at him over her shoulder as she led the way upstairs. "You see, it isn't very often I have the pleasure of taking a visitor into my little nest."

The old girl is slightly dotty, Billy told himself. But at five and sixpence a night, who cares about that? "I should've thought you'd be simply swamped with applicants," he said politely.

"Oh, I am, my dear, I am, of course I am. But the trouble is that I'm inclined to be just a teeny-weeny bit choosy and particular—if you see what I mean."

"Ah, yes."

Comprehension Check

Reread the boxed text. What does the landlady do when she worries that the price might be too expensive for Billy?

_____

_____

_____

_____

_____

Reading Skill

Question Reread the highlighted text. Which is the **best** question to ask while reading to get the most important information from the passage? Check the correct response.

☐ How many floors are there?

☐ Why are there no other guests?

☐ What will Billy's room be like?

Comprehension Check

Reread the text boxed in green. What does the landlady say about Billy? Underline the answer in the text.

Background Info

A hot-water bottle is a container, usually made of rubber, that is filled with very hot water. It can be used to warm a bed or a part of the body (such as a stiff neck).

"But I'm always ready. Everything is always ready day and night in this house just on the off chance that an acceptable young gentleman will come along. And it is such a pleasure, my dear, such a very great pleasure when now and again I open the door and I see someone standing there who is just *exactly* right." She was halfway up the stairs, and she paused with one hand on the stair rail, turning her head and smiling down at him with pale lips. "Like you," she added, and her blue eyes traveled slowly all the way down the length of Billy's body, to his feet, and then up again.

On the second-floor landing she said to him, "This floor is mine."

They climbed up another flight. "And this one is all yours," she said. "Here's your room. I do hope you'll like it." She took him into a small but charming front bedroom, switching on the light as she went in.

"The morning sun comes right in the window, Mr. Perkins. It *is* Mr. Perkins, isn't it?"

"No," he said. "It's Weaver."

"Mr. Weaver. How nice. I've put a water bottle between the sheets to air them out, Mr. Weaver. It's such a comfort to have a hot-water bottle in a strange bed with clean sheets, don't you agree? And you may light the gas fire at any time if you feel chilly."

"Thank you," Billy said. "Thank you ever so much." He noticed that the bedspread had been taken off the bed and that the bedclothes had been neatly turned back on one side, all ready for someone to get in.

"I'm so glad you appeared," she said, looking earnestly into his face. "I was beginning to get worried."

"That's all right," Billy answered brightly. "You mustn't worry about me." He put his suitcase on the chair and started to open it.

"And what about supper, my dear? Did you manage to get anything to eat before you came here?"

"I'm not a bit hungry, thank you," he said. "I think I'll just go to bed as soon as possible because tomorrow I've got to get up rather early and report to the office."

"Very well, then. I'll leave you now so that you can unpack. But before you go to bed, would you be kind enough to pop into the sitting room on the ground floor and sign the book? Everyone has to do that because it's the law of the land, and we don't want to go breaking any laws at *this* stage in the proceedings, do we?" She gave him a little wave of the hand and went quickly out of the room and closed the door.

Now, the fact that his landlady appeared to be slightly off her rocker didn't worry Billy in the least. After all, she not only was harmless—there was no question about that—but she was also quite obviously a kind and generous soul. He guessed that she had probably lost a son in the war, or something like that, and had never gotten over it.

Reading Skill

Evaluate Reread the highlighted text. Evaluate Billy's opinion of the landlady. Do you think he is right about her? Why or why not?

_____

_____

_____

_____

_____

_____

 Stop here for **Break Time** on the next page.

Break Time

As you read "The Landlady," it is important to keep track of clues about what the landlady is like. Think about details the author gives you, like what the landlady says and what Billy thinks of her. Read each question below. Then write the answer in the circle to show what you know about the landlady so far.

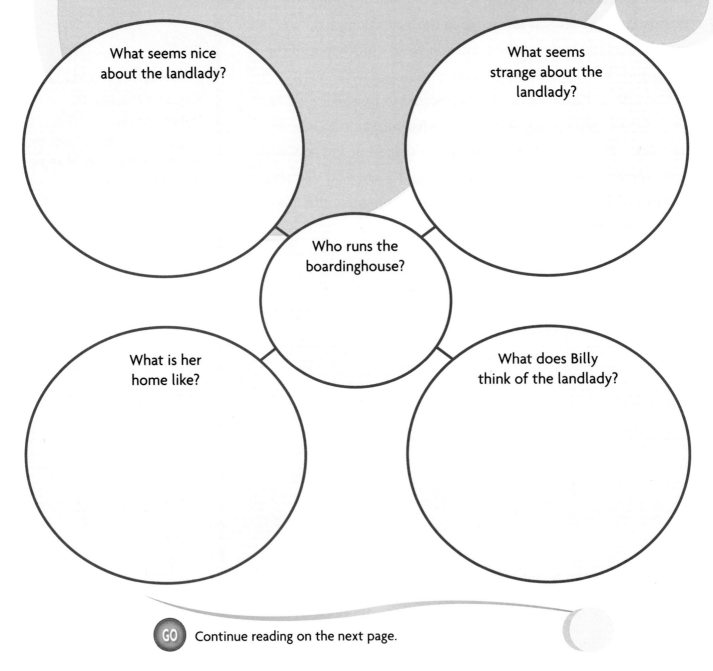

What seems nice about the landlady?

What seems strange about the landlady?

Who runs the boardinghouse?

What is her home like?

What does Billy think of the landlady?

GO Continue reading on the next page.

So a few minutes later, after unpacking his suitcase and washing his hands, he trotted downstairs to the ground floor and entered the living room. His landlady wasn't there, but the fire was glowing in the hearth, and the little dachshund was still sleeping soundly in front of it. The room was wonderfully warm and cozy. I'm a lucky fellow, he thought, rubbing his hands. This is a bit of all right.

He found the guest book lying open on the piano, so he took out his pen and wrote down his name and address. There were only two other entries above his on the page, and as one always does with guest books, he started to read them. One was a Christopher Mulholland from Cardiff. The other was Gregory W. Temple from Bristol.

That's funny, he thought suddenly. Christopher Mulholland. It rings a bell.

Now where on earth had he heard that rather unusual name before?

Was it a boy at school? No. Was it one of his sister's numerous young men, perhaps, or a friend of his father's? No, no, it wasn't any of those. He glanced down again at the book.

Christopher Mulholland
231 Cathedral Road, Cardiff

Gregory W. Temple
27 Sycamore Drive, Bristol

As a matter of fact, now he came to think of it, he wasn't at all sure that the second name didn't have almost as much of a familiar ring about it as the first.

"Gregory Temple?" he said aloud, searching his memory. "Christopher Mulholland? . . ."

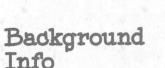

"Such charming boys," a voice behind him answered, and he turned and saw his landlady sailing into the room with a large silver tea tray in her hands. She was holding it well out in front of her, and rather high up, as though the tray were a pair of reins on a frisky horse.

"They sound somehow familiar," he said.

"They do? How interesting."

"I'm almost positive I've heard those names before somewhere. Isn't that odd? Maybe it was in the newspapers. They weren't famous in any way, were they? I mean famous cricketers or footballers or something like that?"

"Famous," she said, setting the tea tray down on the low table in front of the sofa. "Oh no, I don't think they were famous. But they were incredibly handsome, both of them, I can promise you that. They were tall and young and handsome, my dear, just exactly like you."

Once more, Billy glanced down at the book. "Look here," he said, noticing the dates. "This last entry is over two years old."

"It is?"

"Yes, indeed. And Christopher Mulholland's is nearly a year before that—more than *three years* ago."

"Dear me," she said, shaking her head and heaving a dainty little sigh. "I would never have thought it. How time does fly away from us all, doesn't it, Mr. Wilkins?"

"It's Weaver," Billy said. "W-e-a-v-e-r."

"Oh, of course it is!" she cried, sitting down on the sofa. "How silly of me. I do apologize. In one ear and out the other, that's me, Mr. Weaver."

"You know something?" Billy said. "Something that's really quite extraordinary about all this?"

"No, dear, I don't."

"Well, you see, both of these names—Mulholland and Temple—I not only seem to remember each one of them separately, so to speak, but somehow or other, in some peculiar way, they both appear to be sort of connected together as well. As though they were both famous for the same sort of thing, if you see what I mean—like . . . well . . . like Dempsey and Tunney, for example, or Churchill and Roosevelt."

"How amusing," she said. "But come over here now, dear, and sit down beside me on the sofa and I'll give you a nice cup of tea and a ginger biscuit before you go to bed."

"You really shouldn't bother," Billy said. "I didn't mean you to do anything like that." He stood by the piano, watching her as she fussed about with the cups and saucers. He noticed that she had small, white, quickly moving hands and red fingernails.

"I'm almost positive it was in the newspapers I saw them," Billy said. "I'll think of it in a second. I'm sure I will."

There is nothing more **tantalizing** than a thing like this that lingers just outside the borders of one's memory. He hated to give up.

"Now wait a minute," he said. "Wait just a minute. Mulholland . . . Christopher Mulholland . . . wasn't *that* the name of the Eton schoolboy who was on a walking tour through the West Country, and then all of a sudden . . ."

"Milk?" she said. "And sugar?"

"Yes, please. And then all of a sudden . . ."

"Eton schoolboy?" she said. "Oh no, my dear, that can't possibly be right, because *my* Mr. Mulholland was certainly not an Eton schoolboy when he came to me. He was a Cambridge undergraduate. Come over here now and sit next to me and warm yourself in front of this lovely fire. Come on. Your tea's all ready for you." She patted the empty place beside her on the sofa, and she sat there smiling at Billy and waiting for him to come over.

Word Power

tantalizing (tant´ əl īz´ ing) *adj.* teasingly out of reach

Background Info

Gene Tunney was the heavyweight boxing champion from 1926 to 1928. He defeated Jack Dempsey for the title in 1926 and 1927. During World War II, Winston Churchill was prime minister of the United Kingdom, and Franklin D. Roosevelt was president of the United States. They worked together to win the war.

Reading Skill

Evaluate Reread the highlighted sentence and the rest of the page. Think about the way the author writes this conversation. Do you think he does a good job of showing that the landlady is trying to stop Billy from figuring out where he heard Mulholland's name before? Why or why not?

_____

_____

_____

_____

_____

_____

Think about how oddly the landlady is acting. Then look at this picture. Do you think a cozy scene like this helps keep Billy off his guard? Why or why not?

Connect to the Text

Reread the text boxed in purple. Think about a smell that reminds you of a particular person, place, or event. How would you describe the smell? What does it remind you of?

_____

_____

_____

_____

_____

Comprehension Check

Reread the text boxed in green. What does the landlady tell Billy about where Mulholland and Temple are? Underline the answers in the text.

He crossed the room slowly and sat down on the edge of the sofa. She placed his teacup on the table in front of him.

"*There* we are," she said. "How nice and cozy this is, isn't it?"

Billy started sipping his tea. She did the same. For half a minute or so, neither of them spoke. But Billy knew that she was looking at him. Her body was half turned toward him, and he could feel her eyes resting on his face, watching him over the rim of her teacup. Now and again, he caught a whiff of a peculiar smell that seemed to emanate directly from her person. It was not in the least unpleasant, and it reminded him—well, he wasn't quite sure what it reminded him of. Pickled walnuts? New leather? Or was it the corridors of a hospital?

At length, she said, "Mr. Mulholland was a great one for his tea. Never in my life have I seen anyone drink as much tea as dear, sweet Mr. Mulholland."

"I suppose he left fairly recently," Billy said. He was still puzzling his head about the two names. He was positive now that he had seen them in the newspapers—in the headlines.

"Left?" she said, arching her brows. "But my dear boy, he never left. He's still here. Mr. Temple is also here. They're on the fourth floor, both of them together."

Billy set his cup down slowly on the table and stared at his landlady. She smiled back at him, and then she put out one of her white hands and patted him comfortingly on the knee. "How old are you, my dear?" she asked.

"Seventeen."

"Seventeen!" she cried. "Oh, it's the perfect age! Mr. Mulholland was also seventeen. But I think he was a trifle shorter than you are; in fact I'm sure he was, and his teeth weren't *quite* so white. You have the most beautiful teeth, Mr. Weaver, did you know that?"

"They're not as good as they look," Billy said. "They've got simply masses of fillings in them at the back."

"Mr. Temple, of course, was a little older," she said, ignoring his remark. "He was actually twenty-eight. And yet I never would have guessed it if he hadn't told me, never in my whole life. There wasn't a *blemish* on his body."

"A what?" Billy said.

"His skin was *just* like a baby's."

There was a pause. Billy picked up his teacup and took another sip of his tea; then he set it down again gently in its saucer. He waited for her to say something else, but she seemed to have **lapsed** into another of her silences. He sat there staring straight ahead of him into the far corner of the room, biting his lower lip.

"That parrot," he said at last. "You know something? It had me completely fooled when I first saw it through the window. I could have sworn it was alive."

"Alas, no longer."

"It's most terribly clever the way it's been done," he said. "It doesn't look in the least bit dead. Who did it?"

"I did."

"*You* did?"

Reading Skill

Question Reread the highlighted paragraphs. Which is the **best** question to ask yourself to help you understand what is so strange about the landlady's comments? Check the correct response.

☐ How does she know Mr. Temple's body didn't have any marks?

☐ Why does she ignore Billy when he mentions his fillings?

☐ What is a baby's skin like?

Word Power

blemish (blem´ ish) *n.* a mark or stain that causes something to be less pleasing than it could be

lapsed (lapsd) *v.* gradually fell or slipped into a different condition

"Of course," she said. "And have you met my little Basil as well?" She nodded toward the dachshund curled up so comfortably in front of the fire. Billy looked at it. And suddenly, he realized that this animal had all the time been just as silent and motionless as the parrot. He put out a hand and touched it gently on the top of its back. The back was hard and cold, and when he pushed the hair to one side with his fingers, he could see the skin underneath, grayish black and dry and perfectly preserved.

"Good gracious me," he said. "How absolutely fascinating." He turned away from the dog and stared with deep admiration at the little woman beside him on the sofa. "It must be most awfully difficult to do a thing like that."

"Not in the least," she said. "I stuff *all* my little pets myself when they pass away. Will you have another cup of tea?"

"No, thank you," Billy said. The tea tasted faintly of bitter almonds, and he didn't much care for it.

"You did sign the book, didn't you?"

"Oh, yes."

"That's good. Because later on, if I happen to forget what you were called, then I could always come down here and look it up. I still do that almost every day with Mr. Mulholland and Mr. . . . Mr. . . ."

"Temple," Billy said, "Gregory Temple. Excuse my asking, but haven't there been *any* other guests here except them in the last two or three years?"

Holding her teacup high in one hand, **inclining** her head slightly to the left, she looked up at him out of the corners of her eyes and gave him another gentle little smile.

"No, my dear," she said. "Only you."

Did You Know?
Cyanide is a poison that tastes and smells like bitter almonds.
. . . .

Word Power
inclining (in klīn´ ing) *v.* bending or slanting; leaning

Respond to Literature

The Landlady

A Comprehension Check

Answer the following questions in the spaces provided.

1. Why does Billy decide to ring the doorbell of the boardinghouse?

   _____

   _____

2. For what two reasons does the landlady ask Billy to sign the guestbook?

   _____

   _____

B Reading Skills

Answer the following questions in the spaces provided.

1. **Question** When Billy remembers Christopher Mulholland's name, he says Mulholland was a schoolboy who was on a walking tour when "all of a sudden . . ." But Billy never finishes his thought. What is a good question to ask yourself at this point in the story?_____

   _____

   _____

2. **Evaluate** The author ends the story on a mysterious note. He leaves it to the reader to figure out what happens next. Do you think this is a good way to end a story? Why or why not? _____

   _____

   _____

C Word Power

Complete each sentence below, using one of the words in the box.

characteristic	congenial	compelling
tantalizing	blemish	lapsed	inclining

1. When Nazneen looked in the mirror, she noticed an odd
   _____ on her cheek.

2. My friend's best _____ is that she is a very good listener.

3. The dog kept _____ his head toward the door whenever
   he heard footsteps outside.

4. After tossing and turning all night, Arturo finally _____
   into a deep sleep.

5. He looked at the _____ desserts, but decided to
   have a cup of tea instead.

6. My classmates and I were very _____ as we welcomed
   the new student.

7. As she approached the finish line, Donna felt a force _____
   her to keep going.

D Literary Element: Foreshadowing

Read the passages below from "The Landlady." As you read, think about how the author uses foreshadowing to hint at the outcome of the story. Then answer the questions that follow.

"Such charming boys," a voice behind him answered, and he turned and saw his landlady sailing into the room with a large silver tea tray in her hands.[1] She was holding it well out in front of her, and rather high up, as though the tray were a pair of reins on a frisky horse.[2]

"I stuff *all* my little pets myself when they pass away.[3] Will you have another cup of tea?"[4]

"No, thank you," Billy said.[5] The tea tasted faintly of bitter almonds, and he didn't much care for it.[6]

1. Near the end of the story, you learn that the landlady has put poison in Billy's tea. In sentences 1–2 above, how does the author hint that there is something wrong with the tea Billy will drink?

   _____

   _____

   _____

2. What do sentences 3–6 hint about what will happen to Billy?

   _____

   _____

   _____

E An Instant Message from Billy

Pretend you are Billy. You sense you are in danger, so you send an instant message to Mr. Greenslade back in London. Write about what's happened to you and how you feel about it.

BriskBilly: Mr. Greenslade, are you there?

Greenslade: **Good evening, Billy! Are you enjoying your trip?**

BriskBilly: Not really! Something strange is going on. I decided to stay at this boardinghouse because it seemed _____

_____

When I looked in the window, I could see _____

_____

Greenslade: **Well, I usually prefer to stay at a pub, but this boardinghouse sounds charming, I suppose.**

BriskBilly: I thought so too! At first the landlady seemed _____

_____

But things got weird when I signed the guestbook and noticed the names

_____

Greenslade: **Hmm, where have I heard those names before?**

BriskBilly: You won't believe this, but after looking closely at her dog, I discovered her hobby is _____

The worst part was the tea. It tasted _____

I think she may be trying to _____

Greenslade: **Nonsense, my boy! You're tired from your trip.**

Greenslade: **Billy? Billy, are you there?**

Greenslade: **Billy?**

Send

Assessment

Fill in the circle next to each correct answer.

1. Why does Billy end up ringing the bell at the boardinghouse?
   - ○ A. He decides that The Bell and Dragon is too far away.
   - ○ B. He feels mysteriously forced to approach the house.
   - ○ C. He feels cold and needs to get inside.
   - ○ D. He smells delicious eggs cooking.

2. In order to better understand why the boardinghouse is so mysterious, which is the **best** question you can ask about it as you read?
   - ○ A. What street is it on?
   - ○ B. Is it close to the train station?
   - ○ C. How many rooms does it have?
   - ○ D. Why are there no other guests there?

3. How does the landlady keep Billy from figuring out where he heard the names Temple and Mullholland?
   - ○ A. She says she does not remember them at all.
   - ○ B. She leaves the room whenever he asks about them.
   - ○ C. She keeps changing the subject.
   - ○ D. She makes up lies about them.

4. Which quote from the landlady best foreshadows what she will do to Billy?
   - ○ A. "I stuff *all* my little pets myself when they pass away."
   - ○ B. "Do you desire an egg for breakfast?"
   - ○ C. "And you may light the gas fire at any time if you feel chilly."
   - ○ D. "You did sign the book, didn't you?"

5. Which of the following words means the same thing as "friendly and agreeable"?
   - ○ A. tantalizing
   - ○ B. congenial
   - ○ C. compelling
   - ○ D. inclining

Lob's Girl

Meet Joan Aiken

British author Joan Aiken was born in 1924. She began creating poems and stories when she was just five years old. Her first work was published when she was seventeen. Since then, Aiken has written more than eighty books and many short stories. Aiken says that she writes "the sort of thing I should have liked to read myself." She is best known for fiction with mysterious or enchanted characters and places. "Lob's Girl" was first published in 1982.

What You Know

Do you think the bond between an animal and a person can be as strong as the bond between two people?

Reason to Read

Read this short story to find out about the powerful relationship between a young girl and her dog.

Background Info

Dogs have been known to walk hundreds of miles to find their owners or to return to their homes. No one is exactly sure how dogs can do this, but it is clear that a dog's sense of smell is a powerful tool. Dogs seem to remember smells more than they remember sights. For example, dogs remember the arrangement of things in a room by their different scents rather than by how the things look.

Word Power

decisively (di sī′ siv lē) *adv.* in a way that brings a clear decision; p. 26
The coach blew the whistle *decisively* when practice was done.

dutifully (dōō′ ti fəl ē) *adv.* doing something you are supposed to do; p. 28
He *dutifully* returned home at dinnertime.

resolutions (rez′ ə lōō′ shənz) *n.* things that have been decided or determined; p. 28
Every New Year's Day, we make fresh *resolutions*.

accompanied (ə kum′ pə nēd) *v.* went along with; p. 28
Her dog always *accompanied* her on visits to the lake.

objection (əb jek′ shən) *n.* a feeling of dislike; a protest; p. 29
At the meeting, a parent offered an *objection* to the new plan.

assured (ə shoord′) *v.* promised; made a person sure of something; p. 29
The doctor *assured* us that Mom would be fine.

strictly (strikt′ lē) *adv.* following a rule in an exact way; p. 35
Eating in the classroom is *strictly* forbidden.

**Answer the following questions that contain the new words above.
Write your answers in the spaces provided.**

1. If your team's victory is *assured*, would you expect to win or lose? _____

2. If you *decisively* made a choice, are you sure or not sure about the choice?

   _____

3. If you were *accompanied* on a trip, did you go with someone or go alone?

   _____

4. Are *resolutions* actions that you definitely plan to take or actions that you might

   not take? _____

5. If you *strictly* follow a recipe, do you do exactly what it says or follow only some

   of the directions? _____

6. If your father has an *objection* to your plan, is he for your plan or against it?

   _____

7. If you do something *dutifully*, do you do it as you are supposed to or any way you

   want? _____

Staithes, Yorkshire. Dame Laura Knight, 1877–1970. Oil on canvas, 29½ x 24½ in. Private collection.

Adapted from

Lob's Girl

Joan Aiken

Comprehension Check

Reread the boxed text. What happens to Sandy as she lies on the beach?

_____

_____

_____

_____

Did You Know?

Alsatians, also called German shepherds, were originally bred in Germany. They are known for being intelligent and loyal.

Some people choose their dogs, and some dogs choose their people. The Pengelly family had no say in the choosing of Lob; he came to them in the second way, and very **decisively.**

It began on the beach, the summer when Sandy was five, Don, her older brother, twelve, and the twins were three. On this summer day she was lying peacefully reading a comic.

Sandy rolled onto her back to make sure that the twins were not climbing on slippery rocks or getting cut off by the tide.

> At the same moment a large body struck her hard in the stomach and she was covered by flying sand. She shut her eyes and felt the sand being wiped off her face by something that seemed like a warm, rough, damp flannel. She opened her eyes and looked. It was a tongue. Its owner was a large and bouncy young Alsatian, or German shepherd, with light-brown eyes, black-tipped prick ears, a thick, soft coat, and a bushy black-tipped tail.

Word Power

decisively (di sī´ siv lē) *adv.* in a way that brings a clear decision

26

"*Lob!*" shouted a man farther up the beach. "Lob, come here!"

But Lob went on licking the sand off Sandy's face. His owner walked over as quickly as he could and grabbed him by the collar.

"I hope he didn't give you a fright?" the man said to Sandy.

"Oh, no, I think he's *beautiful*," said Sandy truly. She picked up a bit of driftwood and threw it. Lob came back with the stick, beaming, and gave it to Sandy. It was then that Lob fell in love with Sandy. But with Sandy, too, it was love at first sight.

"I wish we could play with him every day," Tess sighed.

"Why can't we?" said Tim.

Sandy explained, "Because Mr. Dodsworth, who owns him, is from Liverpool, and he is only staying at the Fisherman's Arms till Saturday."

"Is Liverpool a long way off?"

"Right at the other end of England from Cornwall, I'm afraid."

It was a Cornish fishing village where the Pengelly family lived, with rocks and cliffs and a strip of beach and a little round harbor, and palm trees growing in the gardens of the little stone houses. The village was approached by a narrow, steep, twisting hill-road, and guarded by a notice that said LOW GEAR FOR 1 1/2 MILES, DANGEROUS TO CYCLISTS.

The whole family was playing cards by the fire in the front room after supper when there was a loud thump and a crash of china in the kitchen.

"My puddings!" exclaimed Jean, and ran out.

"Did you put TNT in them, then?" her husband said.

But it was Lob. Finding the front door shut, he had gone around to the back and bounced in through the open kitchen window, where the puddings were cooling on the sill.

Lob stood on his hind legs and covered Sandy's face with licks. "Where does this friend of yours come from?" asked Mr. Pengelly.

Literary Element

Foreshadowing Reread the text highlighted in blue. What clues hint that Sandy and Lob will find a way to be together?

_____

_____

_____

_____

_____

Reading Skill

Evaluate Reread the paragraph highlighted in green. The author tries to make the Pengelly's village sound far away from other people and very hard to get to. Do you think she does a good job making the village sound lonely and cut off? Why or why not?

_____

_____

_____

_____

_____

_____

_____

Connect to the Text

Reread the boxed text. Has anyone you were close to ever gone far away? How did that make you feel? How do you think the person who was leaving felt?

_____

_____

_____

_____

English Coach

Here, *eyes like stars* means that Sandy's eyes are bright when she sees Lob. This means that Sandy is happy. If a character has "eyes like saucers," what do you think that character is feeling?

_____

_____

_____

_____

_____

"He's staying at the Fisherman's Arms—I mean his owner is."

"Then he must go back there."

"I wonder how he found his way here," Mrs. Pengelly said. "Fisherman's Arms is right round the other side of the harbor."

Lob's owner scolded him and thanked Mr. Pengelly for bringing him back. Jean Pengelly warned the children that they had better not encourage Lob any more if they met him on the beach. So they **dutifully** took no notice of him the next day until he spoiled their good **resolutions** by dashing up to them with joyful barks. They had a happy day, playing on the sand.

The next day was Saturday. Sandy had found out that Mr. Dodsworth was to catch the 9:30 train. She went out secretly, down to the station. She saw Mr. Dodsworth get on the train, **accompanied** by an unhappy-looking Lob with drooping ears and tail.

A week passed. Then, one evening, Mrs. Pengelly and the younger children were in the front room playing snakes and ladders. Suddenly, history repeating itself, there was a crash from the kitchen. Jean Pengelly leaped up, crying, "My blackberry jelly!"

But Sandy was ahead of her mother. With flushed cheeks and eyes like stars she had darted into the kitchen, where she and Lob were hugging one another joyfully.

"Good heavens!" exclaimed Jean. "How in the world did he get here?"

"He must have walked," said Sandy. "Look at his feet."

They were worn, dusty, and tarry. One had a cut on the pad.

"What'll we do about him, Mother?" said Sandy anxiously.

Word Power

dutifully (do͞o′ ti fəl ē) *adv.* doing something you are supposed to do

resolutions (rez′ ə lo͞o′ shənz) *n.* things that have been decided or determined

accompanied (ə kum′ pə nēd) *v.* went along with

28

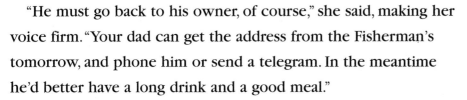

"He must go back to his owner, of course," she said, making her voice firm. "Your dad can get the address from the Fisherman's tomorrow, and phone him or send a telegram. In the meantime he'd better have a long drink and a good meal."

Lob was very grateful for the drink and the meal, and made no **objection** to having his feet washed. Then he flopped down on the rug and slept in front of the fire with his head on Sandy's feet. He was a very tired dog. He had walked all the way from Liverpool to Cornwall, which is more than four hundred miles.

The next day Mr. Pengelly phoned Lob's owner, and the following morning Mr. Dodsworth arrived off the night train to take his pet home. In ten days' time Lob was back—limping this time, with a torn ear and a patch missing out of his furry coat. He looked as if he had met and tangled with an enemy or two in the course of his four-hundred-mile walk.

Bert Pengelly rang up Liverpool again. Mr. Dodsworth, when he answered, sounded weary. He said, "That dog has already cost me two days that I can't spare away from my work. I think we'd better face the fact, Mr. Pengelly, that it's your family he wants to stay with—that is, if you want to have him."

Bert Pengelly gulped. He said cautiously, "How much would you be asking for him?"

"Good heavens, man, I'm not suggesting I'd sell him to you. You must have him as a gift."

"Is he a big eater?" Bert asked doubtfully.

"Oh, not for his size," Lob's owner **assured** Bert. "Two or three pounds of meat a day and some vegetables and gravy and biscuits—he does very well on that."

Reading Skill

Question Reread the highlighted paragraph. Which is the **best** question to ask yourself to help you understand Lob's behavior? Check the correct response.

☐ What enemies did Lob fight on his journey?

☐ Why does Lob keep coming back?

☐ Why doesn't Lob's owner take better care of him?

Comprehension Check

Reread the boxed text. What is Mr. Dodsworth telling Mr. Pengelly about Lob? Circle the answer in the text.

Word Power

objection (əb jek´ shən) *n.* a feeling of dislike; a protest

assured (ə shoord´) *v.* promised; made a person sure of something

Think about how the author has described where the Pengellys live. In what ways is the house in this picture similar to the Pengellys' home?

Reading Skill

Evaluate Reread the highlighted paragraph. Do you think Mr. Pengelly makes the right decision in accepting Lob? Why or why not?

_____

_____

_____

_____

"Well, then, Mr. Dodsworth," he said briskly, "we'll accept your offer and thank you very much. But I can tell you," he ended firmly, "if he wants to settle in with us he'll have to learn to eat a lot of fish."

So that was how Lob came to live with the Pengelly family. Everybody loved him and he loved them all. But there was never any question who came first with him. He was Sandy's dog.

 Stop here for **Break Time** on the next page.

30

Break Time

Lob shows he really wants to be Sandy's dog! Think about the times Lob and Sandy get separated and then how Lob always returns. Then look at the boxes below. The boxes on the left tell about the times they are separated. In the boxes on the right, fill in the details about the way Lob returns to Sandy. The first row has been completed for you. Save the two boxes at the bottom until you have finished the story. Then come back and fill them in.

Separation	Return
Lob returns to the hotel after meeting Sandy on the beach.	Lob comes from the hotel across the harbor to Sandy's home.
Lob returns to Liverpool with his owner.	
Lob's owner comes to take Lob back to Liverpool.	

GO Turn the page to continue reading.

Literary Element

Foreshadowing Reread the text highlighted in blue. Think about how the author describes the scene: Sandy does not want to go; it is getting dark; the wind is howling. What do you think the author is foreshadowing?

_____

_____

_____

_____

_____

Reading Skill

Question Reread the paragraphs highlighted in green. Which is the **best** question to ask yourself to help you understand what might have happened to the child by the wall? Check the correct response.

☐ Why are Dr. Travers and his wife out driving?

☐ What kind of doctor is Dr. Travers?

☐ Why does the author keep mentioning the dangerous hill?

In the course of nine years Lob changed less than Sandy. As she went into her teens he became a little slower, a little stiffer, there was a touch of gray on his nose, but he was still a handsome dog. He and Sandy still loved one another faithfully.

One evening in October when the children came home from school Jean Pengelly said, "Sandy, your Aunt Rebecca says she's lonely, and she wants one of you to go and spend the evening with her. You go, dear; you can take your homework with you."

"Can I take Lob with me?"

"Oh, very well." Mrs. Pengelly sighed.

Unwillingly Sandy put on the damp raincoat she had just taken off, fastened Lob's lead to his collar, and set off to walk through the dusk to Aunt Becky's cottage, which was five minutes' climb up the steep hill.

The wind was howling.

"Put some cheerful music on, do," said Jean Pengelly. "Anything to drown that terrible sound while I make your dad's supper." So Don put on some rock music, loud. Which was why the Pengellys did not hear the truck race down the hill and crash against the post office wall a few minutes later.

Dr. Travers was driving through Cornwall with his wife, taking a late holiday. He saw the sign that said STEEP HILL. LOW GEAR FOR 1 1/2 MILES. Dutifully he changed into second gear.

"We must be nearly there," said his wife. "I noticed a sign on the coast road that said the Fisherman's Arms was two miles. What a narrow, dangerous hill! Oh, Frank, stop, stop! There's a child, I'm sure it's a child—by the wall over there!"

A little stream ran down by the road in a shallow stone drain, and half in the water lay something that looked, in the dusk, like a pile of clothes. Mrs. Travers was out of the car in a flash, but her husband was quicker.

"Don't touch her, Emily!" he said sharply. "She's been hit. Remember that truck that passed us half a mile back, speeding like the devil? Here, quick, go into that cottage and phone for an ambulance. I'll stay here and do what I can to stop the bleeding."

This Dr. Travers was able to do, but he didn't dare do more. The girl was lying in an oddly crumpled heap. He guessed she had a number of bones broken and that it would be highly dangerous to move her.

Mrs. Travers was very quick. The first cottage she tried had a phone. In four minutes she was back, and in six an ambulance was wailing down the hill.

The ambulance sped off to Plymouth and Dr. Travers went down to the police station to report what he had done.

He found that the police already knew about the speeding truck—which had suffered from loss of brakes and ended up with its radiator halfway through the post office wall. The driver had a head injury and was in shock, but the police thought he was the only person injured.

At half-past nine that night Aunt Rebecca Hoskins was sitting by her fire when she was startled by a neighbor, who burst in exclaiming, "Have you heard about Sandy Pengelly? Terrible thing, poor little soul, and they don't know if she's likely to live." Horrified, Aunt Rebecca put on a coat and went down to her brother's house. Bert and Jean were about to drive off to the hospital where Sandy had been taken. Lob was nowhere to be seen.

"Thank the lord you've come, Beck," said her brother. "Will you stay the night with Don and the twins? Don's out looking for Lob and heaven knows when we'll be back."

That night seemed to last forever. Don came home very late and grim-faced. Bert and Jean sat in a waiting room of the Western Counties Hospital, but Sandy was unconscious. All that could be done for her was done.

"Is she a healthy girl?" the emergency doctor asked.

Comprehension Check

Reread the boxed text. What happened to the girl who is lying by the side of the road? How does Dr. Travers help her?

_____

_____

_____

_____

_____

Reading Skill

Evaluate Reread the highlighted sentences. What do you think about the way the neighbor tells Aunt Rebecca about Sandy's condition? Do you think she is being sensitive?

_____

_____

_____

_____

_____

_____

Literary Element

Foreshadowing Reread the text highlighted in blue. The author makes it sound like Sandy might not recover. Then the author writes about a dog trying to get into the hospital. What do you think the author is foreshadowing here?

_____

_____

_____

_____

_____

English Coach

Here, *agitated* means "excited; feeling a lot of worry." Write a sentence below using the word *agitated*.

_____

_____

_____

_____

"Aye, doctor, she is that," Bert said hoarsely.

"Then she ought to have a chance. But I won't hide that her condition is very serious, unless she shows signs of coming out from this coma."

But as hour after hour passed, Sandy showed no signs of recovering consciousness. At noon next day Dr. and Mrs. Travers went to the Pengelly cottage to inquire how Sandy was doing, but the report was gloomy.

The Western Counties Hospital is a large one, with five or six connected buildings, each with three or four entrances. By that afternoon it became obvious that a dog seemed to have taken up position outside the hospital, with the fixed intention of getting in. Patiently he would try first one entrance and then another, all the way around, and then begin again. Sometimes he would get a little way inside, following a visitor, but he was always kindly but firmly turned out again. Sometimes the guard at the main entrance gave him a pat or offered him a bit of sandwich—he looked so wet and pleading and desperate. But he never ate the sandwich. At tea time Granny Pearce came through the pouring rain to bring a bottle of hot tea to her daughter and son-in-law. Just as she reached the main entrance the guard was gently but forcibly shoving out a large, agitated, soaking-wet Alsatian dog.

"No, old fellow, you can *not* come in."

"Why, bless me," exclaimed old Mrs. Pearce. "That's Lob! Here, Lob. Lobby boy!"

Lob ran to her, whining. Mrs. Pearce walked up to the desk.

"I'm sorry, madam, you can't bring that dog in here," the guard said.

"Now, see here, young man. That dog has walked twenty miles from St. Killan to get to my granddaughter. Heaven knows how he knew she was here, but it's plain he knows. He ought to get to see her! Do you know," she went on, bristling, "that dog has walked the length of England—*twice*—to be with that girl?"

"I'll have to ask the medical officer," the guard said weakly.

"You do that, young man." Granny Pearce sat down in a determined manner, shutting her umbrella, and Lob sat patiently dripping at her feet. Every now and then he shook his head, as if to remove something heavy that was tied around his neck.

Presently a tired, thin, intelligent-looking man in a white coat came downstairs, with a silver-haired man in a dark suit. There was a low-voiced discussion. "Frankly... not much to lose," said the older man. The man in the white coat approached Granny Pearce.

"It's **strictly** against every rule, but as it's such a serious case we are making an exception," he said to her quietly. "But only *outside* her bedroom door—and only for a moment or two."

Without a word, Granny Pearce rose and went upstairs. Lob followed close to her skirts.

They waited in the green-floored hallway outside Sandy's room. Bert and Jean were inside. A nurse came out and left the door open. Sandy lay there, in a narrow bed with lots of gadgets around it, very flat under the covers, very still. All Lob's attention was focused on the bed. He strained toward it, but Granny Pearce held his collar firmly.

Lob let out a faint whine, anxious and pleading.

At the sound of that whine Sandy **stirred** just a little. Lob whined again. And then Sandy turned her head. Her eyes opened, looking at the door.

"Lob?" she murmured—no more than a breath of sound. "Lobby boy?"

The doctor by Granny Pearce drew a quick, sharp breath. Sandy moved her left arm—the one that was not broken—from below the covers and let her hand dangle down, feeling, as she always did in the mornings, for Lob's furry head. The doctor nodded slowly.

Word Power

strictly (strikt´ lē) *adv.* following a rule in an exact way

Reading Skill

Question Reread the paragraph highlighted in green. Which is the **best** question to ask yourself to help you understand what is important here? Check the correct response.

- ☐ Why is Granny Pearce so mean to the guard?
- ☐ Why is Lob shaking his head like that?
- ☐ Are Granny Pearce and Lob friends?

English Coach

Here, *stirred* means "changed one's position." What is another meaning of *stirred*?

_____

_____

_____

_____

Comprehension Check

Reread the boxed text. How does Sandy respond to Lob?

_____

_____

_____

_____

_____

Reading Skill

Evaluate Reread the highlighted sentences and the rest of the page. Here, the author suggests that the dog that comes to the hospital is Lob. Do you think the author does a good job explaining that the dog is really Lob? Why or why not?

_____

_____

_____

_____

_____

_____

"All right," he whispered. "Let him go to the bedside." Granny Pearce and Lob moved to the bedside. She looked at the smile on her granddaughter's face as the groping fingers found Lob's wet ears and gently pulled them. "Good boy," whispered Sandy, and fell asleep again.

Granny Pearce led Lob out into the passage again. There she let go of him and he ran off swiftly down the stairs. She would have followed him, but Bert and Jean had come out into the passage, and she spoke to Bert fiercely.

"I don't know why you were so foolish as not to bring the dog before! Leaving him to find the way here himself—"

"But, Mother!" said Jean Pengelly. "That can't have been Lob."

"Not Lob? I've known that dog nine years! I suppose I ought to know my own granddaughter's dog?"

"Listen, Mother," said Bert. "Lob was killed by the same truck that hit Sandy. Don found him—when he went to look for Sandy's schoolbag. He was—he was dead. No question of that. Don told me on the phone—he and Will Hoskins rowed a half mile out to sea and sank the dog with a lump of concrete tied to his collar."

"_Sank him at sea?_ Then what—?"

Slowly old Mrs. Pearce, and then the other two, turned to look at the trail of dripping-wet footprints that led down the hospital stairs.

In the Pengellys' garden they have a stone, under the palm tree. It says: "Lob. Sandy's dog. Buried at sea."

Respond to Literature

Lob's Girl

A Comprehension Check

Answer the following questions in the spaces provided.

1. Where do Lob and Sandy first meet? _____

2. Why does Mr. Dodsworth give Lob to the Pengelly family? _____

_____

B Reading Skills

Answer the following questions in the spaces provided.

1. **Evaluate** Think about how far Lob travels to be with Sandy. Does it seem
   realistic to you that a dog would travel so far to be with someone? Why or

   why not? _____

   _____

2 **Question** Ask yourself the question: "Why was the dog in the hospital
   shaking his head as if to remove something?" How does asking this question

   help you understand the ending? _____

   _____

   _____

3. **Evaluate** Do you believe that a pet could actually help someone who is

   hurt or sick to feel better? Why or why not? _____

   _____

   _____

C Word Power

Complete each sentence below, using one of the words in the box.

decisively	dutifully	resolutions
accompanied	objection	assured	strictly

1. It is _____ against the rules to stay out after dark.

2. The children kept their _____ about eating their vegetables and doing their chores every day.

3. The players _____ the coach that they would do their best.

4. After much discussion, Judge Santos said firmly and _____ that the man was guilty of the crime.

5. When the rules were changed to make sure the game was fair to everyone, there was no _____.

6. Mrs. Johnson _____ her daughter on her first trip to the dentist.

7. When its owner whistled, the dog _____ trotted over.

D Literary Element: Foreshadowing

Read the passages below from "Lob's Girl." The first passage is from the moment right after Sandy and Lob first meet. The second passage is from the moment right before Sandy and Lob leave the house one stormy night. As you read, think about how the passages hint at what will happen in the story. Then answer the questions that follow.

"Oh, no, I think he's *beautiful*," said Sandy truly.[1] She picked up a bit of driftwood and threw it.[2] Lob came back with the stick, beaming, and gave it to Sandy.[3] It was then that Lob fell in love with Sandy.[4] But with Sandy, too, it was love at first sight.[5]

Unwillingly Sandy put on the damp raincoat she had just taken off, fastened Lob's lead to his collar, and set off to walk through the dusk to Aunt Becky's cottage, which was five minutes' climb up the steep hill.[6] The wind was howling.[7]

1. In sentences 1–5, Lob does not yet belong to Sandy. How does this passage hint that they will be together? _____

_____

_____

_____

2. How do sentences 6–7 hint that something bad is going to happen?

_____

_____

_____

E A Letter from Sandy

Imagine that you are Sandy. Write a thank you letter to the hospital for allowing Lob to come and visit you. In your letter, explain why you are sure that the dog was Lob.

Dear Doctors,

Thank you for the good care you gave me. My mother said that when I arrived, I was _____

_____

Then you allowed my dog to see me. When I heard him whine, I

_____

_____

_____

I know that the dog was Lob because _____

_____

_____

Thank you again for letting the dog come to see me.

Sincerely,
Sandy Pengelly

Assessment

Fill in the circle next to each correct answer.

1. Who is Lob closest to in the story?
   - ○ A. Jean Pengelly
   - ○ B. Sandy Pengelly
   - ○ C. Tess Pengelly
   - ○ D. Granny Pearce

2. Which question would **best** help you understand how Lob comes to live with the Pengellys?
   - ○ A. Why does Lob keep coming back to Sandy?
   - ○ B. How long has Mr. Dodsworth owned Lob?
   - ○ C. Does Mr. Pengelly want a dog?
   - ○ D. Why do the children like Lob?

3. Which detail from the story **best** foreshadows that there might be an accident?
   - ○ A. The name of the hotel is Fisherman's Arms.
   - ○ B. The sign says the road is steep and dangerous.
   - ○ C. Mr. Dodsworth offers Lob to the Pengellys.
   - ○ D. Lob ruins Mrs. Pengelly's puddings and jelly.

4. Who finds Sandy right after the accident?
   - ○ A. Mr. Dodsworth
   - ○ B. Aunt Rebecca
   - ○ C. Lob
   - ○ D. Dr. Travers

5. Which of the following words means "a protest"?
   - ○ A. accompanied
   - ○ B. decisively
   - ○ C. objection
   - ○ D. strictly

Get Ready to Read!

Meet Piri Thomas

Piri Thomas was born in 1928. He first started to write while he was in prison for attempting an armed robbery. Thomas wrote as a way to deal with prison life. He wrote about the lives of African Americans and Puerto Ricans. He continued to write after he got out of prison. He also worked in centers to help people stay off drugs and start new lives. "Amigo Brothers" was first published in 1978.

What You Know

Think about your closest friend. What qualities make that person such a good friend?

Reason to Read

Read to find out how two friends respond to a test of their friendship.

Background Info

The Golden Gloves tournament began in Chicago in the 1920s. Young amateur boxers competed in different weight classes. The winners of each class received a small golden glove as their reward. The Golden Gloves programs continue today. These programs often provide opportunities for young men and women who have had difficult lives. The goals of the programs are to encourage positive values for young people and to help them develop physical and social skills.

Word Power

barrage (bə räzh´) *n.* a heavy attack; p. 45
The president faced a *barrage* of questions.

psyching (sī´ king) *v.* getting into the right state of mind; p. 47
The tennis star was *psyching* herself to win by picturing herself making great shots.

escorted (es kor´ tid) *v.* traveled with someone to show support or to honor; p. 51
The judges *escorted* the contest winner to the stage.

piston (pis´ tən) *n.* part of an engine that goes up and down very fast; p. 53
His fists hit the punching bag like a *piston*.

feinted (fān´ tid) *v.* made a tricky move to draw attention away from the real attack;
p. 54
Jesse *feinted* a run in one direction, but then ran in another direction.

mute (mūt) *adj.* silent; p. 55
Everyone in the classroom was *mute* during the test.

embraced (em brāsd´) *v.* hugged; p. 56
The two old friends *embraced* when they met again after many years.

**Answer the following questions, using one of the new words above.
Write your answers in the spaces provided.**

1. Which word goes with "faked a punch"? _____

2. Which word goes with "hugged a baby"? _____

3. Which word goes with "not making a sound"? _____

4. Which word goes with "walked with someone"? _____

5. Which word goes with "thinking about how you're going to win"? _____

6. Which word goes with "a lot of punches being thrown"? _____

7. Which word goes with "something that moves up and down"? _____

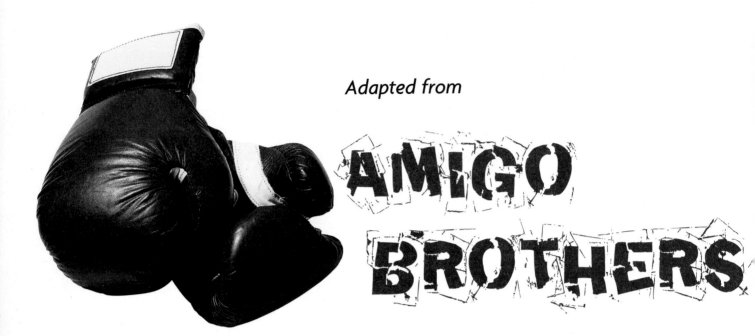

Adapted from

AMIGO BROTHERS

Piri Thomas

Antonio Cruz and Felix Vargas were both seventeen years old. They were so together in friendship that they felt themselves to be brothers. They had known each other since childhood on the lower east side of Manhattan. They grew up in the same apartment building on Fifth Street between Avenue A and Avenue B.

Antonio was fair, lean, and lanky, while Felix was dark, short, and husky. Antonio's hair was always falling over his eyes, while Felix wore his black hair in a natural Afro style.

Each youngster had a dream of someday becoming lightweight champion of the world. Early morning sunrises would find them running along the East River Drive, wrapped in sweat shirts, short towels around their necks, and handkerchiefs Apache style around their foreheads.

Antonio and Felix slept, ate, rapped, and dreamt positive. Between them, they had a huge collection of *Fight* magazines, plus a scrapbook filled with torn tickets to every boxing match they had ever attended, and some clippings of their own.

Each had fought many bouts representing their community and had won two gold-plated medals plus a silver and bronze medallion. Antonio's lean form and long reach made him the better boxer, while Felix's short and muscular frame made him the better slugger. Now, after a series of elimination bouts, they had been informed that they were to meet each other in the division finals that were scheduled for the seventh of August, two weeks away—the winner to represent the Boys Club in the Golden Gloves Championship Tournament.

One morning less than a week before their bout, they met as usual for their daily workout. They fooled around with a few jabs at the air, slapped skin, and then took off, running lightly along the dirty East River's edge.

Antonio glanced at Felix who kept his eyes purposely straight ahead, pausing from time to time to do some fancy leg work while throwing one-twos followed by upper cuts to an imaginary jaw. Antonio then beat the air with a **barrage** of body blows and short destructive lefts with an overhand jaw-breaking right.

After a mile or so, Felix puffed and said, "Let's stop a while, bro. I think we both got something to say to each other."

Antonio nodded.

Felix leaned heavily on the river's railing and stared across to the shores of Brooklyn. Finally, he broke the silence.

Word Power
barrage (bə räzh´) *n.* a heavy attack

Literary Element

Conflict Reread the highlighted sentence and the rest of the paragraph. What is the conflict between the two friends? Is this an internal or an external conflict? How do you know?

_____

_____

_____

_____

Comprehension Check

Reread the boxed paragraph. Antonio and Felix are practicing boxing moves. Circle the different phrases that tell you what punches they are practicing.

Reading Skill

Question Reread the highlighted sentences. What is the **best** question to ask yourself to help you understand the conversation between Felix and Antonio? Check the correct response.

☐ Where are the boys talking?

☐ Why does each boy tell the other he wants to win?

☐ How will the boys train for the big fight?

Comprehension Check

Reread the boxed text. How do the two boys decide to train before the fight? Underline the answer in the text.

"Man, I don't know how to come out with it."

Antonio helped. "It's about our fight, right?"

"Yeah, right." Felix's eyes squinted at the rising orange sun.

"I've been thinking about it too, *panin*. In fact, since we found out it was going to be me and you, I've been awake at night, pulling punches on you, trying not to hurt you."

"Same here. It ain't natural not to think about the fight. I mean, we both are *cheverote* fighters and we both want to win. But only one of us can win. There ain't no draws in the eliminations."

Felix tapped Antonio gently on the shoulder. "I don't mean to sound like I'm bragging, bro. But I wanna win, fair and square."

Antonio nodded quietly. "Yeah. We both know that in the ring the better man wins. Friend or no friend, brother or no..."

Did You Know?

A boxing ring is not shaped like a ring at all. It is a square platform with horizontal ropes on each side.
. . . .

Felix finished it for him. "Brother. Tony, let's promise something right here. Okay?"

"If it's fair, *hermano*, I'm for it."

"It's fair, Tony. When we get into the ring, it's gotta be like we never met. You understand, don'tcha?"

"*Sí*, I know." Tony smiled. "No pulling punches. We go all the way."

"Yeah, that's right. Listen, Tony. Don't you think it's a good idea if we don't see each other until the day of the fight? I'm going to stay with my Aunt Lucy in the Bronx. I can use Gleason's Gym for working out."

Tony scratched his nose thoughtfully. "Yeah, it would be better for our heads." He held out his hand, palm upward. "Deal?"

"Deal." Felix lightly slapped open skin.

"You ain't worried, are you?" Tony asked.

"No way, man." Felix laughed out loud. "I got too much smarts for that. I just think it's cooler if we split right here."

The *amigo* brothers were not ashamed to hug each other tightly.

"Guess you're right. Watch yourself, Felix. I hear there's some pretty heavy dudes up in the Bronx. *Suavecito*, okay?"

"Okay. You watch yourself too, sabe?"

Tony jogged away. Felix watched his friend disappear from view, throwing rights and lefts.

The evening before the big fight, Tony made his way to the roof of his building. He tried not to think of Felix, feeling he had succeeded in **psyching** his mind. But only in the ring would he really know. To spare Felix hurt, he would have to knock him out, early and quick.

Up in the South Bronx, Felix decided to take in a movie in an effort to keep Antonio's face away from his fists. The flick was *The Champion* with Kirk Douglas, the third time Felix was seeing it.

Felix became the champ and Tony the challenger.

Felix saw himself in the ring, blasting Antonio against the ropes. The champ had to be forcibly held back. The challenger fell slowly to the canvas.

When Felix finally left the theatre, he had figured out how to psyche himself for tomorrow's fight. It was Felix the Champion vs. Antonio the Challenger.

Word Power

psyching (sī´ king) *v.* getting into the right state of mind

Background Info

Suavecito (swä´ vä sē´ tō) is an American Spanish slang expression meaning "Take it easy." *Sabe* (sä´ bā) is Spanish for "You know?"

Connect to the Text

Reread the boxed text. To prepare himself for the fight, Felix pictures himself as the champion in a movie. Have you ever imagined yourself as a character in a movie or a book? Write about it below.

_____

_____

_____

_____

Reading Skill

Evaluate Look at the painting. Do you think this fighter shows the same determination as the amigo brothers? Why or why not?

_____

_____

_____

_____

_____

_____

Vinny Pazienza, 1996. Bill Angresano. Oil on canvas, 24 x 20 in. Big Fights Boxing Memorabilia, New York.

He walked up some dark streets, deserted except for small pockets of nervous-looking kids wearing gang colors. He let himself quietly into his Aunt Lucy's apartment and went straight to bed, falling into an unsteady sleep with sounds of the gong for Round One.

Antonio was passing some heavy time on his rooftop. How would the fight tomorrow affect his relationship with Felix? Felix, his *amigo* brother, was not going to be Felix at all in the ring. Just an opponent with another face. Antonio went to sleep, hearing the opening bell for the first round. Like his friend in the South Bronx, he prayed for victory, with a quick clean knockout in the first round.

Literary Element

Conflict Reread the highlighted paragraph. Is this an internal or an external conflict? How do you know?

_____

_____

_____

_____

_____

STOP Stop here for **Break Time** on the next page.

Break Time

Antonio Cruz and Felix Vargas share a dream. Yet the two boxers are different from each other in some ways. Think about the ways they are alike and different. In the middle of the diagram below, list three ways they are alike. Then under each of their names, list three ways each boy is different from the other.

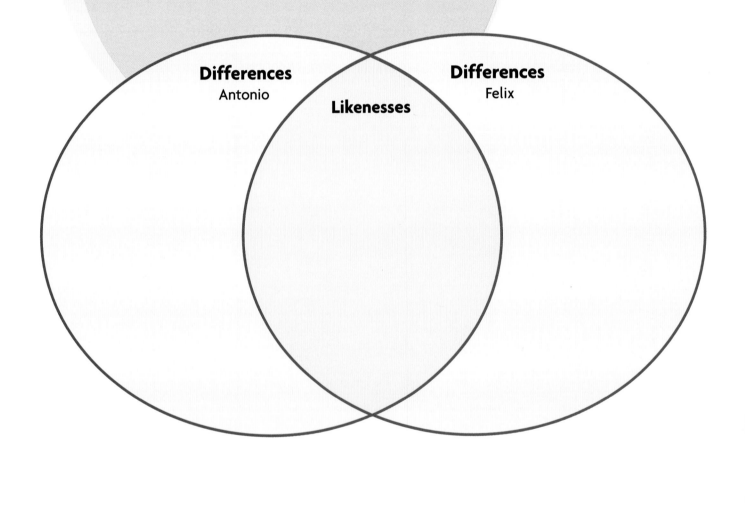

Differences
Antonio

Likenesses

Differences
Felix

GO Continue reading on the next page.

The fight had created great interest in the neighborhood. Antonio and Felix were well-liked and respected. Each had his own loyal following.

The fight was scheduled to take place in Tompkins Square Park. It had been decided that the gymnasium of the Boys Club was not large enough to hold all the people who were sure to attend. In Tompkins Square Park, everyone who wanted could view the fight from ringside or window fire escapes or apartment building rooftops.

The junior high school across from Tompkins Square Park served as the dressing room for all the fighters. Each was given a separate classroom with desktops, covered with mats, serving as resting tables.

The fighters changed from their street clothes into fighting gear. Antonio wore white trunks, black socks, and black shoes. Felix wore sky blue trunks, red socks, and white boxing shoes. Each had dressing gowns to match their fighting trunks with their names neatly stitched on the back.

The loudspeakers blared into the open windows of the school. There were speeches by honored guests, community leaders, and great boxers of yesteryear. Mixed with the speeches were the sounds of other boxing events. After the sixth bout, Felix was much relieved when his trainer Charlie said, "Time change. Quick knockout. This is it. We're on."

Waiting time was over. Felix was **escorted** from the classroom by a dozen fans in white T-shirts with the word FELIX across their fronts. Antonio was escorted down a different stairwell and guided through a roped-off path.

Word Power

escorted (es kor´ tid) v. traveled with someone to show support or to honor

English Coach

A *bilingual* person can speak two languages. Sometimes when a word starts with *bi-*, it means "two of something." In *bicycle*, the *bi-* tells you that it has two of something, in this case wheels. How many wheels does a tricycle have? What part of the word tells you that?

_____

_____

_____

Background Info

Reread the boxed text. This means that each boy made the Sign of the Cross by touching his forehead, his chest, and then each shoulder. This is something Roman Catholics do before they say a prayer.

As the two climbed into the ring, the crowd exploded with a roar. Antonio and Felix both bowed gracefully and then raised their arms in greeting.

Antonio tried to be cool, but even as the roar began, he turned slowly to meet Felix's eyes looking directly into his. Felix nodded his head and Antonio nodded back. And both as one, just as quickly, turned away to face his own corner.

Bong! Bong! Bong! The roar turned to stillness.

"Ladies and Gentlemen, *Señores y Señoras.*"

The announcer spoke slowly, pleased at his bilingual efforts.

"Now the moment we have all been waiting for—the main event between two fine young Puerto Rican fighters, products of our lower east side.

"In this corner, weighing 134 pounds, Felix Vargas. And in this corner, weighing 133 pounds, Antonio Cruz. The winner will represent the Boys Club in the tournament of champions, the Golden Gloves. There will be no draw. May the best man win."

The cheering of the crowd shook the window panes of the old buildings surrounding Tompkins Square Park. At the center of the ring, the referee was giving instructions to the youngsters.

"Keep your punches up. No low blows. No punching on the back of the head. Keep your heads up. Understand. Let's have a clean fight. Now shake hands and come out fighting."

Both youngsters touched gloves and nodded. They turned and danced quickly to their corners. Their head towels and dressing gowns were lifted neatly from their shoulders by their trainers. Antonio crossed himself. Felix did the same.

Bong! Bong! Round one. Felix and Antonio turned and faced each other squarely in a fighting pose. Felix wasted no time. He came in fast, head low, half hunched toward his right shoulder, and lashed out with a straight left. He missed a right cross as Antonio moved quickly aside and came back with one-two-three lefts that snapped Felix's head back, sending a mild shock through him. Antonio danced, a joy to behold. His left hand was like a **piston** pumping jabs one right after another with seeming ease. Felix bobbed and weaved and never stopped pushing in. He knew that he was not his best at long range. Antonio had too much reach on him. Only by coming in close could Felix hope to achieve the dreamed-of knockout.

Antonio knew the dynamite that was stored in his *amigo* brother's fist. Felix trapped him against the ropes just long enough to pour some punishing rights and lefts to Antonio's hard midsection. Antonio slipped away from Felix, crashing two lefts to his head, which set Felix's right ear to ringing.

Bong! Both *amigos* froze a punch well on its way, sending up a roar of approval for good sportsmanship.

Felix walked briskly back to his corner. His right ear had not stopped ringing. Antonio danced his way toward his stool still fine, except for glowing glove burns that looked angry red against the whiteness of his midribs.

"Watch that right, Tony." His trainer talked into his ear. "Remember Felix always goes to the body. He'll want you to drop your hands for his overhand left or right. Got it?"

Word Power
piston (pis´ tən) *n.* part of an engine that goes up and down very fast

Reading Skill

Evaluate Reread the highlighted text. Earlier in the story, the author mentions Antonio's and Felix's different boxing styles. Do you think he does a good job here showing how their fighting styles are different? Why or why not?

_____

_____

_____

_____

_____

_____

Comprehension Check

Reread the boxed text. What do Felix and Antonio do when the bell sounds to end the round? Check the correct response.
- [ ] They stop mid-punch.
- [ ] They keep punching past the bell.
- [ ] They fall to the floor of the ring.

Reading Skill

Evaluate Reread the paragraphs highlighted in green. Does the author's detailed description of the fight make it seem real and exciting? Why or why not?

_____

_____

_____

_____

_____

_____

English Coach

A possum is an animal that pretends to be dead to trick an animal that is threatening it. Felix is *playing possum,* or pretending to be hurt, to trick Antonio. Write a sentence using the phrase *playing possum.*

_____

_____

Felix's corner was also busy.

"You gotta get in there, fella." Felix's trainer poured water over his curly Afro locks. "Get in there or he's gonna chop you up from way back."

Bong! Bong! Round two. Felix was off his stool and rushed Antonio like a bull, sending a hard right to his head. Beads of water exploded from Antonio's long hair.

Antonio, hurt, sent back a blurring barrage of lefts and rights that only meant pain to Felix. He returned with a short left to the head followed by a looping right to the body.

Antonio waited for the rush that was sure to come. Felix closed in and **feinted** with his left shoulder and threw his right instead.

Lights suddenly exploded inside Felix's head as Antonio moved quickly to one side and hit him with a piston-like left, catching him squarely on the point of his chin.

The crowd went wild as Felix's legs momentarily buckled. He fought off a series of rights and lefts and came back with a strong right that taught Antonio respect.

Antonio danced in carefully. He knew Felix had the habit of playing possum when hurt, to trick an opponent into coming within reach of the powerful bombs he carried in each fist.

Antonio, a bit too eager, moved in too close and Felix had him tangled in a rip-roaring, punching toe-to-toe slugfest that brought the whole Tompkins Square Park screaming to its feet.

Suddenly a short right caught Antonio squarely on the chin. His long legs turned to jelly and his arms swung out desperately. Felix, grunting like a bull, threw wild punches from every direction. Antonio, groggy, bobbed and weaved, escaping most of the blows. Suddenly his head cleared. His left flashed out hard and straight catching Felix on the bony part of his nose.

Word Power

feinted (fān′ tid) *v.* made a tricky move to draw attention away from the real attack

Felix lashed back with a haymaker, right off the ghetto streets. At the same instant, his eye caught another left hook from Antonio. Felix swung out trying to clear the pain. Only the frenzied screaming of those along ringside let him know that he had dropped Antonio.

Fighting off the growing haze, Antonio struggled to his feet, got up, ducked, and threw a smashing right that dropped Felix flat on his back.

Felix got up as fast as he could in his own corner, groggy but still game. His head cleared to hear the bell sound at the end of the round. He was very glad. In his corner, Antonio was doing what all fighters do when they are hurt. They sit and smile at everyone.

The referee signaled the ring doctor to check the fighters out. He did so and then gave his okay.

Bong! Round three—the final round. Up to now it had been tic-tac-toe, pretty much even. But everyone knew there could be no draw and that this round would decide the winner.

This time, to Felix's surprise, it was Antonio who came out fast, charging across the ring. Felix braced himself but couldn't ward off the barrage of punches. Antonio drove Felix hard against the ropes.

The crowd ate it up.

Both pounded away. Neither gave an inch and neither fell to the canvas. Felix's left eye was tightly closed. Dark, purplish-red blood poured from Antonio's nose. They fought toe-to-toe.

The sounds of their blows were loud in contrast to the silence of a crowd gone completely **mute.**

Bong! Bong! Bong! The bell sounded over and over again.

Felix and Antonio were past hearing. Their blows continued to pound on each other like hailstones.

Word Power

mute (mūt) *adj.* silent

My Workspace

Background Info

A haymaker is a very strong punch designed to knock a boxer down. The punch gets its name from the motion that farmers use to cut hay.

Reading Skill

Question Reread the highlighted paragraphs. What is the **best** question to ask yourself while reading to get the most information from the passage? Check the correct response.

☐ What are hailstones?

☐ Why are the boys fighting so hard?

☐ Does the crowd like one boxer more than the other?

55

Reading Skill

Evaluate Reread the highlighted text. Why do you think the author chooses not to reveal the result of the fight? How does the word *champions* in the last sentence give you a clue to the author's reason?

_____

_____

_____

_____

_____

_____

Finally the referee and the two trainers pried Felix and Antonio apart. Cold water was poured over them to bring them back to their senses.

They looked around and then rushed toward each other. A cry of alarm went up from the crowd. Was this a fight to the death instead of a boxing match?

The fear soon gave way to wave upon wave of cheering as the two *amigos* **embraced.**

No matter what the decision, they knew they would always be champions to each other.

BONG! BONG! BONG! "Ladies and Gentlemen. *Señores* and *Señoras.* The winner and representative to the Golden Gloves Tournament of Champions is..."

The announcer turned to point to the winner and found himself alone.

Arm in arm, the champions had already left the ring.

Boxing. G. Cominetti. 75.3 x 92 cm. Private collection.

Does the artist's style of painting fit the feeling of the story? Why or why not?

_____

Word Power

embraced (em brāsd´) *v.* hugged

Respond to Literature

AMIGO BROTHERS

A Comprehension Check

Answer the following questions in the spaces provided.

1. What hope do Antonio and Felix share? _____

   _____

2. How does the fight end? _____

   _____

B Reading Skills

Answer the following questions in the spaces provided.

1. **Question** What question could you ask about the boys' friendship that
   would help you understand the end of the story? _____

   _____

   _____

2. **Evaluate** After the boxing match, Antonio and Felix are still best friends.
   Do you think this is realistic? Why or why not? _____

   _____

   _____

3. **Evaluate** As the author describes the fight, he makes it sound pretty even.
   Does this make reading about the fight more exciting? Why or why not?

   _____

   _____

C Word Power

Complete each sentence below, using one of the words in the box.

barrage	psyching	escorted	piston
feinted	mute	embraced	

1. Sally _____ to the left and took a jump shot.

2. The parents _____ the children to their classrooms on the first day of school.

3. Jeff worked each leg like a _____ as he rode his bike up the hill.

4. The little girl tightly _____ her favorite doll.

5. There was a _____ of rain on the roof when the storm started.

6. The children were still and _____ during the movie.

7. Jaime was _____ himself to win the race by picturing himself crossing the finish line first.

D Literary Element: Conflict

Read the passages below from "Amigo Brothers." As you read, think about the types of conflict that are being described. Then answer the questions that follow.

Antonio was passing some heavy time on his rooftop.[1] How would the fight tomorrow affect his relationship with Felix?[2] Felix, his *amigo* brother, was not going to be Felix at all in the ring.[3] Just an opponent with another face.[4] Antonio went to sleep, hearing the opening bell for the first round.[5] Like his friend in the South Bronx, he prayed for victory, with a quick clean knockout in the first round.[6]

As the two climbed into the ring, the crowd exploded with a roar.[7] Antonio and Felix both bowed gracefully and then raised their arms in greeting.[8]

Antonio tried to be cool, but even as the roar began, he turned slowly to meet Felix's eyes looking directly into his.[9]

1. In sentences 1-6, what kind of conflict is being described: internal or external? How can you tell? How does Antonio try to resolve this conflict?

   _____

   _____

   _____

2. What kind of conflict is being described in sentences 7–9? How can you tell? How will this conflict be resolved? _____

   _____

   _____

   _____

E Boxing Match Article

Pretend you are a sportswriter writing an article about the fight between Antonio and Felix. Write about what the boxers look like, what happens in the fight, and who you think won the fight.

SPORTS   *Tompkins Square Times*

THE FIGHT AT TOMPKINS SQUARE PARK

Felix and Antonio are both good friends. They look like good boxers too.

Felix is _____

Antonio is _____

They both fight very well throughout the match. When the bell rings at the end of the fight, _____

_____

_____

They leave before a winner is announced. Finally, the announcer says the winner of the fight is _____

However, after seeing today's match between these two friends, I believe they are both champions because _____

_____

_____

Article written by _____

Assessment

Fill in the circle next to each correct answer.

1. What does each boy dream of becoming?
   - ○ A. a boxing trainer
   - ○ B. President of the Boys Club
   - ○ C. a movie star like Kirk Douglas
   - ○ D. lightweight champion of the world

2. Where does Felix go to live before the fight?
   - ○ A. Tompkins Square
   - ○ B. the Boys Club
   - ○ C. his Aunt Lucy's place in the Bronx
   - ○ D. the apartment building on Fifth Street

3. Which question would **best** help you understand why Felix and Antonio decide not to see each other before the fight?
   - ○ A. Is each boy worried about fighting his best friend?
   - ○ B. Does each boy worry the other will see his best moves?
   - ○ C. Is the gym in the Bronx a better gym?
   - ○ D. Does each boy really prefer to train alone?

4. Which is **not** a conflict in the story?
   - ○ A. the fight between the two friends
   - ○ B. Antonio's feelings about fighting Felix
   - ○ C. Felix's feelings about fighting Antonio
   - ○ D. the choice of where to hold the fight

5. Which of the following words means "traveled with someone"?
   - ○ A. embraced
   - ○ B. escorted
   - ○ C. barrage
   - ○ D. feinted

Get Ready to Read!

Broken Chain

Meet Gary Soto

Gary Soto was born in 1952. He grew up in a Spanish-speaking neighborhood much like the neighborhood in this story. Like his parents and grandparents, Soto worked for a time picking fruit at different farms and orchards. His love of writing came later. "Writing is my one talent," he says. "There are a lot of people who never discover what their talent is. . . . I am very lucky to have found mine." "Broken Chain" was first published in 1990.

What You Know

Are you completely happy with how you look? Most young people are not. Why do you think some young people spend so much time thinking about how they look, what they wear, and what other people think of them?

Reason to Read

Read to find out about a seventh-grade boy who is very concerned about his looks.

Background Info

Your body image is the way you feel about how you look to yourself and to others. Ads and images in magazines and on TV can shape the way people think they should look. Sometimes ads make it hard for people to feel comfortable with their own looks because they don't look like the people in the images they see around them.

Word Power

swaggered (swag′ ərd) *v.* walked in a bold, superior way; p. 65
The famous singer *swaggered* across the stage.

winced (winst) *v.* pulled back slightly in pain or fear; p. 68
The batter *winced* when the ball hit her arm.

wadded (wod′ əd) *adj.* something made into the shape of a ball; p. 71
The child rolled the *wadded* clay on the floor.

frustrated (frus′ trāt əd) *adj.* unhappy because something is not working as hoped or expected; p. 73
The fans are *frustrated* because their team lost again.

retrieved (ri trēvd′) *v.* brought back; p. 73
Using a long pole, Sally *retrieved* her hat from the water.

desperation (des′ pə rā′ shən) *n.* a hopeless feeling; p. 74
Another day of rain on our vacation caused us to feel great *desperation*.

trudging (truj′ ing) *v.* walking heavily or slowly; p. 74
After the flood, everyone was *trudging* through mud-covered streets.

Answer the following questions that contain the new words above. Write your answers in the spaces provided.

1. If you show *desperation*, are you feeling hopeful or discouraged? _____

2. If you *retrieved* something, did you send it somewhere or get it back? _____

3. If a piece of tissue is *wadded*, is it shaped like a ball or ripped into shreds?

   _____

4. If you are *trudging* uphill, are you walking slowly or quickly? _____

5. When you feel *frustrated*, are you feeling happy or unhappy? _____

6. If a child *winced*, was the child feeling joy or pain? _____

7. If someone *swaggered* into a room, was the person feeling bold or afraid?

   _____

Broken Chain

Gary Soto

Background Info

In the 1400s and early 1500s, the Aztec people ruled what is now central and southern Mexico. The Aztec Empire ended when it was defeated by the Spanish in 1521.

Connect to the Text

Reread the boxed sentences. Who are some musicians or famous people you admire?

_____

_____

_____

_____

Alfonso sat on the porch trying to push his crooked teeth to where he thought they belonged. He hated the way he looked. Last week he did fifty sit-ups a day, thinking that he would burn those already apparent ripples on his stomach to even deeper ripples, dark ones, so when he went swimming at the canal next summer, girls in cut-offs would notice. And the guys would think he was tough, someone who could take a punch and give it back. He wanted "cuts" like those he had seen on a calendar of an Aztec warrior standing on a pyramid with a woman in his arms. (Even she had cuts he could see beneath her thin dress.) The calendar hung above the cash register at La Plaza. Orsua, the owner, said Alfonso could have the calendar at the end of the year if the waitress, Yolanda, didn't take it first.

Alfonso studied the magazine pictures of rock stars for a hairstyle. He liked the way Prince looked—and the bass player from Los Lobos. Alfonso thought he would look cool with his hair razored into a V in the back and streaked purple. But he knew his mother wouldn't go for it. And his father, who was *puro Mexicano,* would sit in his chair after work, sullen as a toad, and call him "sissy."

Alfonso didn't dare color his hair. But one day he had had it butched on the top, like in the magazines. His father had come home that evening from a softball game, happy that his team had drilled four homers in a thirteen-to-five bashing of Color Tile. He'd **swaggered** into the living room, but had stopped cold when he saw Alfonso and asked, not joking but with real concern, "Did you hurt your head at school? *Qué pasó?*"

Alfonso had pretended not to hear his father and had gone to his room, where he studied his hair from all angles in the mirror. He liked what he saw until he smiled and realized for the first time that his teeth were crooked, like a pile of wrecked cars. He grew depressed and turned away from the mirror. He sat on his bed and leafed through the rock magazine until he came to the rock star with the butched top. His mouth was closed, but Alfonso was sure his teeth weren't crooked.

Alfonso didn't want to be the handsomest kid at school, but he was determined to be better-looking than average. The next day he spent his lawn-mowing money on a new shirt, and, with a pocket-knife, scooped the moons of dirt from under his fingernails.

He spent hours in front of the mirror trying to herd his teeth into place with his thumb. He asked his mother if he could have braces, like Frankie Molina, her godson, but he asked at the wrong time. She was at the kitchen table licking the envelope to the house payment. She glared up at him. "Do you think money grows on trees?"

His mother clipped coupons from magazines and newspapers, kept a vegetable garden in the summer, and shopped at Penney's and K-Mart. Their family ate a lot of *frijoles*, which was OK because nothing else tasted so good, though one time Alfonso had had Chinese pot stickers and thought they were the next best food in the world.

Word Power

swaggered (swag´ ərd) *v.* walked in a bold, superior way

Comprehension Check

Reread the boxed text. How does Alfonso try to fix his teeth? Why does he try to fix them this way?

_____

_____

_____

_____

_____

English Coach

Here, *too* means "more than enough." It is important to tell the difference between the words *to*, *too*, and *two*. *To* often means "in the direction of." *Two* refers to the number. Read the sentences below and fill in *to*, *too*, or *two* where they belong.

1. He went _____ the store.
2. She ate _____ scoops of ice cream.
3. The weather is _____ hot.

He didn't ask his mother for braces again, even when she was in a better mood. He decided to fix his teeth by pushing on them with his thumbs. After breakfast that Saturday he went to his room, closed the door quietly, turned the radio on, and pushed for three hours straight.

He pushed for ten minutes, rested for five, and every half hour, during a radio commercial, checked to see if his smile had improved. It hadn't.

Eventually he grew bored and went outside with an old gym sock to wipe down his bike, a ten-speed from Montgomery Ward. His thumbs were tired and wrinkled and pink, the way they got when he stayed in the bathtub too long.

Alfonso's older brother, Ernie, rode up on his Montgomery Ward bicycle looking depressed. He parked his bike against the peach tree and sat on the back steps, keeping his head down and stepping on ants that came too close.

Alfonso knew better than to say anything when Ernie looked mad. He turned his bike over, balancing it on the handlebars and seat, and flossed the spokes with the sock. When he was finished, he pressed a knuckle to his teeth until they tingled.

Ernie groaned and said, "Ah, man."

Alfonso waited a few minutes before asking, "What's the matter?" He pretended not to be too interested. He picked up a wad of steel wool and continued cleaning the spokes.

Ernie hesitated, not sure if Alfonso would laugh. But it came out. "Those girls didn't show up. And you better not laugh."

"What girls?"

Then Alfonso remembered his brother bragging about how he and Frostie met two girls from Kings Canyon Junior High last week on Halloween night. They were dressed as gypsies, the costume for all poor *Chicanas*—they just had to borrow scarves and gaudy red lipstick from their *abuelitas*.

Alfonso walked over to his brother. He compared their two bikes: his gleamed like a handful of dimes, while Ernie's looked dirty.

"They said we were supposed to wait at the corner. But they didn't show up. Me and Frostie waited and waited like fools. They were playing games with us."

Alfonso thought that was a pretty dirty trick but sort of funny too. He would have to try that some day.

"Were they cute?" Alfonso asked.

"I guess so."

"Do you think you could recognize them?"

"If they were wearing red lipstick, maybe."

Alfonso sat with his brother in silence, both of them smearing ants with their floppy high tops. Girls could sure act weird, especially the ones you meet on Halloween.

Later that day, Alfonso sat on the porch pressing on his teeth. Press, relax; press, relax. His portable radio was on, but not loud enough to make Mr. Rojas come down the steps and wave his cane at him.

Alfonso's father drove up. Alfonso could tell by the way he sat in his truck, a Datsun with a different-colored front fender, that his team had lost their softball game. Alfonso got off the porch in a hurry because he knew his father would be in a bad mood. He went to the backyard, where he unlocked his bike, sat on it with the kickstand down, and pressed on his teeth. He punched himself in the stomach, and growled, "Cuts." Then he patted his butch and whispered, "Fresh."

After a while Alfonso pedaled up the street, hands in his pockets, toward Foster's Freeze, where he was chased by a ratlike Chihuahua. At his old school, John Burroughs Elementary, he found a kid hanging upside down on the top of a barbed-wire fence with a girl looking up at him.

Did You Know?
The Chihuahua is the world's smallest breed of dog.

Reading Skill
Evaluate Reread the highlighted paragraphs. What do you think of the girls' trick? What do you think of Ernie's and Alfonso's reactions to the trick?

Reading Skill

Question Reread the highlighted sentences. Which is the **best** question to ask yourself to help you understand more about Alfonso? Check the correct response.

☐ Why does Alfonso help the kid?

☐ Who needs Alfonso's help?

☐ Do Alfonso and the kid know each other?

Connect to the Text

Reread the boxed paragraph. Think about your own experiences trying to get to know someone you like. What tips would you give Alfonso to help him talk to Sandra?

_____

_____

_____

_____

_____

Alfonso skidded to a stop and helped the kid untangle his pants from the barbed wire. The kid was grateful. He had been afraid he would have to stay up there all night. His sister, who was Alfonso's age, was also grateful. If she had to go home and tell her mother that Frankie was stuck on a fence and couldn't get down, she would get scolded.

"Thanks," she said. "What's your name?"

Alfonso remembered her from his school and noticed that she was kind of cute, with ponytails and straight teeth. "Alfonso. You go to my school, huh?"

"Yeah. I've seen you around. You live nearby?"

"Over on Madison."

"My uncle used to live on that street, but he moved to Stockton."

"Stockton's near Sacramento, isn't it?"

"You been there?"

"No." Alfonso looked down at his shoes. He wanted to say something clever the way people do on TV. But the only thing he could think to say was that the governor lived in Sacramento. As soon as he shared this observation, he **winced** inside.

Alfonso walked with the girl and the boy as they started for home. They didn't talk much. Every few steps, the girl, whose name was Sandra, would look at him out of the corner of her eye, and Alfonso would look away. He learned that she was in seventh grade, just like him, and that she had a pet terrier named Queenie. Her father was a mechanic at Rudy's Speedy Repair, and her mother was a teacher's aide at Jefferson Elementary.

When they came to the street, Alfonso and Sandra stopped at her corner, but her brother ran home. Alfonso watched him stop in the front yard to talk to a lady he guessed was their mother. She was raking leaves into a pile.

Word Power

winced (winst) *v.* pulled back slightly in pain or fear

"I live over there," she said, pointing.

Alfonso looked over her shoulder for a long time, trying to muster enough nerve to ask her if she'd like to go bike riding tomorrow.

Shyly, he asked, "You wanna go bike riding?"

"Maybe." She played with a ponytail and crossed one leg in front of the other. "But my bike has a flat."

"I can get my brother's bike. He won't mind."

She thought for a moment before she said, "OK. But not tomorrow. I have to go to my aunt's."

"How about after school on Monday?"

"I have to take care of my brother until my mom comes home from work. How 'bout four-thirty?"

"OK," he said. "Four-thirty." Instead of parting immediately, they talked for a while, asking questions like, "Who's your favorite group?" "Have you ever been on the Big Dipper at Santa Cruz?" and "Have you ever tasted pot stickers?" But the question-and-answer period ended when Sandra's mother called her home.

Alfonso took off as fast as he could on his bike, jumped the curb, and, cool as he could be, raced away with his hands stuffed in his pockets. But when he looked back over his shoulder, the wind raking through his butch, Sandra wasn't even looking. She was already on her lawn, heading for the porch.

Reading Skill

Evaluate Reread the highlighted paragraphs. Do you think it is a good idea for Alfonso to say that he will be able to get his brother's bike? Why or why not?

_____

_____

_____

_____

_____

_____

STOP Stop here for **Break Time** on the next page.

Break Time

Alfonso is at the center of this story, so it important to understand him and remember things he says and does. What have you learned about Alfonso so far? Answer the question in each circle.

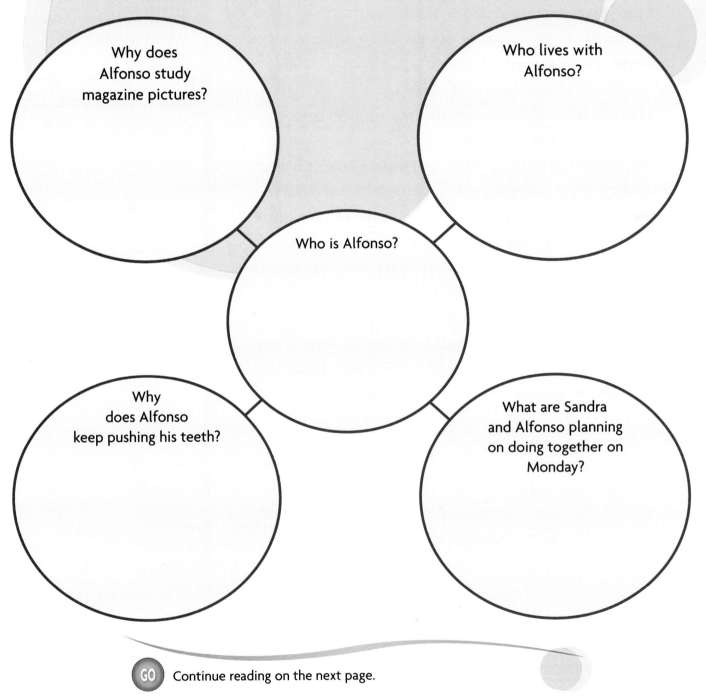

Why does Alfonso study magazine pictures?

Who lives with Alfonso?

Who is Alfonso?

Why does Alfonso keep pushing his teeth?

What are Sandra and Alfonso planning on doing together on Monday?

GO Continue reading on the next page.

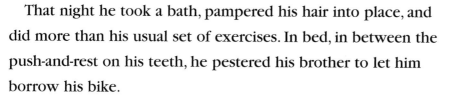

That night he took a bath, pampered his hair into place, and did more than his usual set of exercises. In bed, in between the push-and-rest on his teeth, he pestered his brother to let him borrow his bike.

"Come on, Ernie," he whined. "Just for an hour."

"*Chale*, I might want to use it."

"Come on, man, I'll let you have my trick-or-treat candy."

"What you got?"

"Three baby Milky Ways and some Skittles."

"Who's going to use it?"

Alfonso hesitated, then risked the truth. "I met this girl. She doesn't live too far."

Ernie rolled over on his stomach and stared at the outline of his brother, whose head was resting on his elbow. "You got a girlfriend?"

"She ain't my girlfriend, just a girl."

"What does she look like?"

"Like a girl."

"Come on, what does she look like?"

"She's got ponytails and a little brother."

"Ponytails! Those girls who messed with Frostie and me had ponytails. Is she cool?"

"I think so."

Ernie sat up in bed. "I bet you that's her."

Alfonso felt his stomach knot up. "She's going to be my girlfriend, not yours!"

"I'm going to get even with her!"

"You better not touch her," Alfonso snarled, throwing a **wadded** Kleenex at him. "I'll run you over with my bike."

Word Power

wadded (wod′ əd) *adj.* something made into the shape of a ball

Sibling Rivals, 1989. Phoebe Beasley. Collage, 32 x 41 in. Stella Jones Gallery, New Orleans.

What does this picture say about conflict? Do these figures remind you of Alfonso and Ernie? Why or why not?

Reading Skill

Evaluate Reread the highlighted paragraph. Do you think Ernie is right to suspect that Sandra is one of the girls who stood him up? Why or why not?

_____

_____

_____

_____

_____

For the next hour, until their mother threatened them from the living room to be quiet or else, they argued whether it was the same girl who had stood Ernie up. Alfonso said over and over that she was too nice to pull a stunt like that. But Ernie argued that she lived only two blocks from where those girls had told them to wait, that she was in the same grade, and, the clincher, that she had ponytails. Secretly, however, Ernie was jealous that his brother, two years younger than himself, might have found a girlfriend.

Sunday morning, Ernie and Alfonso stayed away from each other, though over breakfast they fought over the last tortilla. Their mother, sewing at the kitchen table, warned them to knock it off. At church they made faces at one another when the priest, Father Jerry, wasn't looking. Ernie punched Alfonso in the arm, and Alfonso, his eyes wide with anger, punched back.

Monday morning they hurried to school on their bikes, neither saying a word, though they rode side by side. In first period, Alfonso worried himself sick. How would he borrow a bike for her? He considered asking his best friend, Raul, for his bike. But Alfonso knew Raul, a paper boy with dollar signs in his eyes, would charge him, and he had less than sixty cents, counting the soda bottles he could cash.

Between history and math, Alfonso saw Sandra and her girlfriend huddling at their lockers. He hurried by without being seen.

During lunch Alfonso hid in metal shop so he wouldn't run into Sandra. What would he say to her? If he weren't mad at his brother, he could ask Ernie what girls and guys talk about. But he was mad, and anyway, Ernie was pitching nickels with his friends.

Alfonso hurried home after school. He did the morning dishes as his mother had asked and raked the leaves. After finishing his chores, he did a hundred sit-ups, pushed on his teeth until they hurt, showered, and combed his hair into a perfect butch. He then stepped out to the patio to clean his bike. On an impulse, he removed the chain to wipe off the gritty oil. But while he was unhooking it from the back sprocket, it snapped. The chain lay in his hand like a dead snake.

Alfonso couldn't believe his luck. Now, not only did he not have an extra bike for Sandra, he had no bike for himself. **Frustrated,** and on the verge of tears, he flung the chain as far as he could. It landed with a hard slap against the back fence and spooked his sleeping cat, Benny. Benny looked around, blinking his soft gray eyes, and went back to sleep.

Alfonso **retrieved** the chain, which was hopelessly broken. He cursed himself for being stupid, yelled at his bike for being cheap, and slammed the chain onto the cement. The chain snapped in another place and hit him when it popped up, slicing his hand like a snake's fang.

Word Power

frustrated (frus′ trāt əd) *adj.* unhappy because something is not working as hoped or expected

retrieved (ri trēvd′) *v.* brought back

Reading Skill

Question Reread the paragraphs highlighted in green. What is the **best** question to ask yourself to help you understand Alfonso's behavior here? Check the correct response.

☐ Why is Alfonso mad at his brother?

☐ Why is Alfonso avoiding Sandra?

☐ What are Sandra and her friend talking about?

Literary Element

Conflict Reread the paragraph highlighted in blue. Would you describe the conflicts here as internal, external, or both? Why?

_____

_____

_____

_____

Comprehension Check

Reread the boxed paragraph. How does Ernie feel about Alfonso's trouble? Why doesn't he help him? Underline the phrases that best answer these questions.

Background Info

Menso (men´ sō) is a Spanish word for "foolish."

"Ow!" he cried, his mouth immediately going to his hand to suck on the wound.

After a dab of iodine, which only made his cut hurt more, and a lot of thought, he went to the bedroom to plead with Ernie, who was changing to his after-school clothes.

"Come on, man, let me use it," Alfonso pleaded. "Please, Ernie, I'll do anything."

Although Ernie could see Alfonso's **desperation,** he had plans with his friend Raymundo. They were going to catch frogs at the Mayfair canal. He felt sorry for his brother, and gave him a stick of gum to make him feel better, but there was nothing he could do. The canal was three miles away, and the frogs were waiting.

Alfonso took the stick of gum, placed it in his shirt pocket, and left the bedroom with his head down. He went outside, slamming the screen door behind him, and sat in the alley behind his house. A sparrow landed in the weeds, and when it tried to come close, Alfonso screamed for it to scram. The sparrow responded with a squeaky chirp and flew away.

At four he decided to get it over with and started walking to Sandra's house, **trudging** slowly, as if he were waist-deep in water. Shame colored his face. How could he disappoint his first date? She would probably laugh. She might even call him *menso*.

He stopped at the corner where they were supposed to meet and watched her house. But there was no one outside, only a rake leaning against the steps.

Word Power

desperation (des´ pə rā´ shən) *n.* a hopeless feeling
trudging (truj´ ing) *v.* walking heavily or slowly

Alfonso takes very good care of his bike. Look at the bike in the picture. Do you think the owner of this bike takes good care of it? Why or why not?

Why did he have to take the chain off? he scolded himself. He always messed things up when he tried to take them apart, like the time he tried to repad his baseball mitt. He had unlaced the mitt and filled the pocket with cotton balls. But when he tried to put it back together, he had forgotten how it laced up. Everything became tangled like kite string. When he showed the mess to his mother, who was at the stove cooking dinner, she scolded him but put it back together and didn't tell his father what a dumb thing he had done.

Reading Skill

Evaluate Reread the highlighted sentence and the rest of the paragraph. Do you think Alfonso is right to be so angry with himself? Why or why not?

_____

_____

_____

_____

_____

Now he had to face Sandra and say, "I broke my bike, and my stingy brother took off on his."

He waited at the corner for a few minutes, hiding behind a hedge for what seemed like forever. Just as he was starting to think about going home, he heard footsteps and knew it was too late. His hands, moist from worry, hung at his sides, and a thread of sweat raced down his armpit.

He peeked through the hedge. She was wearing a sweater with a checkerboard pattern. A red purse was slung over her shoulder. He could see her looking for him, standing on tiptoe to see if he was coming around the corner.

What have I done? Alfonso thought. He bit his lip, called himself *menso*, and pounded his palm against his forehead. Someone slapped the back of his head. He turned around and saw Ernie.

"We got the frogs, Alfonso," he said, holding up a wiggling plastic bag. "I'll show you later."

Ernie looked through the hedge, with one eye closed, at the girl. "She's not the one who messed with Frostie and me," he said finally. "You still wanna borrow my bike?"

Alfonso couldn't believe his luck. What a brother! What a pal! He promised to take Ernie's turn next time it was his turn to do the dishes. Ernie hopped on Raymundo's handlebars and said he would remember that promise. Then he was gone as they took off without looking back.

Free of worry now that his brother had come through, Alfonso emerged from behind the hedge with Ernie's bike, which was mud-splashed but better than nothing. Sandra waved.

Comprehension Check

Reread the boxed paragraphs. Why does Ernie decide to lend Alfonso his bike? Write two reasons below.

_____

_____

_____

_____

_____

Literary Element

Conflict Reread the highlighted paragraph. Alfonso's internal conflict about breaking his bike has ended. Underline the phrase in this paragraph that tells you this.

"Hi," she said.

"Hi," he said back.

She looked cheerful. Alfonso told her his bike was broken and asked if she wanted to ride with him.

"Sounds good," she said, and jumped on the crossbar.

It took all of Alfonso's strength to steady the bike. He started off slowly, gritting his teeth, because she was heavier than he thought. But once he got going, it got easier. He pedaled smoothly, sometimes with only one hand on the handlebars, as they sped up one street and down another. Whenever he ran over a pothole, which was often, she screamed with delight, and once, when it looked like they were going to crash, she placed her hand over his, and it felt like love.

English Coach

Sometimes the suffix *-ful* means "full of something." The word *cheerful* means "full of cheer." Write the word that means "full of grace."

_____

Broken Chain

A Comprehension Check

Answer the following questions in the spaces provided.

1. What parts of his appearance does Alfonso want to change?

   _____

2. How does Sandra react when Alfonso shows up with just one bicycle?

   _____

B Reading Skills

Answer the following questions in the spaces provided.

1. **Question** Ask yourself: "Why does Alfonso hesitate before telling Ernie about the girl?" How does asking this question help you understand

   Alfonso better? _____

   _____

   _____

2. **Evaluate** Several times the author describes how Alfonso tries to straighten his teeth. Do you think this shows you how important straight

   teeth are to Alfonso? Why or why not? _____

   _____

   _____

3. **Evaluate** Think about how Alfonso takes such good care of his bike and keeps it looking good. Does it seem realistic that someone like Alfonso

   would do this? Why or why not? _____

   _____

   _____

C Word Power

Complete each sentence below, using one of the words in the box.

swaggered	winced	wadded	frustrated
retrieved	desperation	trudging	

1. The traffic jam made the _____ drivers honk their horns.

2. Timmy _____ the book his friend had borrowed.

3. I picked up the _____ piece of paper and tossed it into the trash.

4. Dad _____ when Mom touched the sunburn on his neck.

5. We were tired after _____ through the snow.

6. The winning fighter _____ through the crowd.

7. After locking myself in the closet, I yelled in _____ for help.

D Literary Element: Conflict

Read the passages below from "Broken Chain." In the first passage, Alfonso and Ernie are talking. In the second passage, Alfonso breaks the chain on his bike. As you read, think about Alfonso's conflicts. Then answer the questions that follow.

Alfonso felt his stomach knot up.[1] "She's going to be my girlfriend, not yours!"[2]

"I'm going to get even with her!"[3]

"You better not touch her," Alfonso snarled, throwing a wadded Kleenex at him.[4] "I'll run you over with my bike."[5]

Why did he have to take the chain off?[6] he scolded himself.[7] He always messed things up when he tried to take them apart, like the time he tried to repad his baseball mitt.[8]

1. In sentences 1–5, is Alfonso experiencing an internal or external conflict? How do you know? _____

_____

_____

2. In sentences 6–8, how do you know that the conflict Alfonso is experiencing is internal? In what way is Alfonso's reaction to this conflict similar to the reaction he has to the conflict in sentences 1–5?

_____

_____

_____

_____

E Instant Messages

Pretend that Alfonso and Sandra are writing instant messages to each other. What would they say after their day together? Complete their instant-message conversation below.

Sandra: Hi, Alfonso! I enjoyed the bike ride today. You're very nice. Just like when we first met and you _____

_____

Alfonso: I hope it was okay using my brother's bike. He almost didn't let me borrow it because _____

_____

Sandra: But he finally let you borrow it! It's a nice bike!
I liked riding _____

_____

Alfonso: At first I was mad at my brother, but now I think he's _____

_____

Sandra: I have to go now. I just wanted to say I like your haircut. It reminds me of _____

_____

Alfonso: Wow, thanks! I like your hair too! Especially _____

_____

Sandra: Thanks! I also like your smile! Okay, bye!

Send

Assessment

Fill in the circle next to each correct answer.

1. Which is the **best** question to ask yourself to help you understand the reason Alfonso pushes his teeth?
   - ○ A. Who else has teeth like Alfonso?
   - ○ B. Why doesn't Alfonso get braces?
   - ○ C. Why is Alfonso so bothered by his teeth?
   - ○ D. What happened to make Alfonso's teeth crooked?

2. When Ernie first appears in the story, he is upset and angry because
   - ○ A. he thinks two girls tricked him and his friend.
   - ○ B. he did not catch any frogs in the canal.
   - ○ C. his bike is not as clean as Alfonso's bike.
   - ○ D. Alfonso laughs at him for being easily fooled.

3. What is Sandra's reaction when Alfonso shows up with only one bike?
   - ○ A. She gets angry and leaves.
   - ○ B. She suggests they go riding another day.
   - ○ C. She sits on the crossbar.
   - ○ D. She asks to borrow her own brother's bike.

4. Which of the following is an internal conflict?
   - ○ A. Alfonso and Ernie argue about Sandra.
   - ○ B. Alfonso gets mad at himself when the chain breaks.
   - ○ C. Alfonso helps Sandra's brother when he is stuck.
   - ○ D. Alfonso does not like Ernie's haircut.

5. Which of the following words means "walked in a bold way"?
   - ○ A. retrieved
   - ○ B. winced
   - ○ C. wadded
   - ○ D. swaggered

Wrap-up

Compare and Contrast

Conflict is an important literary element in both "Amigo Brothers" and "Broken Chain." Although Antonio and Felix in "Amigo Brothers" and Alfonso in "Broken Chain" face different conflicts, their conflicts have some similarities. Think about the conflicts in both stories and how these conflicts affect the relationships between the characters.

Use the Venn diagram below to tell how the conflicts in "Amigo Brothers" and "Broken Chain" are alike and different. In the outer parts of the circles, write about the ways in which the conflicts are different. In the overlapping part, write about how these conflicts are alike. Don't forget to label each conflict as internal or external. An example in each section has been done for you.

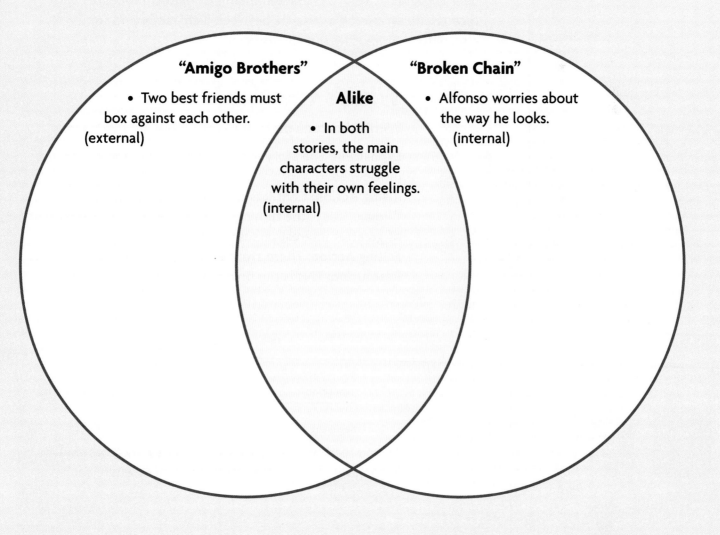

"Amigo Brothers"

- Two best friends must box against each other. (external)

Alike

- In both stories, the main characters struggle with their own feelings. (internal)

"Broken Chain"

- Alfonso worries about the way he looks. (internal)

UNIT 2

Short Story

How Is a Short Story Organized?

Now that you have read a few short stories, let's stop for a moment to take a closer look at how a short story is put together. Understanding the parts of a story can help you be a better reader.

A short story always has a **beginning,** a **middle,** and an **end.**

Most stories also include a conflict. As discussed in Unit 1, conflict can be a struggle between a character and his or her own thoughts and feelings. It can also be a struggle between a character and someone else, nature, or another outside force.

What's the Plan?

Within the three parts of a story, there are five stages:

Exposition: The story is set up. Characters and places are introduced.
Rising Action: Conflicts or problems occur in the story.
Climax: This is the turning point in the story. It is the point of greatest interest or suspense.
Falling Action: These are the events that follow the climax.
Resolution: This is the final outcome.

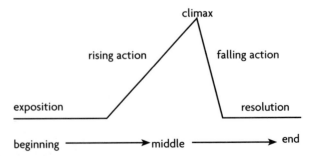

As you read the next four stories, try to find these stages in each story. In the text, mark the places where each stage occurs.

How Do I Read Short Stories?

Focus on key **literary elements** and **reading skills** to get the most out of reading the four short stories in this unit. Here are two key literary elements and two key reading skills that you will practice in this unit.

Key Literary Elements

• Character

A **character** is an actor in a story. Characters can be people, animals, robots, or whatever the writer chooses. A story is usually built around a main character. That character is often described in detail. He or she may change because of events that occur in the story. Many stories also have minor characters. You can learn about characters by looking at how they act, think, talk, and feel. You can also use what other characters say about them to learn about them.

• Theme

A **theme** is the message the reader can take from a story. A story may have more than one theme, but one message will probably be the strongest. A theme may be stated very clearly. However, sometimes a theme is suggested by the words, thoughts, and actions of the characters. Readers usually need to look at what the characters do and say to figure out the theme.

Key Reading Skills

• Predict

Get involved in the story! Use story clues and what you already know to **predict,** or guess, what will happen next. Suppose you are reading about a baseball player who always strikes out. You might predict that he will get a hit by the end of the story. As you read, you can check your predictions by finding out what really happens. Don't worry if what you predict isn't right. You can change your predictions as you get more details from the story.

• Infer

Authors do not always directly state information. Instead, an author sometimes gives clues that can help you **infer,** or figure out, what he or she wants you to know. For example, suppose a character looks down at her feet when someone talks to her. You can use that clue to infer that the character is shy. Instead of telling you directly that the character is shy, the author uses details to show the character acting shyly.

Get Ready to Read!

Thank You, M'am

Meet
Langston Hughes

Langston Hughes was born in 1902. He was one of the first African Americans to make a living as a writer. He once said his subjects are "people up today and down tomorrow, working this week and fired the next, beaten and baffled, but determined not to be wholly beaten." Hughes is known for his poems, stories, plays, and essays. Hughes died in 1967. "Thank You, M'am" was first published in 1958.

What You Know

Think of someone you trust. Think about your reasons for trusting that person.

Reason to Read

Read this short story to find out how two characters come to trust each other, despite unlikely circumstances.

Background Info

The setting of "Thank You, M'am" starts on a street and ends up in a rooming house, probably in a large city. A rooming house is a place where people rent rooms to live in. Rooming houses are often found in urban areas and are inexpensive places to live. They provide homes for people who cannot afford an apartment or house of their own.

Word Power

slung (slung) *adj.* hung or thrown loosely; p. 88
I carried my heavy backpack *slung* over my shoulder.

permit (pər mit´) *v.* to allow; p. 88
Our school does not *permit* students to wear hats inside the building.

frail (frāl) *adj.* weak; thin; easily broken; p. 89
The woman held the *frail* baby carefully.

presentable (pri zen´ tə bəl) *adj.* looking nice, clean, or neat; p. 91
We cleaned the house to make it *presentable* for company.

barren (bar´ ən) *adj.* empty; bare; p. 92
The fields were *barren* because there was not enough rain to grow crops.

Answer the following questions, using one of the new words above. Write your answers in the spaces provided.

1. Which word goes with "something that you need to handle carefully"?_____

2. Which word goes with "how you carried a bag over your arm"? _____

3. Which word goes with "to allow someone to leave the room"? _____

4. Which word goes with "wearing clothes that are clean and unwrinkled"?

_____

5. Which word goes with "a cabinet that has no food"? _____

Thank You, M'am

Langston Hughes

Reading Skill

Predict Reread the sentence highlighted in green and the rest of the paragraph. Then reread the title. What do you predict the woman will do with the boy?

_____

_____

_____

_____

_____

Literary Element

Character Reread the text highlighted in blue. The boy says he didn't mean to steal the purse and that he will run away if the woman lets him go. What do these details tell you about his character?

_____

_____

_____

_____

She was a large woman with a large purse that had everything in it but hammer and nails. It had a long strap and she carried it **slung** across her shoulder. It was about eleven o'clock at night, and she was walking alone, when a boy ran up behind her and tried to snatch her purse. The strap broke with the single tug the boy gave it from behind. But the boy's weight, and the weight of the purse combined caused him to lose his balance so, instead of taking off full blast as he had hoped, the boy fell on his back on the sidewalk, and his legs flew up. The large woman simply turned around and kicked him right square in his blue jeaned sitter. Then she reached down, picked the boy up by his shirt front, and shook him until his teeth rattled.

After that the woman said, "Pick up my pocketbook, boy, and give it here."

She still held him. But she bent down enough to **permit** him to stoop and pick up her purse. Then she said, "Now ain't you ashamed of yourself?"

Firmly gripped by his shirt front, the boy said, "Yes'm."

The woman said, "What did you want to do it for?"

The boy said, "I didn't aim to."

She said, "You a lie!"

By that time two or three people passed, stopped, turned to look, and some stood watching.

"If I turn you loose, will you run?" asked the woman.

"Yes'm," said the boy.

Word Power

slung (slung) *adj.* hung or thrown loosely
permit (pər mit´) *v.* to allow

"Then I won't turn you loose," said the woman. She did not release him.

"I'm very sorry, lady, I'm sorry," whispered the boy.

"Um-hum! And your face is dirty. I got a great mind to wash your face for you. Ain't you got nobody home to tell you to wash your face?"

"No'm," said the boy.

"Then it will get washed this evening," said the large woman starting up the street, dragging the frightened boy behind her.

He looked as if he were fourteen or fifteen, **frail** and willow-wild, in tennis shoes and blue jeans.

The woman said, "You ought to be my son. I would teach you right from wrong. Least I can do right now is to wash your face. Are you hungry?"

"No'm," said the being-dragged boy. "I just want you to turn me loose."

"Was I bothering *you* when I turned that corner?" asked the woman.

"No'm."

"But you put yourself in contact with *me*," said the woman. "If you think that that contact is not going to last awhile, you got another thought coming. When I get through with you, sir, you are going to remember Mrs. Luella Bates Washington Jones."

Sweat popped out on the boy's face and he began to struggle. Mrs. Jones stopped, jerked him around in front of her, put a half nelson about his neck, and continued to drag him up the street. When she got to her door, she dragged the boy inside, down a hall, and into a large kitchenette-furnished room at the rear of the house. She switched on the light and left the door open. The boy could hear other roomers laughing and talking in the large house.

Word Power
frail (frāl) *adj.* weak; thin; easily broken

Connect to the Text

Reread the boxed text. Think about a time you were caught doing something you weren't supposed to be doing. How did you feel after you got caught?

_____

_____

_____

_____

English Coach

Sometimes the suffix -*ette* means "little one." The word *kitchenette* means "little kitchen." What word can you think of that means "small statue"?

_____

Reading Skill

Infer Reread the highlighted text. Why do you think Roger looks back and forth between the woman and the door?

_____

_____

_____

_____

Comprehension Check

Mrs. Jones tells the boy he didn't have to steal her pocketbook to get money. What does she say he could have done instead?

_____

_____

_____

Did You Know?

Blue suede shoes are men's shoes made of soft leather. These shoes became popular in the late 1950s after Elvis Presley recorded a hit song called "Blue Suede Shoes."
....

Some of their doors were open, too, so he knew he and the woman were not alone. The woman still had him by the neck in the middle of her room.

She said, "What is your name?"

"Roger," answered the boy.

"Then, Roger, you go to that sink and wash your face," said the woman, whereupon she turned him loose—at last. Roger looked at the door—looked at the woman—looked at the door—_and went to the sink._

"Let the water run until it gets warm," she said. "Here's a clean towel."

"You gonna take me to jail?" asked the boy, bending over the sink.

"Not with that face, I would not take you nowhere," said the woman. "Here I am trying to get home to cook me a bite to eat and you snatch my pocketbook! Maybe you ain't been to your supper either, late as it be. Have you?"

"There's nobody home at my house," said the boy.

"Then we'll eat," said the woman. "I believe you're hungry—or been hungry—to try to snatch my pocketbook."

"I wanted a pair of blue suede shoes," said the boy.

"Well, you didn't have to snatch _my_ pocketbook to get some suede shoes," said Mrs. Luella Bates Washington Jones. "You could of asked me."

"M'am?"

The water dripping from his face, the boy looked at her. There was a long pause. A very long pause. After he had dried his face and not knowing what else to do dried it again, the boy turned around, wondering what next. The door was open. He could make a dash for it down the hall. He could run, run, run, run, _run!_

The woman was sitting on the daybed. After a while she said, "I were young once and I wanted things I could not get."

There was another long pause. The boy's mouth opened. Then he frowned, but not knowing he frowned.

The woman said, "Um-hum! You thought I was going to say *but*, didn't you? You thought I was going to say, *but I didn't snatch people's pocketbooks.* Well, I wasn't going to say that." Pause. Silence. "I have done things, too, which I would not tell you, son— neither tell God, if he didn't already know. So you set down while I fix us something to eat. You might run that comb through your hair so you will look **presentable.**"

In another corner of the room behind a screen was a gas plate and an icebox. Mrs. Jones got up and went behind the screen. The woman did not watch the boy to see if he was going to run now, nor did she watch her purse which she left behind her on the daybed. But the boy took care to sit on the far side of the room where he thought she could easily see him out of the corner of her eye, if she wanted to. He did not trust the woman *not* to trust him. And he did not want to be mistrusted now.

Portrait of a Woman, 1932. John Wesley Hardrick. Oil on board, 30 x 24 in. Hampton University Museum, Hampton, VA. Indianapolis Museum of Art in cooperation with Indiana University Press.

Does the woman in the painting remind you of Mrs. Jones? Explain why you think Mrs. Jones is similar to or different from the woman in the picture.

Word Power

presentable (pri zen´ tə bəl) *adj.* looking nice, clean, or neat

English Coach

A *daybed* is a sofa that can also be used as a bed. You usually think of a bed as something for night, but the word *day* in front of it tells you it can be used during the day too. What do you think a *daydream* is?

_____

_____

_____

Comprehension Check

Reread the boxed paragraph. What does the boy do while Mrs. Jones cooks some food? Why does he do this?

_____

_____

_____

_____

_____

_____

Literary Element

Character Reread the highlighted text. Which words best describe Mrs. Jones? Check all the responses that apply.
- ☐ mean
- ☐ nosy
- ☐ thoughtful
- ☐ understanding

Reading Skill

Predict Did you accurately predict what would happen to the boy at the end of the story? What details did you use to help you make your prediction? (Don't worry if your prediction doesn't match how the story ends! Remember, as you read a story and get new information, you can change your predictions.)

_____

_____

_____

_____

"Do you need somebody to go to the store," asked the boy, "maybe to get some milk or something?"

"Don't believe I do," said the woman, "unless you just want sweet milk yourself. I was going to make cocoa out of this canned milk I got here."

"That will be fine," said the boy.

She heated some lima beans and ham she had in the icebox, made the cocoa, and set the table. The woman did not ask the boy anything about where he lived, or his folks, or anything else that would embarrass him. Instead, as they ate, she told him about her job in a hotel beauty shop that stayed open late, what the work was like, and how all kinds of women came in and out, blondes, red-heads, and Spanish. Then she cut him a half of her ten-cent cake.

"Eat some more, son," she said.

When they were finished eating she got up and said, "Now, here, take this ten dollars and buy yourself some blue suede shoes. And next time, do not make the mistake of latching onto *my* pocketbook *nor nobody else's*—because shoes come by devilish like that will burn your feet. I got to get my rest now. But I wish you would behave yourself, son, from here on in." She led him down the hall to the front door and opened it. "Goodnight! Behave yourself, boy!" she said, looking out into the street.

The boy wanted to say something else other than, "Thank you, m'am," to Mrs. Luella Bates Washington Jones, but he couldn't do so as he turned at the **barren** stoop and looked back at the large woman in the door. He barely managed to say, "Thank you," before she shut the door. And he never saw her again.

Word Power
barren (bar´ ən) *adj.* empty; bare

Thank You, M'am*✳

A Comprehension Check

Answer the following questions in the spaces provided.

1. What does Roger want to do with the money he tries to steal?

   _____

2. What does Mrs. Jones tell Roger he should have done to get the money
   he wanted? _____

   _____

   _____

B Reading Skills

Answer the following questions in the spaces provided.

1. **Infer** Roger has a dirty face and seems hungry. He is trying to steal money
   to buy fancy shoes. What can you infer about Roger's home life from
   these clues? _____

   _____

   _____

   _____

2. **Predict** Do you think that Roger will ever try to steal money again?
   Why or why not? _____

   _____

   _____

C Word Power

Complete each sentence below, using one of the words in the box.

slung	permit	frail
presentable		barren

1. I got a haircut before the wedding so I would look _____.

2. The shelves were _____ of any food.

3. Tom arrived at school with his bag _____ over the shoulder.

4. I let go of the leash to _____ the dog to run around the yard.

5. My grandmother is ill and has become very _____.

Circle the word that best completes each sentence.

6. The boy shined his shoes to make them **(frail, presentable)**.

7. Sometimes the teacher will **(barren, permit)** the students to talk quietly during class.

8. The plain white walls looked **(barren, presentable)** in the evening light.

9. The man's jacket was **(slung, permit)** over the back of the chair.

10. The little dog looked unhealthy and **(frail, slung)**.

D Literary Element: Character

Read the passages below from "Thank You, M'am." Think about what it tells you about the characters. Then answer the questions that follow.

> The woman was sitting on the daybed.[1] After a while she said, "I were young once and I wanted things I could not get."[2]
>
> The woman did not watch the boy to see if he was going to run now, nor did she watch her purse which she left behind her on the daybed.[3] But the boy took care to sit on the far side of the room where he thought she could easily see him out of the corner of her eye, if she wanted to.[4] He did not trust the woman *not* to trust him.[5] And he did not want to be mistrusted now.[6]

1. What do sentences 1–2 tell you about the woman? Do they show that she understands why the boy tries to steal? Why or why not?

   _____

   _____

   _____

   _____

2. How does sentence 3 show you that the woman is a trusting person? What does the boy's reaction in sentences 4–6 tell you about him?

   _____

   _____

   _____

   _____

E A Thank-You Letter

Roger wants to say more than just "thank you" when he leaves Mrs. Jones. Pretend you are Roger leaving a letter (and a special gift) for Mrs. Jones on her doorstep. Finish writing the letter below.

Dear Mrs. Jones,

    I want to tell you how I feel about meeting you. At first, I felt _____

_____

    When we got to your home, I looked at the door and thought about _____

But I changed my mind when you _____

_____

_____

    Thank you for feeding me. And thank you for the money. I decided not to buy _____

Instead, I want to give you a gift, so I bought you

_____

Sincerely,
Roger

P.S. Most of all, thank you for _____

_____

Assessment

Fill in the circle next to each correct answer.

1. Why does Roger want to steal a purse?
   - ○ A. He wants money to buy food.
   - ○ B. He wants money to buy blue suede shoes.
   - ○ C. He wants keys to someone's car.
   - ○ D. He wants keys to someone's apartment.

2. Which quote from Mrs. Jones would **best** help you predict that she won't punish Roger?
   - ○ A. "You a lie!"
   - ○ B. "Then I won't turn you loose."
   - ○ C. "Least I can do right now is to wash your face."
   - ○ D. "Pick up my pocketbook, boy, and give it here."

3. What clue from the story **best** helps you figure out that Mrs. Jones trusts Roger?
   - ○ A. She drags him down the street.
   - ○ B. She offers him food.
   - ○ C. She leaves her purse on the daybed.
   - ○ D. She tells him to behave.

4. Which of the following actions shows that Mrs. Jones is a generous person?
   - ○ A. She gives money to Roger.
   - ○ B. She kicks Roger in the pants.
   - ○ C. She asks Roger what his name is.
   - ○ D. She asks Roger why he wanted to steal.

5. Which word means the same thing as "allow"?
   - ○ A. barren
   - ○ B. frail
   - ○ C. slung
   - ○ D. permit

DUFFY'S JACKET

Meet Bruce Coville

Bruce Coville was born in New York in 1950. He worked as a toymaker, a salesman, an assembly-line worker, and a schoolteacher on his way to becoming a popular writer of young adult fiction. Coville has said, "The first time I can remember thinking that I would like to be a writer came in sixth grade, when our teacher . . . gave us an extended period of time to write a long story. I loved doing it." "Duffy's Jacket" was first published in 1994.

What You Know

Think of someone you know who is always forgetting something. Do you always need to remind this person to remember things?

Reason to Read

Read this short story to find out what happens to a forgetful boy and his cousins.

Background Info

This story takes place on a family camping trip. Camping is especially popular with people who live in cities. City dwellers like going camping because they can get away from the crowded streets. They like to enjoy the peace and quiet of nature. One of the most popular activities to do on a camping trip is to tell stories around a campfire. Campfire tales are usually spooky stories that become even spookier when told out in the wilderness. Sometimes these stories involve mysterious creatures or scary monsters that are supposed to live in the very forest where the tale is told.

Word Power

scatterbrained (skat´ ər brānd´) *adj.* unable to pay attention; forgets things; p. 100
My *scatterbrained* older brother forgot his keys again.

allergic (ə lur´ jik) *adj.* having a condition that causes reactions like sneezing or sensitive skin after contact with certain things; p. 102
I am *allergic* to cats, so I sneeze if one comes anywhere near me.

sentinel (sent´ ən əl) *n.* a person or animal that stands guard and keeps watch; p. 102
We asked Kim to be the *sentinel* outside our secret clubhouse.

sabotage (sab´ ə tazh´) *v.* to harm something in order to get it to fail; p. 103
I tried to *sabotage* my mother's plan to take me to the dentist.

lurking (lurk´ ing) *v.* waiting in a hidden place, usually for a sneaky purpose; p. 105
I saw my little sister *lurking* in the bushes and knew she was following me.

frantically (fran´ tik lē) *adv.* in a fast, nervous, and anxious manner; p. 105
I searched *frantically* for my book but couldn't find it anywhere.

glimpse (glimps) *n.* a brief look at something; p. 106
I caught a *glimpse* of my friend wandering through the crowded park.

Answer the following questions, using one of the new words above. Write your answers in the spaces provided.

1. Which word goes with "quickly and nervously"? _____

2. Which word goes with "trying to mess up a plan"? _____

3. Which word goes with "staying hidden somewhere"? _____

4. Which word goes with "a quick glance at something"? _____

5. Which word goes with "sneezing because a dog is nearby"? _____

6. Which word goes with "unable to keep track of things"? _____

7. Which word goes with "a guard who warns others of danger"? _____

Adapted from

DUFFY'S JACKET

Bruce Coville

Literary Element

Character Reread the text highlighted in blue. What does the narrator say Duffy is like? What does his mother say about Duffy?

_____

_____

_____

_____

_____

_____

Reading Skill

Predict Reread the text highlighted in green. Think about the title of the story. Think about what you know about Duffy. What do you predict will cause "the mess" the narrator is talking about?

_____

_____

_____

If my cousin Duffy had the brains of a turnip, it never would have happened. But as far as I'm concerned, Duffy makes a turnip look bright. My mother disagrees. According to her, Duffy is actually very bright. She claims the reason he's so **scatterbrained** is that he's too busy being brilliant inside his own head to remember everyday things. Maybe. But hanging around with Duffy means you spend a lot of time saying, "Your glasses, Duffy," or "Your coat, Duffy," or—well, you get the idea: a lot of three-word sentences that start with "Your," end with "Duffy," and have words like _book_, _radio_, _wallet_, or whatever it is he's just put down and left behind, stuck in the middle.

Me, I think turnips are brighter.

But since Duffy's my cousin, and since my mother and her sister are both single parents, we tend to do a lot of things together— like camping, which is how we got into the mess I want to tell you about.

Personally, I thought camping was a big mistake. But since Mom and Aunt Elise are raising the three of us—me, Duffy, and my little sister, Marie—on their own, they're convinced they have to do man-stuff with us every once in a while. I think they read some book that said me and Duffy would come out weird if they don't. You can take him camping all you want. It ain't gonna make Duffy normal.

Word Power

scatterbrained (skat´ ər brānd´) _adj._ unable to pay attention; forgets things

Anyway, the fact that our mothers were getting ready to do something fatherly combined with the fact that Aunt Elise's boss had a friend who had a friend who said we could use his cabin, added up to the five of us bouncing along this horrible dirt road late one Friday in October.

It was late because we had lost an hour going back to get Duffy's suitcase. I suppose it wasn't actually Duffy's fault. No one remembered to say, "Your suitcase, Duffy," so he couldn't really have been expected to remember it.

"Oh, Elise," cried my mother, as we got deeper into the woods. "Aren't the leaves beautiful?"

That's why it doesn't make sense for them to try to do man-stuff with us. If it had been our fathers, they would have been drinking beer and burping and maybe telling dirty stories instead of talking about the leaves. So why try to fake it?

Anyway, we get to this cabin, which is about eighteen million miles from nowhere, and to my surprise, it's not a cabin at all. It's a house. A big house.

"Oh, my," said my mother as we pulled into the driveway.

"Isn't it great?" said Aunt Elise. "It's almost a hundred years old, back from the time when they used to build big hunting lodges up here. It's the only one in the area still standing. Horace said he hasn't been able to get up here in some time. That's why he was glad to let us use it. He said it would be good to have someone go in and air the place out."

Leave it to Aunt Elise. This place didn't need airing out—it needed fumigating. I never saw so many spiderwebs in my life. From the sounds we heard coming from the walls, hundreds of mice seemed to have made it their home. We found a total of two working lightbulbs: one in the kitchen, and one in the dining room, which was covered with dark wood and had a big stone fireplace at one end.

Comprehension Check

Reread the boxed text. Why does the family decide to take a trip together? Check the correct responses.

☐ Someone lets them use a cabin in the woods.

☐ They always go camping in October.

☐ The mothers want to do something "fatherly" with the boys.

English Coach

The word *driveway* is a compound word made from the two smaller words *drive* and *way*. Write two other compound words you know of that end with *way*.

_____

_____

English Coach

The phrase *hit the hay* means "to go to bed." What does the phrase "hit the road" mean?

_____

_____

Reading Skill

Infer Reread the text highlighted in green. Sometimes information is not directly stated. You have to use clues and details to infer, or figure out, what is really being said. Who is the narrator suggesting is also frightened?

_____

_____

_____

_____

"Oh, my," said my mother again.

Duffy, who is **allergic** to about fifteen different things, started to sneeze.

"Isn't it charming?" asked Aunt Elise hopefully.

No one answered her.

Four hours later we had managed to get three bedrooms clean enough to sleep in without getting the heebie-jeebies—one for Mom and Aunt Elise, one for Marie, and one for me and Duffy. After a supper of beans and franks we hit the hay, which I think is what our mattresses were stuffed with. As I was drifting off, which took about thirty seconds, it occurred to me that four hours of housework wasn't all that much of a man-thing, something it might be useful to remember the next time Mom got one of these plans into her head.

Things looked better in the morning when we went outside and found a stream where we could go wading. ("Your sneakers, Duffy.")

Later we went back and started looking around the house, which really was enormous.

That was when things started getting a little spooky. In the room next to ours I found a message scrawled on the wall. BEWARE OF THE **SENTINEL,** it said in big black letters.

When I showed Mom and Aunt Elise, they said it was just a joke and got mad at me for frightening Marie.

Marie wasn't the only one who was frightened.

We decided to go out for another walk. ("Your lunch, Duffy.") We went deep into the woods. It was a hot day, even in the deep woods, and after a while we decided to take off our coats.

Word Power

allergic (ə lur′ jik) *adj.* having a condition that causes reactions like sneezing or sensitive skin after contact with certain things

sentinel (sent′ ən əl) *n.* a person or animal that stands guard and keeps watch

Imagine that you saw this written on the wall of a house in the woods. What would you think? Would you be afraid?

When we got back and Duffy didn't have his jacket, did they get mad at him? My mother actually had the nerve to say, "Why didn't you remind him? You know he forgets things like that."

What do I look like, a walking memo pad?

Anyway, I had other things on my mind—like the fact that I was convinced someone had been following us while we were in the woods.

I tried to tell my mother about it, but first she said I was being ridiculous, and then she accused me of trying to **sabotage** the trip.

So I shut up. But I was pretty nervous, especially when Mom and Aunt Elise announced that they were going into town—which was twenty miles away—to pick up some supplies (like lightbulbs).

"You kids will be fine on your own," said Mom cheerfully. "You can make popcorn and play Monopoly. And there's enough soda here for you to make yourselves sick on."

And with that they were gone.

Word Power

sabotage (sab′ ə tazh′) *v.* to harm something in order to get it to fail

Reading Skill

Predict Reread the highlighted text. Did you predict that Duffy would lose his jacket? Now think about the words the narrator sees in one room of the cabin. What do you predict will happen with Duffy's jacket?

_____

_____

_____

_____

_____

Literary Element

Character Reread the highlighted text. What detail lets you know that the narrator is someone who is easily frightened?

_____

_____

_____

_____

_____

It got dark.

We played Monopoly.

They didn't come back. That didn't surprise me. Since Duffy and I were both fifteen, they felt it was okay to leave us on our own, and Mom had warned us they might decide to have dinner at the little inn we had seen on the way up.

But I would have been happier if they had been there.

Especially when something started scratching on the door.

"What was that?" asked Marie.

"What was what?" asked Duffy.

"That!" she said, and this time I heard it too. My stomach rolled over, and the skin at the back of my neck started to prickle.

"Maybe it's the Sentinel!" I hissed.

"Andrew!" yelled Marie. "Mom told you not to say that."

"She said not to try to scare you," I said. "I'm not. *I'm* scared! I told you I heard something following us in the woods today."

Scratch, scratch.

"But you said it stopped," said Duffy. "So how would it know where we are now?"

"I don't know. I don't know what it is. Maybe it tracked us, like a bloodhound."

Scratch, scratch.

"Don't bloodhounds have to have something to give them a scent?" asked Marie. "Like a piece of clothing, or—"

We both looked at Duffy!

"Your jacket, Duffy!"

Duffy turned white.

Did You Know?

A bloodhound is a breed of dog that is well known for its ability to track scents over long distances.

· · · · · · · · · · · · · · · · · · · ·

"That's silly," he said after a moment.

"There's something at the door," I said. "Maybe it's been **lurking** around all day, waiting for our mothers to leave. Maybe it's been waiting for years for someone to come back here."

Scratch, scratch.

"I don't believe it," said Duffy. "It's just the wind moving a branch. I'll prove it."

He got up and headed for the door. But he didn't open it. Instead he peeked through the window next to it. When he turned back, his eyes looked as big as the hardboiled eggs we had eaten for supper.

"There's something out there!" he hissed. *"Something big!"*

"I told you," I cried. "Oh, I knew there was something there."

"Andrew, are you doing this just to scare me?" said Marie. "Because if you are—"

Scratch, scratch.

"Come on," I said, grabbing her by the hand. "Let's get out of here."

I started to lead her up the stairs.

"Not there!" said Duffy. "If we go up there, we'll be trapped."

"You're right," I said. "Let's go out the back way!"

The thought of going outside scared the daylights out of me. But at least out there we would have somewhere to run. Inside—well, who knew what might happen if the thing found us inside.

We went into the kitchen.

I heard the front door open.

"Let's get out of here!" I hissed.

We scooted out the back door. "What now?" I wondered, looking around **frantically.**

Word Power

lurking (lurk´ ing) *v.* waiting in a hidden place, usually for a sneaky purpose
frantically (fran´ tik lē) *adv.* in a fast, nervous, and anxious manner

Reading Skill

Infer Reread the highlighted text. What is the narrator suggesting in his description of Duffy?

_____

_____

_____

_____

Comprehension Check

Reread the boxed text. Why do Duffy, Andrew, and Marie decide to go outside? Check the correct response.

☐ It's almost daylight, so it's safer outside.

☐ They might find some help in the woods.

☐ If they stay in the house, they could be trapped.

Comprehension Check

Reread the boxed text. Why don't the kids go into the barn? Why do they decide to go back into the house? Circle the answers in the text.

"The barn," whispered Duffy. "We can hide in the barn."

"Good idea," I said. Holding Marie by the hand, I led the way to the barn. But the door was held shut by a huge padlock.

The wind was blowing harder, but not hard enough to hide the sound of the back door of the house opening, and then slamming shut.

"Quick!" I whispered, "It knows we're out here. Let's sneak around front. It will never expect us to go back into the house."

Duffy and Marie followed me as I led them behind a hedge. I caught a **glimpse** of something heading toward the barn and swallowed nervously. It was big. Very big.

"I'm scared," whispered Marie.

"*Shhhh!*" I hissed. "We can't let it know where we are."

Look at the picture. Imagine that you are with the characters. Do you think you would feel safer inside this house or out in the woods? Why?

_____

Word Power

glimpse (glimps) *n.* a brief look at something

We slipped through the front door. We locked it, just like people always do in the movies, though what good that would do I couldn't figure, since if something really wanted to get at us, it would just break the window and come in.

"Upstairs," I whispered.

We tiptoed up the stairs. Once we were in our bedroom, I thought we were safe.

Crawling over the floor, I raised my head just enough to peek out the window. My heart almost stopped. Standing in the moonlight was an enormous, manlike creature. It had a scrap of cloth in its hands. It was looking around—looking for us. I saw it lift its head and sniff the wind. To my horror, it started back toward the house.

"It's coming back!" I yelped, more frightened than ever.

"How does it know where we are?" asked Marie.

I knew how. It had Duffy's jacket. It was tracking us down, like some giant bloodhound.

We huddled together in the middle of the room, trying to think of what to do.

A minute later we heard it.

Scratch, scratch.

None of us moved.

Scratch, scratch.

We stopped breathing, then jumped up in alarm at a terrible crashing sound.

The door was down.

We hunched back against the wall as heavy footsteps came clomping up the stairs.

I wondered what our mothers would think when they got back. Would they find our bodies? Or would there be nothing left of us at all?

Connect to the Text

Reread the boxed text. The narrator says they do something they've seen characters do in the movies. This scene feels very much like a scene in a scary movie. Do you like scary movies? Why or why not?

_____

_____

_____

_____

_____

Reading Skill

Infer Reread the highlighted paragraph. What is the narrator suggesting here?

_____

_____

_____

_____

Thump. Thump. Thump.

It was getting closer.

Thump. Thump. Thump.

It was outside the door.

Knock, knock.

"Don't answer!" hissed Duffy.

Like I said, he doesn't have the brains of a turnip.

It didn't matter. The door wasn't locked. It came swinging open. In the shaft of light I saw a huge figure. The Sentinel of the Woods! It had to be. I thought I was going to die.

The figure stepped into the room. Its head nearly touched the ceiling.

Marie squeezed against my side.

The huge creature sniffed the air. It turned in our direction. Its eyes seemed to glow. Moonlight glittered on its fangs.

Slowly the Sentinel raised its arm. I could see Duffy's jacket dangling from its fingertips.

And then it spoke.

"You forgot your jacket, stupid."

It threw the jacket at Duffy, turned around, and stomped down the stairs.

Which is why, I suppose, no one has had to remind Duffy to remember his jacket, or his glasses, or his math book, for at least a year now.

After all, when you leave stuff lying around, you never can be sure just who might bring it back.

Reading Skill

Predict Reread the highlighted text. Think back to the predictions you made throughout the story. Did you accurately predict what would happen with Duffy's jacket? What clues did you use to make your prediction? (When you read a story, don't worry if your predictions don't match what actually happens! You can always change your predictions as you get new information while reading.)

_____

_____

_____

_____

_____

Respond to Literature

DUFFY'S JACKET

A Comprehension Check

Answer the following questions in the spaces provided.

1. What is Duffy known for doing all the time? _____

_____

2. How do the characters first learn about the Sentinel? _____

_____

B Reading Skills

Answer the following questions in the spaces provided.

1. **Infer** What does the narrator mean when he says "Duffy makes a turnip look bright"? (Hint: A turnip is a kind of vegetable.) _____

_____

2. **Infer** At the end of the story the narrator says, "no one has had to remind Duffy to remember his jacket, or his glasses, or his math book, for at least a year now." What is the narrator suggesting about Duffy's reaction to the experience with the Sentinel? _____

_____

_____

3. **Predict** Do you predict that Duffy will eventually go back to his old ways? Will he start losing and forgetting things again? Why or why not?

_____

_____

C Word Power

Complete each sentence below, using one of the words in the box.

scatterbrained	allergic	sentinel	sabotage
lurking	frantically	glimpse	

1. The train was about to leave the station, so we rushed _____ to catch it.

2. Jamal caught a _____ of a smile on the principal's face and knew he was not in trouble.

3. Emily's brother constantly tries to _____ her band rehearsals by hiding her drumsticks.

4. I am feeling so _____ today that I almost can't remember my own name!

5. If Maria eats even one peanut, she has a terrible _____ reaction.

6. She stood outside the door of the secret meeting room, acting as a _____.

7. As Casey was hiking, he thought he saw a wolf _____ in the woods.

D Literary Element: Character

Read the passages below from "Duffy's Jacket." As you read, think about clues the author gives about the characters. Then answer the questions that follow.

If my cousin Duffy had the brains of a turnip, it never would have happened.[1] But as far as I'm concerned, Duffy makes a turnip look bright.[2] My mother disagrees.[3] According to her, Duffy is actually very bright.[4] She claims the reason he's so scatterbrained is that he's too busy being brilliant inside his own head to remember everyday things.[5]

When we got back and Duffy didn't have his jacket, did they get mad at him?[6] My mother actually had the nerve to say, "Why didn't you remind him?[7] You know he forgets things like that."[8]

What do I look like, a walking memo pad?[9]

1. In sentences 1–5, how does the narrator describe Duffy? How is this different from what the narrator's mother thinks of Duffy?

_____

_____

_____

2. What do sentences 6–9 tell you about the narrator? Do you think the narrator is patient and likes looking after Duffy? Why or why not?

_____

_____

_____

E The Sentinel Speaks!

Pretend you are the Sentinel doing a press conference to explain what happened with Duffy and his cousins. Fill in the lines below to finish what the Sentinel says.

I tell ya, it's not easy being the Sentinel of the _____

There was this family from the city. I heard their car bumping all the way down the road. They go into the woods to do stuff, like _____

_____

Now, I get pretty upset when people mess up my woods. So I left messages in all the nearby houses. In big letters, I wrote:

_____

You think it worked? Uh-uh. When they were out in the woods, the one kid forgot his _____

So I gotta bring it back to this kid. I didn't know where they were, so I tracked them like a _____

When I found them, they were running around like scared chickens. All I wanted to do was _____

Finally I got 'em cornered. I said to the kid, _____

_____

Then I was on my way. And that's the story. And now I have just one question—who left those shoes sitting by the stream?

Assessment

Fill in the circle next to each correct answer.

1. How are Duffy and the narrator related?
   - ○ A. They are brothers.
   - ○ B. They are cousins.
   - ○ C. They are close friends.
   - ○ D. They are half brothers.

2. Which of the following lines from the story gives you the **best** clue about what the narrator thinks Duffy is like?
   - ○ A. "What was what?" asked Duffy.
   - ○ B. You can take him camping all you want.
   - ○ C. Duffy turned white.
   - ○ D. Duffy makes a turnip look bright.

3. What is the narrator suggesting when he says, "Marie wasn't the only one who was frightened"?
   - ○ A. He likes frightening Marie.
   - ○ B. He thinks it is funny that Marie is frightened.
   - ○ C. Marie is not really frightened at all.
   - ○ D. He is frightened as well.

4. Which line from the story **best** helps you predict that the Sentinel is using Duffy's jacket to find the kids?
   - ○ A. It had a scrap of cloth in its hands.
   - ○ B. Moonlight glittered on its fangs.
   - ○ C. It turned in our direction.
   - ○ D. Its head nearly touched the ceiling.

5. Which of the following words means almost the same thing as "forgetful"?
   - ○ A. sentinel
   - ○ B. allergic
   - ○ C. scatterbrained
   - ○ D. sabotage

Home

Meet Gwendolyn Brooks

Gwendolyn Brooks was born in Kansas in 1917. Her family moved to Chicago after her birth. Her stories are usually set in cities. Her characters are ordinary people trying to make it from day to day. In 1950 Brooks became the first African American author to win the Pulitzer Prize for Poetry. The story "Home" is taken from Gwendolyn Brooks's novel *Maud Martha*, which was first published in 1953. Brooks died in 2000.

What You Know

When you hear the word *home*, what do you think about? What are some things that make a home important to the people who live there?

Reason to Read

As you read this story, look for what makes home important to the characters.

Background Info

The story "Home" is set on Chicago's South Side, where Gwendolyn Brooks grew up. By the 1920s, most of Chicago's African American population lived on the South Side. Since African Americans were usually prevented from moving into other neighborhoods, South Side residents set up their own churches, businesses, and entertainment centers. In time, the South Side of Chicago became one of the most active African American communities in the United States.

Word Power

obstinate (ob´ stə nit) *adj.* stubborn; not willing to give in; p. 116
The *obstinate* child refused to eat the carrots.

extension (iks ten´ shən) *n.* an additional amount of time; p. 116
The students were given an *extension* to finish their project.

flat (flat) *n.* an apartment; p. 116
We rented a *flat* on the third floor of a building downtown.

firing (fīr´ ing) *n.* starting up a fire; lighting up something; p. 117
The early settlers in America had to do a lot of *firing* for cooking.

casually (kazh´ o͞o ə lē) *adv.* in a way that happens by chance; not planned; p. 118
Anita's mother *casually* mentioned that they would have a surprise visitor at dinner.

Answer the following questions, using one of the new words above.
Write your answers in the spaces provided.

1. Which word goes with "the act of turning on the oven"? _____

2. Which word goes with "refusing to give in"? _____

3. Which word goes with "an extra day to finish something"? _____

4. Which word goes with "walking through the park without planning a route"?

    _____

5. Which word goes with "a place where you live"?_____

Home

Gwendolyn Brooks

Reading Skill

Predict Reread the title and the highlighted sentences. What is the family worried about losing? What do you predict will happen?

_____

_____

_____

_____

_____

Comprehension Check

Reread the boxed text. What will the family have to do if Papa does not get an extension on the loan? Circle the answers in the text.

What had been wanted was this always, this always to last, the talking softly on this porch, with the snake plant in the jardiniere in the southwest corner, and the **obstinate** slip from Aunt Eppie's magnificent Michigan fern at the left side of the friendly door. Mama, Maud Martha and Helen rocked slowly in their rocking chairs, and looked at the late afternoon light on the lawn, and at the emphatic iron of the fence and at the poplar tree. These things might soon be theirs no longer. Those shafts and pools of light, the tree, the graceful iron, might soon be viewed possessively by different eyes.

Papa was to have gone that noon, during his lunch hour, to the office of the Home Owners' Loan. If he had not succeeded in getting another **extension,** they would be leaving this house in which they had lived for more than fourteen years. There was little hope. The Home Owners' Loan was hard. They sat, making their plans.

"We'll be moving into a nice **flat** somewhere," said Mama. "Somewhere on South Park, or Michigan, or in Washington Park Court." Those flats, as the girls and Mama knew well, were burdens on wages twice the size of Papa's. This was not mentioned now.

Word Power

obstinate (ob′ stə nit) *adj.* stubborn; not willing to give in
extension (iks ten′ shən) *n.* an additional amount of time
flat (flat) *n.* an apartment

"They're much prettier than this old house," said Helen. "I have friends I'd just as soon not bring here. And I have other friends that wouldn't come down this far for anything, unless they were in a taxi."

Yesterday, Maud Martha would have attacked her. Tomorrow she might. Today she said nothing. She merely gazed at a little hopping robin in the tree, her tree, and tried to keep the fronts of her eyes dry.

"Well, I do know," said Mama, turning her hands over and over, "that I've been getting tireder and tireder of doing that **firing.** From October to April, there's firing to be done."

"But lately we've been helping, Harry and I," said Maud Martha. "And sometimes in March and April and in October, and even in November, we could build a little fire in the fireplace. Sometimes the weather was just right for that."

She knew, from the way they looked at her, that this had been a mistake. They did not want to cry.

But she felt that the little line of white, somewhat ridged with smoked purple, and all that cream-shot saffron, would never drift across any western sky except that in back of this house. The rain would drum with as sweet a dullness nowhere but here. The birds on South Park were mechanical birds, no better than the poor caught canaries in those "rich" women's sun parlors.

"It's just going to kill Papa!" burst out Maud Martha. "He loves this house! He *lives* for this house!"

"He lives for us," said Helen. "It's us he loves. He wouldn't want the house, except for us."

"And he'll have us," added Mama, "wherever."

"You know," Helen sighed, "if you want to know the truth, this is a relief. If this hadn't come up, we would have gone on, just dragged on, hanging out here forever."

Word Power
firing (fīr′ ing) *n.* starting up a fire; lighting up something

English Coach

The grammatically correct way to say *tireder and tireder* is "more and more tired." Sometimes you can add *-er* to words to mean "more." What word can you make to mean "more tall"? Write another word that ends with *-er* and means "more" of something.

_____

_____

Literary Element

Theme Reread the text highlighted in blue. Think about what Helen and Mama say about what Papa really loves. Which sentence **best** represents the theme? Check the correct response.

☐ A house is the only important thing for a family.

☐ A home cannot be wherever you want it to be.

☐ Being with family is the most important part of a home.

Reading Skill

Predict Reread the first highlighted passage. Look back at the prediction you made earlier. Did you predict that the family was worried about losing their house? Do you think Papa is bringing them good news? Why or why not?

_____

_____

_____

_____

Reading Skill

Infer Reread the second highlighted passage. What can you infer about Helen's feelings when she says why she wants to throw a party? Check the correct response.

☐ She is proud that they own their own home.

☐ She wants to have a party because she's bored.

☐ She is sad that her friends don't live closer.

"It might," allowed Mama, "be an act of God. God may just have reached down, and picked up the reins."

"Yes," Maud Martha cracked in, "that's what you always say— that God knows best."

Her mother looked at her quickly, decided the statement was not suspect, looked away.

Helen saw Papa coming. "There's Papa," said Helen.

They could not tell a thing from the way Papa was walking. It was that same dear little staccato walk, one shoulder down, then the other, then repeat, and repeat. They watched his progress. He passed the Kennedys', he passed the vacant lot, he passed Mrs. Blakemore's. They wanted to hurl themselves over the fence, into the street, and shake the truth out of his collar. He opened his gate—the gate—and still his stride and face told them nothing.

"Hello," he said.

Mama got up and followed him through the front door. The girls knew better than to go in too.

Presently Mama's head emerged. Her eyes were lamps turned on.

"It's all right," she exclaimed. "He got it. It's all over. Everything is all right."

The door slammed shut. Mama's footsteps hurried away.

"I think," said Helen, rocking rapidly, "I think I'll give a party. I haven't given a party since I was eleven. I'd like some of my friends to just **casually** see that we're homeowners."

Children Dancing, 1948. Robert Gwathmey (1903–1988). Oil on canvas, 32 x 40 in. The Butler Institute of American Art, Youngstown, OH.

Imagine that this is a scene from "Home." What part of the story do you think it would be from?

_____

Word Power

casually (kazh´ o͞o ə lē) *adv.* in a way that happens by chance; not planned

Home

A Comprehension Check

Answer the following questions in the spaces provided.

1. What problem does the family in the story face? _____

   _____

   _____

2. At the end of the story, what news does Papa bring home? _____

   _____

   _____

B Reading Skills

Answer the following questions in the spaces provided.

1. **Predict** After Mama speaks to Papa when he comes home, her eyes are "lamps turned on." How does this clue help you predict how the story

   will end? _____

   _____

   _____

2. **Infer** When the characters talk of losing their home, the narrator says Maud Martha "tried to keep the fronts of her eyes dry." What is the

   narrator suggesting about Maud Martha's feelings? _____

   _____

   _____

C Word Power

Complete each sentence below, using one of the words in the box.

obstinate	extension	flat
firing	casually	

1. Before winter comes, we always need to do the _____ for the furnace.

2. I need an _____ on my assignment because I'm not finished.

3. Maria was _____ and insisted that she was right.

4. Julian _____ said that he could not make it to the party.

5. Dara lives in a _____ that has a great view of the park.

Circle the word that best completes each sentence.

6. His mother woke up early to start the **(casually, firing)** for the oven.

7. Amelia **(casually, extension)** walked through the lunchroom looking for a place to sit.

8. Damien likes living on a high floor because his **(flat, obstinate)** receives a lot of sunlight.

9. She needed the book for the weekend, so the librarian gave her the **(extension, flat)** she had requested.

10. Barbara is often **(firing, obstinate)** when she does not get her way.

D Literary Element: Theme

Read the passage below from "Home." As you read, think about what the sentences reveal about the theme of the story that being together is the most important part of having a home. Then answer the questions that follow.

"It's just going to kill Papa!" burst out Maud Martha.[1] "He loves this house![2] He *lives* for this house!"[3]

"He lives for us," said Helen.[4] "It's us he loves.[5] He wouldn't want the house, except for us."[6]

"And he'll have us," added Mama, "wherever."[7]

1. How do sentences 1–6 show that it's not the house Papa loves, it's the family in it that he loves? _____

_____

_____

_____

_____

_____

2. How does sentence 7 show that even if they lose their house, the family will still have a home? _____

_____

_____

_____

_____

_____

E Party Invitation

Imagine you are Helen writing the party invitation. Explain what has happened and why you are throwing the party. Tell your guests what you will provide, and ask them to bring something.

PARTY!

Dear Friends!

Good news! Papa got the _____

We were worried we would have to _____

_____

But we're staying put . . . and throwing a party to celebrate!
We will provide _____

We would be very grateful if you would bring _____

_____

But most important, bring yourselves! We want to
share with everyone what we learned: the most
important part of a home is _____

_____

We can't wait to see you!

Assessment

Fill in the circle next to each correct answer.

1. Which sentence from the story **best** helps you predict what the story will be about?
   - ○ A. There was little hope.
   - ○ B. They sat, making their plans.
   - ○ C. The girls knew better than to go in too.
   - ○ D. These things might soon be theirs no longer.

2. When the author writes that Mama's eyes "were lamps turned on," what is she suggesting about Mama?
   - ○ A. Mama is excited and happy.
   - ○ B. Mama is sad and crying.
   - ○ C. Mama is not looking at anyone.
   - ○ D. Mama can't see very well.

3. What news does Mama deliver to the girls at the end of the story?
   - ○ A. Mama is going to sell the house.
   - ○ B. Helen is going to have a party.
   - ○ C. The family will have to move.
   - ○ D. Papa got the home loan extension.

4. Which statement **best** tells the theme of "Home"?
   - ○ A. Apartments make the best homes.
   - ○ B. Home is wherever the family lives.
   - ○ C. New homes are better than old homes.
   - ○ D. You need a loan to own a home.

5. Which of the following words means "an additional amount of time"?
   - ○ A. flat
   - ○ B. obstinate
   - ○ C. extension
   - ○ D. firing

A Crush

Meet
Cynthia Rylant

Cynthia Rylant (rī′lənt) was born in West Virginia in 1954. She faced hard times growing up, so her stories often deal with ordinary people who face difficult times. She says she likes writing about "people who don't get any attention in the world." She wants to make these people important in her stories. Today Cynthia Rylant lives in Oregon. "A Crush" was first published in 1990.

What You Know

Think about someone your age whom you wish you knew better. How could you let that person know you are interested?

Reason to Read

Read this short story to find out how one person shows that he likes another person.

Background Info

Some people are born with mental disabilities. This means that it may take them longer to learn to do certain things, like speak. There may be some things that they cannot learn or do, so they may need extra help taking care of themselves. Other people dedicate their time to helping those with special needs. They help people with mental disabilities learn to take care of themselves and feel more comfortable in the world.

Word Power

excess (ek´ses) *adj.* more than usual or necessary; p. 126
The *excess* glue made the paper very sticky.

taut (tôt) *adj.* stretched tight; p. 127
He pulled the rope to make it straight and *taut*.

illuminated (i lōō´mə nāt´id) *v.* lit up; p. 128
The lamp *illuminated* the room.

eventually (i ven´chōō ə lē) *adv.* in the end; finally; p. 129
She looked at the books for a long time and *eventually* chose a mystery.

intently (in tent´lē) *adv.* in a firmly focused way; with concentration; p. 130
He stared *intently* at the map to find the street.

hardy (här´dē) *adj.* strong and sturdy; able to hold up under bad conditions; p. 132
The *hardy* plants lived through the winter.

**Answer the following questions that contain the new words above.
Write your answers in the spaces provided.**

1. Is a *hardy* person someone who is strong or weak? _____

2. If you have *excess* popcorn, do you have too much popcorn or

   too little? _____

3. When Lee looked *intently* at a painting, did he study it or glance at it?

   _____

4. If a rope is *taut*, is it loose or tight? _____

5. When Paula *illuminated* the room, did she turn on a light or turn off a light?

   _____

6. If Sandy *eventually* showed up, did she show up right away or at a later time?

   _____

Adapted from

A Crush

Cynthia Rylant

Connect to the Text

Reread the boxed sentence. Do you live in a small town or a friendly neighborhood? Do you think most people in a small town or neighborhood know each other very well?

_____

_____

_____

_____

_____

Did You Know?

Stan Laurel was part of the comedy team Laurel and Hardy. Stan is the thin man with the long face. Laurel and Hardy made movies together from the late 1920s to 1951.

> When the windows of Stan's Hardware started filling up with flowers, everyone in town knew something had happened.

Excess flowers usually mean death, but since these were all real flowers and since they stood bunched in clear mason jars, everyone knew nobody had died. So they all figured somebody had a crush and kept quiet.

There wasn't really a Stan of Stan's Hardware. Dick Wilcox was the owner. Since he'd never liked his own name, he gave his store half the name of his childhood hero, Stan Laurel in the movies. Dick had been married for twenty-seven years. Once, his wife Helen had dropped a German chocolate cake on his head at a Lion's Club dance. So Dick and Helen were probably not the ones for whom the flowers lining the windows of Stan's Hardware were meant. That left Dolores.

Word Power

excess (ek´ses) *adj.* more than usual or necessary

126

Dolores was the assistant manager at Stan's. She had worked there for twenty years, since high school. She knew the store like a mother knows her baby. Dick—who had trouble keeping up with things like prices—tried to keep himself busy in the back and give Dolores the run of the floor. This worked fine because the carpenters and plumbers and painters in town trusted Dolores and took her advice to heart. They also liked her tattoo.

Dolores was the only woman in town with a tattoo. On the days she went sleeveless, one could see it on the **taut** brown skin of her upper arm:"Howl at the Moon."The picture was of a baying coyote. Nobody had gotten out of Dolores the true story behind the tattoo. Some of the men who came in liked to show off their own. All of them had gotten their tattoos when they were in the service. Dolores had never been in the service and there wasn't a tattoo parlor anywhere near. They couldn't figure why or where any woman would have a howling coyote ground into the soft skin of her upper arm. But Dolores wasn't telling.

That the flowers in Stan's front window had anything to do with Dolores seemed completely unlikely. As far as anyone knew, Dolores had never been in love nor had anyone ever been in love with her. Some believed it was the tattoo which kept admirers away. Some felt it was because Dolores was just more of a man than most of the men in town. Fellows couldn't figure out how to date someone who knew more about the carburetor of a car or the back side of a washing machine than they did. Others thought Dolores simply didn't want love.

English Coach

Reread the sentence highlighted in red. The author is comparing Dolores and the store to a mother and her baby. A mother knows her baby very well, so Dolores must know the store very well. Think of something you know really well. Now write a sentence about it below and use the phrase *like a mother knows her baby.*

_____

_____

_____

Reading Skill

Predict Reread the title of the story and the sentence highlighted in green. Predict why someone is leaving flowers. Whom are the flowers for?

_____

_____

_____

_____

Word Power

taut (tôt) *adj.* stretched tight

127

Reading Skill

Predict Reread the highlighted text. Did you accurately predict why someone is leaving flowers and whom they are for? What details from the story helped you make your prediction? (Don't worry if your prediction doesn't match what happens! You can change your predictions as you get new information from the story.)

_____

_____

_____

_____

Background Info

W. Atlee Burpee & Company is the world's largest mail-order seed company. It was started in 1876 by eighteen-year-old W. Atlee Burpee. He borrowed $1,000 from his mother to start the business.

Did You Know?

Zinnias, cornflowers, nasturtiums, marigolds, asters, and four-o'clocks are colorful types of flowers.

The man who was in love with Dolores and who brought her zinnias and cornflowers and nasturtiums and marigolds and asters and four-o'clocks in clear mason jars did not know any of this. He did not know that men showed Dolores their tattoos. He did not know that Dolores understood how to use and to sell a belt sander. The man who brought flowers to Dolores on Wednesdays when the hardware opened its doors at 7:00 A.M. didn't care who Dolores had ever been or what anyone had ever thought of her. He loved her and he wanted to bring her flowers.

Ernie had lived in this town all of his life and had never before met Dolores. He was thirty-three years old. For thirty-one of those years he had lived at home with his mother in a small, dark house on the edge of town. Ernie had been a perfectly beautiful baby, with shining black hair and large blue eyes and a round, wise face. But as he had grown, it had become clearer and clearer that his mind had not developed as perfectly. Ernie would not be able to speak in sentences until he was six years old. He would not be able to count the apples in a bowl until he was eight. By the time he was ten, he could sing a simple song. At age twelve, he understood what a joke was. And when he was twenty, something he saw on television made him cry.

Ernie's mother kept him in the house with her because it was easier. Ernie knew nothing of the world except this house. They lived, the two of them, in tiny dark rooms always **illuminated** by the glow of a television set. Ernie's bags of cookies littered the floor, his baseball cards were scattered across the sofa, his heavy winter coat was thrown over the arm of a chair so he could wear it whenever he wanted, and his box of Burpee seed packages sat in the middle of the kitchen table.

Word Power

illuminated (i lōō′mə nāt′id) _v._ lit up

These Ernie loved. The seeds had been delivered to his home by mistake. One day a woman wearing a brown uniform had pulled up in a brown truck, walked quickly to the front porch of Ernie's house, set a box down, and with a couple of toots of her horn, driven off again. The box didn't have their name on it. But the brown truck was gone, so whatever was in the box was theirs to keep. Ernie pulled off the heavy tape and found inside the box more little packages of seeds than he could count. He lifted them out, one by one, and examined the beautiful photographs of flowers on each. Ernie sat down at the kitchen table and quietly looked at each package for a long time. His fingers outlined the shapes of zinnias and cornflowers and nasturtiums and marigolds and asters and four-o'clocks. His eyes drank up their colors.

Two months later Ernie's mother died. People from the county courthouse came out to get Ernie. As they led him from the home, he picked up the box of seed packages from his kitchen table.

Eventually Ernie was moved to a large white house near the main street of town. This house was called a group home, because in it lived a group of people who could not live on their own. There were six of them. Each had his own room. When Ernie was shown the room that would be his, he put the box of Burpee seeds on the little table beside the bed. Then he sat down on the bed and cried.

Ernie cried every day for nearly a month. And then he stopped. He dried his tears. He learned how to bake refrigerator biscuits and how to dust mop and what to do if the indoor plants looked brown. Ernie loved watering the indoor plants.

One of the young men who worked at the group home—a college student named Jack—grew a large garden in the back of the house. During his first summer, Ernie would stand at the kitchen window, watching Jack move among the vegetables. Ernie was curious, but too afraid to go into the garden.

Word Power
eventually (i venˊcho͞o ə lē) *adv.* in the end; finally

Comprehension Check

Reread the boxed text. How does Ernie get the seeds? Check the correct response.

- ☐ A. He wins them in a contest.
- ☐ B. His mother gives them to him.
- ☐ C. He buys them with his own money.
- ☐ D. A truck driver delivers them by mistake.

English Coach

Reread the sentence with the highlighted phrase. This does not mean Ernie actually *drinks* the colors. Here, *drank up* means that Ernie stares at the flowers in admiration. Do you think this means that Ernie likes the colorful flowers or does not like them?

_____

_____

_____

Reading Skill

Infer Reread the highlighted sentences. Why do you think Ernie panics when he sees Jack putting seeds into the ground?

_____

_____

_____

Connect to the Text

Reread the boxed sentences. Think about a time you went somewhere new and felt nervous. Why do you think you felt that way? Do you think going back to a place again and again makes you feel more comfortable? Why or why not?

_____

_____

_____

_____

Then one day when Ernie was watching, he noticed that Jack was ripping open several slick little packages and emptying them into the ground. Ernie panicked and ran to his room. But the box of Burpee seeds was still there on his table, untouched. He grabbed it and slid it under his bed. Then he went back through the house and out into the garden as if he had done this every day of his life.

He stood beside Jack, watching him empty seed packages into the soft black soil. As the packages were emptied, Ernie asked for them, holding out his hand. Jack handed the empty packages over with a smile and became Ernie's first friend.

Jack tried to explain to Ernie that the seeds would grow into vegetables. Ernie could not believe this until he saw it come true. And when it did, he looked even more **intently** at the packages of flowers hidden beneath his bed. He thought more deeply about them, but he could not let the garden have his seeds.

That was the first year in the large white house.

The second year, Ernie saw Dolores. After that he thought of nothing else but her and of the photographs of flowers beneath his bed.

Jack had decided to take Ernie downtown for breakfast every Wednesday morning to ease him into the world outside. They left very early, at 5:45 A.M., so there would be few people and almost no traffic to frighten Ernie. Jack and Ernie drove to the restaurant which sat across the street from Stan's Hardware. Their first time in the restaurant, Ernie was too nervous to eat. The second time, he could eat but he couldn't look up. The third time, he not only ate everything on his plate, but he lifted his head and he looked out the window of the restaurant toward Stan's Hardware. There he saw a dark-haired woman in jeans and a black T-shirt unlocking the front door of the building. That was the moment Ernie started loving Dolores and thinking about giving up his seeds to the soft black soil of Jack's garden.

Word Power

intently (in tent′lē) *adv.* in a firmly focused way; with concentration

Boulevard Diner—Worcester, MA, 1992. John Baeder. Oil on canvas, 30¼ x 48¼ in. OK Harris Works of Art, New York.

Look at the diner in the picture. When you picture the diner Ernie and Jack go to, is it similar to this one? Why or why not?

Love is such a mystery. When it strikes the heart of one as mysterious as Ernie himself, it can hardly be spoken of. Ernie could not explain to Jack why he went directly to his room later that morning, pulled the box of Burpee seeds from under his bed, grabbed Jack's hand in the kitchen and walked with him to the garden. Ernie handed the packets of seeds one by one to Jack, who asked Ernie several times, "Are you sure you want to plant these?" Ernie was sure.

That was in June. For the next several Wednesdays at 7:00 A.M. Ernie watched every movement of the dark-haired woman behind the lighted windows of Stan's Hardware. Jack watched Ernie watch Dolores, and wisely said nothing.

Literary Element

Theme Reread the highlighted sentences. After Ernie falls in love, he decides to plant his seeds. How does this action help you understand the theme that love can make people do things they normally would not do?

_____

_____

_____

_____

_____

_____

_____

Comprehension Check

Reread the boxed sentences. How does Ernie know the flowers are ready to be picked? Underline the phrase that best answers the question.

Reading Skill

Infer Reread the highlighted text. What can you infer about what Dolores is thinking or feeling when she smells the flowers and puts them in the window?

_____

_____

_____

_____

_____

When Ernie's flowers began growing in July, Ernie spent most of his time in the garden. The flowers grew fast and **hardy.** One early Wednesday morning when they looked as big and bright as their pictures on the empty packages, Ernie pulled a glass canning jar off a dusty shelf in the basement of his house. He washed the jar and half filled it with water. Then he carried it to the garden where he placed in it one of every kind of flower he had grown. He met Jack at the car and rode off to the restaurant with the jar of flowers held tight between his small hands. Jack told him it was a beautiful bouquet.

When they reached the door of the restaurant, Ernie stopped and pulled at Jack's arm, pointing to the building across the street. "OK," Jack said, and he led Ernie to the front door of Stan's Hardware. It was 6:00 A.M. and the building was still dark. Ernie set the jar full of flowers under the sign that read "Closed." Then he smiled at Jack and followed him back across the street to get breakfast.

When Dolores arrived at seven and picked up the jar of zinnias and cornflowers and nasturtiums and marigolds and asters and four-o'clocks, Ernie and Jack were watching her. Each had a wide smile on his face as Dolores put her nose to the flowers. Ernie giggled. They watched the lights of the hardware store come up and saw Dolores place the jar on the ledge of the front window. They drove home still smiling.

All the rest of that summer Ernie left a jar of flowers every Wednesday morning at the front door of Stan's Hardware. Neither Dick Wilcox nor Dolores could figure out why the flowers kept coming. Each of them thought that somebody had a crush on the other.

Word Power

hardy (här′ dē) *adj.* strong and sturdy; able to hold up under bad conditions

132

If a person were to receive flowers like these, what kind of effect do you think it would have on him or her?

But the flowers had an effect on them anyway. Dick started spending more time making conversation with the customers, while Dolores stopped wearing T-shirts to work. Instead she wore crisp white blouses with the sleeves rolled back off her wrists. Occasionally she put on a bracelet.

By summer's end Jack and Ernie had become very good friends. When the flowers in the garden began to wither, and Ernie's face began to grow gray as he watched them, Jack brought home a great long box. Ernie followed Jack as he carried it down to the basement. He watched as Jack pulled a long glass tube from the box and attached this tube to the wall above a table. When Jack plugged in the tube's electric cord, a soft, lavender light filled the room.

"Sunshine," said Jack.

Then he went back to his car for a smaller box. He carried this down to the basement where Ernie still stood staring at the strange light. Jack handed Ernie the small box. When Ernie opened it he found more little packages of seeds than he could count, with new kinds of photographs on the slick paper.

"Violets," Jack said, pointing to one of them.

Then he and Ernie went outside to get some dirt.

Literary Element

Theme Reread the sentences highlighted in blue. Love can change people. It can make them act better toward each other and themselves. Dick is talking more to customers. What does Dolores do that shows love has changed her?

_____

_____

_____

_____

Reading Skill

Predict Reread the text highlighted in green. What do you think is the purpose of the light?

_____

_____

_____

_____

Respond to Literature

A Crush

A Comprehension Check

Answer the following questions in the spaces provided.

1. How is Dolores different from the other women in town? _____

   _____

2. Whom do Dolores and Dick Wilcox think the flowers are for? _____

   _____

3. What two things does Jack buy for Ernie when the summer ends and the flowers stop growing? _____

   _____

B Reading Skills

Answer the following questions in the spaces provided.

1. **Infer** Why do you think Ernie finally plants his seeds? _____

   _____

2. **Infer** Why do you think Dick and Dolores change when Ernie leaves the flowers at their store? _____

   _____

3. **Predict** The light Jack gives Ernie at the end will help the flowers continue to grow. Predict how Ernie will continue to change and grow as well.

   _____

   _____

C Word Power

Complete each sentence below, using one of the words in the box.

excess	taut	illuminated
eventually	intently	hardy

1. He tightened his guitar strings to make them _____ .

2. Time passed and the flowers _____ wilted.

3. It takes a very _____ hiker to climb the steep mountain.

4. Mark studied the map _____, hoping to find his friend's street.

5. The _____ water spilled over the top of the glass.

6. The fireworks _____ the dark sky.

D Literary Element: Theme

Read the two passages below from "A Crush." As you read, think about what the sentences reveal about the theme of the story that love can change people. Then answer the questions that follow.

> There he saw a dark-haired woman in jeans and a black T-shirt unlocking the front door of the building.[1] That was the moment Ernie started loving Dolores and thinking about giving up his seeds to the soft black soil of Jack's garden.[2]
>
> But the flowers had an effect on them anyway.[3] Dick started spending more time making conversation with the customers, while Dolores stopped wearing T-shirts to work.[4] Instead she wore crisp white blouses with the sleeves rolled back off her wrists.[5] Occasionally she put on a bracelet.[6]

1. How do sentences 1–2 show that love changes Ernie and makes him do something he did not want to do before? _____

_____

_____

2. How do sentences 3–6 show that love can have a good effect on people?

_____

_____

_____

E An Advice Column

Imagine that you write an advice column to help people with their problems. A reader has written you a letter. The reader has a crush on someone and wants to know how to get to know that person better. Give some advice to this reader.

Dear Reader,

There are many ways that you can show that you are interested in a person. You can _____

_____

_____

Perhaps the best way to show this person how you feel is by _____

_____

_____

Maybe the other person will respond by _____

_____

_____

It's always nice to let people know how important they are to you. Good luck!

Assessment

Fill in the circle next to each correct answer.

1. Which sentence from the story **best** helps you predict that the flowers are for Dolores?
   - ○ A. Dolores was the assistant manager at Stan's.
   - ○ B. Dolores was the only woman in town with a tattoo.
   - ○ C. Dolores had never been in love nor had anyone ever been in love with her.
   - ○ D. Nobody had gotten out of Dolores the true story behind the tattoo.

2. How does Ernie first get the packages of seeds?
   - ○ A. He wins them in a contest.
   - ○ B. His mother gives them to him.
   - ○ C. He buys them with his own money.
   - ○ D. A truck driver delivers them by mistake.

3. Why do you think Ernie gets upset when he first sees Jack planting seeds in the ground?
   - ○ A. Ernie suspects that Jack likes Dolores.
   - ○ B. Ernie worries that Jack is planting his seeds.
   - ○ C. Ernie thinks it is too cold for the seeds to grow.
   - ○ D. Ernie does not want Jack to work in the garden without him.

4. What message does the author want us to learn from the story?
   - ○ A. Love can change people for the better.
   - ○ B. It is important to plant seeds in a garden.
   - ○ C. People should not live alone.
   - ○ D. Flowers have no place in a hardware store.

5. Which of the following words means the **opposite** of "weak and frail"?
   - ○ A. intently
   - ○ B. hardy
   - ○ C. excess
   - ○ D. illuminated

Wrap-up

Compare and Contrast

Theme is an important literary element in "Home" and "A Crush." Although the themes in these short stories are different, they both relate to the importance of love and being with those you love. Think about the themes in each story. Think about what the characters value most. Finally, think about how these values influence the characters and their relationships with others.

Under each title below, write the theme. In the middle column, explain what the themes have in common. An example has been done for you.

"Home"	Alike	"A Crush"
	• Both themes show that love helps people deal with hard times.	

Drama

What's Drama?

If you've ever seen a drama, you know that it can grab you. Drama, whether it is a play, a movie, or a TV show, brings literature to life.

A **drama** is a story that is performed by actors for an audience. The printed form of a drama is called a script. When you read a script, you can use your imagination to see the stage, the scenery, and the actors. A script has different parts that help you imagine what you are reading:

- The **cast of characters** tells you who is in the play. Sometimes a brief description is given for each character.

- **Dialogue** is the conversation between the characters. The name of the character speaking appears before each line of dialogue.

- **Stage directions** describe the setting and the characters. They also tell actors how to move or speak. Stage directions are often in *italics*.

- Longer dramas are divided into sections called **acts.** Each act may be divided into smaller sections called **scenes.**

What kinds of drama do you like to watch? Do you have a favorite movie, play, or TV series? What is it?

_____

_____

Why Read Drama?

Dramas amuse, teach, and inspire us. When we watch characters or read their words in a play, we can learn something about other people, and sometimes even learn something about ourselves. Drama, like other literature, can take us to different worlds or give us a new view of our own world.

How Do I Read Drama?

Focus on a key **literary element** and **reading skills** to get the most out of reading the drama in this unit. Here are one key literary element and two key reading skills that you will practice in this unit.

Key Literary Element

Science Fiction

Science fiction is a kind of fiction that uses ideas from science. Sometimes it is about imaginary worlds and may include creatures from a different planet. Often science fiction explores our own world as it may be in the future. Most science fiction stories have details that are both familiar and unfamiliar to readers. For example, science fiction stories may involve time travel or inventions that we don't have today. However, many science fiction stories feature characters who must deal with issues and problems that are familiar to us, like fear and loneliness.

Key Reading Skills

• Respond

Whenever you stop to consider your thoughts and feelings about something you've read, you are **responding** to the text. Think about and express what you like or don't like, what surprises you or scares you or makes you laugh out loud. You can share how you feel about what you have read. You can also respond by putting yourself in a character's place. As you read, think about how what you are reading is making you feel.

• Cause and Effect

A **cause** is a condition or an event that makes something happen. What happens as a result of a cause is an **effect.** Many events in stories are connected by cause-and-effect relationships. A cause can have more than one effect. For example, a character may do something wrong (cause) and then feel guilty (effect). The character may then try to correct the wrong that was done (a new effect caused by the character's feelings of guilt). As you read, ask yourself: Did what just happened occur because of something that happened earlier?

THE MONSTERS ARE DUE ON MAPLE STREET

Meet Rod Serling

Rod Serling was born in New York in 1924. He is best known as the creator of the popular fantasy and science fiction TV series *The Twilight Zone*. The shows are famous for having a surprising twist at the end of the episode. The series ran from 1959 to 1964. Serling wrote nearly two out of every three of the show's 156 plays. Serling died in 1975. "The Monsters Are Due on Maple Street" first aired in 1959.

What You Know

Imagine that strange things start happening on your street: lights flicker on and off, telephones ring and go dead, cars start and stop by themselves. Would you be afraid? How do you think you and your neighbors would react?

Reason to Read

Read this television play to see how the people on Maple Street react when strange things start happening.

Background Info

"The Monsters Are Due on Maple Street" is a play written especially for the television series *The Twilight Zone*. As you read, you will see many passages in italics and brackets. These are the stage directions. Every play has stage directions, but the directions are a little different when they are for television. Not only are there notes for the actors, there are also notes for the camera. For instance, the direction *cut* means to switch from one scene to another. A *close-up* means the camera should move closer to what it is focusing on, such as a person's face.

Word Power

legitimate (li jit´ ə mit) *adj.* that which follows the rules; lawful; p. 145
I was sick, so I had a *legitimate* excuse for missing school.

defiantly (di fī´ ənt lē) *adv.* in a way that boldly resists; p. 147
When his father told him to clean out the garage, Ben *defiantly* refused to do it.

scapegoat (skāp´ gōt´) *n.* a person who is blamed for the mistakes of others; p. 148
When the plan failed, the committee made its newest member a *scapegoat*.

apprehensive (ap´ ri hen´ siv) *adj.* anxious or fearful that something bad will happen; p. 150
I was very *apprehensive* about going down the swift river on a raft.

converging (kən vurj´ ing) *v.* coming together at a place or point; p. 152
We could see firefighters *converging* on the burning house.

explicit (eks plis´ it) *adj.* very clear; p. 155
The safety rules posted at the swimming pool are very *explicit*.

prejudices (prej´ ə dis iz) *n.* critical opinions that are formed unfairly; p. 156
It isn't fair to have *prejudices* against people just because they look different from you.

**Answer the following questions that contain the new words above.
Write your answers in the spaces provided.**

1. If you feel *apprehensive,* are you relaxed or fearful? _____

2. If two rivers are *converging,* are they coming together or flowing away from
   each other? _____

3. If something is *legitimate,* does it go against the rules or follow the rules?

   _____

4. When Kianna spoke *defiantly* to her father, was she agreeing or disagreeing
   with him? _____

5. If someone gives you *explicit* instructions, are the instructions clearly expressed or
   difficult to understand? _____

6. If someone is a *scapegoat,* is that person being rewarded for the actions of others
   or blamed for the actions of others? _____

7. If Roberto has *prejudices,* does he have fair opinions or unfair opinions?

   _____

THE MONSTERS ARE DUE ON MAPLE STREET

Rod Serling

Comprehension Check

Reread the boxed text. This is a list of the characters who will be in the television play. This list can tell you how the characters are related to one another. How is Sally related to Tommy? Circle the answer in the text.

Literary Element

Science Fiction Reread the highlighted text. What details tell you that Tommy's story is science fiction?

_____

_____

_____

_____

_____

CHARACTERS

NARRATOR	FIGURE ONE	FIGURE TWO
STEVE BRAND	CHARLIE'S WIFE	MRS. GOODMAN
MRS. BRAND	TOMMY	WOMAN
DON MARTIN	SALLY, TOMMY'S MOTHER	MAN ONE
PETE VAN HORN	LES GOODMAN	MAN TWO
CHARLIE		

Summary of ACT I

After a mysterious roar and a flash of light, all the homes on Maple Street, a small-town street, lose power. The batteries in cars and radios also go dead. People come out to the street and discuss the situation. One man, Pete Van Horn, leaves to check the next street to see if they have power. Tommy, a 14-year-old boy, tells the people about a story he read that sounds very similar to what is happening on Maple Street. In the story, monsters from outer space are responsible. Tommy explains that the space monsters take the shapes of humans.

Suddenly Les Goodman's car starts by itself. The neighbors become suspicious of Goodman. When they find out that he likes looking at the stars at night, they become even more suspicious. They wonder if Goodman is responsible for the blackout or is helping the space monsters who are responsible.

ACT II

[*We see a* medium shot *of the Goodman entry hall at night. On the side table rests an unlit candle. MRS. GOODMAN walks into the scene, a glass of milk in hand. She sets the milk down on the table, lights the candle with a match from a box on the table, picks up the glass of milk, and starts out of scene. MRS. GOODMAN comes through her porch door, glass of milk in hand. The entry hall, with table and lit candle, can be seen behind her.*

Outside, the camera slowly pans *down the sidewalk, taking in little knots of people who stand around talking in low voices. At the end of each conversation they look toward LES GOODMAN's house. From the various houses we can see candlelight but no electricity, and there's an all-pervading quiet that blankets the whole area, disturbed only by the almost whispered voices of the people as they stand around. The camera pans over to one group where CHARLIE stands. He stares across at GOODMAN's house.*

We see a long shot *of the house. Two men stand across the street in almost sentry-like poses. Then we see a medium shot of a group of people.*]

SALLY.   [*A little timorously*] It just doesn't seem right, though, keeping watch on them. Why . . . he was right when he said he was one of our neighbors. Why, I've known Ethel Goodman ever since they moved in. We've been good friends—

CHARLIE.   That don't prove a thing. Any guy who'd spend his time lookin' up at the sky early in the morning—well, there's something wrong with that kind of person. There's something that ain't **legitimate.** Maybe under normal circumstances we could let it go by, but these aren't normal circumstances. Why, look at this street! Nothin' but candles. Why, it's like goin' back into the dark ages or somethin'!

Word Power

legitimate (li jit′ ə mit) *adj.* that which follows the rules; lawful

Reading Skill

Cause and Effect Reread the highlighted text. What has caused Goodman to worry that people want to give him trouble?

_____

_____

_____

_____

Reading Skill

Respond Reread the highlighted text near the bottom of the page. If you were Steve, how would you be feeling right now?

_____

_____

_____

_____

[*STEVE walks down the steps of his porch, walks down the street over to LES GOODMAN's house, and then stops at the foot of the steps. GOODMAN stands there, his wife behind him, very frightened.*]

GOODMAN.   Just stay right where you are, Steve. We don't want any trouble, but this time if anybody sets foot on my porch, that's what they're going to get—trouble!

STEVE.   Look, Les—

GOODMAN.   I've already explained to you people. I don't sleep very well at night sometimes. I get up and I take a walk and I look up at the sky. I look at the stars!

MRS. GOODMAN.   That's exactly what he does. Why this whole thing, it's . . . it's some kind of madness or something.

STEVE.   [*Nods grimly.*] That's exactly what it is—some kind of madness.

CHARLIE'S VOICE.   [*Shrill, from across the street.*] You best watch who you're seen with, Steve! Until we get this all straightened out, you ain't exactly above suspicion yourself.

STEVE.   [*Whirling around toward him.*] Or you, Charlie. Or any of us, it seems. From age eight on up.

WOMAN.   What I'd like to know is—what are we gonna do? Just stand around here all night?

CHARLIE.   There's nothin' else we can do! [*He turns back looking toward STEVE and GOODMAN again.*] One of 'em'll tip their hand. They got to.

STEVE.   [*Raising his voice.*] There's something you can do, Charlie. You could go home and keep your mouth shut. You could quit strutting around like a self-appointed hanging judge and just climb into bed and forget it.

CHARLIE.   You sound real anxious to have that happen, Steve. I think we better keep our eye on you too!

DON.   [*As if he were taking the bit in his teeth, takes a hesitant step to the front.*] I think everything might as well come out now. [*He turns toward STEVE.*] Your wife's done plenty of talking, Steve, about how odd you are!

CHARLIE. [*Picking this up, his eyes widening.*] Go ahead, tell us what she's said.

[*We see a long shot of STEVE as he walks toward them from across the street.*]

STEVE. Go ahead, what's my wife said? Let's get it all out. Let's pick out every idiosyncrasy of every single man, woman, and child on the street. And then we might as well set up some kind of kangaroo court. How about a firing squad at dawn, Charlie, so we can get rid of all the suspects? Narrow them down. Make it easier for you.

DON. There's no need gettin' so upset, Steve. It's just that . . . well . . . Myra's talked about how there's been plenty of nights you spent hours down in your basement workin' on some kind of radio or something. Well, none of us have ever seen that radio—

[*By this time STEVE has reached the group. He stands there **defiantly** close to them.*]

CHARLIE. Go ahead, Steve. What kind of "radio set" you workin' on? I never seen it. Neither has anyone else. Who you talk to on that radio set? And who talks to you?

STEVE. I'm surprised at you, Charlie. How come you're so dense all of a sudden? [*A pause.*] Who do I talk to? I talk to monsters from outer space. I talk to three-headed green men who fly over here in what look like meteors.

[*STEVE's wife steps down from the porch, bites her lip, calls out.*]

Did You Know?

A meteor is a piece of debris from space that enters Earth's atmosphere. It is also called a shooting star because it leaves a streak of light.

. . . .

Word Power

defiantly (di fī′ ənt lē) *adv.* in a way that boldly resists

Background Info

A kangaroo court is an irregular, unfair trial in which the final decision is usually made before the trial even starts.

Comprehension Check

Reread the boxed text. What has Myra said about Steve that is making people upset?

_____

_____

_____

_____

_____

_____

Background Info

Ham radio is a hobby in which a person operates his or her own radio station.

English Coach

The author uses the phrase *clickety-clack* to help the reader hear the sound of footsteps. Look at the words below. Check any word that imitates a sound.

☐ boom
☐ door
☐ screech
☐ telephone

MRS. BRAND. Steve! Steve, please. [*Then looking around, frightened, she walks toward the group.*] It's just a ham radio set, that's all. I bought him a book on it myself. It's just a ham radio set. A lot of people have them. I can show it to you. It's right down in the basement.

STEVE. [*Whirls around toward her.*] Show them nothing! If they want to look inside our house—let them get a search warrant.

CHARLIE. Look, buddy, you can't afford to—

STEVE. [*Interrupting.*] Charlie, don't tell me what I can afford! And stop telling me who's dangerous and who isn't and who's safe and who's a menace. [*He turns to the group and shouts.*] And you're with him, too—all of you! You're standing here all set to crucify—all set to find a **scapegoat**—all desperate to point some kind of a finger at a neighbor! Well now look, friends, the only thing that's gonna happen is that we'll eat each other up alive—

[*He stops abruptly as CHARLIE suddenly grabs his arm.*]

CHARLIE. [*In a hushed voice.*] That's not the only thing that can happen to us.

[*Cut to a long shot looking down the street. A figure has suddenly materialized in the gloom and in the silence we can hear the clickety-clack of slow, measured footsteps on concrete as the figure walks slowly toward them. One of the women lets out a stifled cry. The young mother grabs her boy as do a couple of others.*]

TOMMY. [*Shouting, frightened.*] It's the monster! It's the monster!

 Stop here for **Break Time** on the next page.

Word Power

scapegoat (skāp′ gōt′) *n.* a person who is blamed for the mistakes of others

Break Time

When reading any story or drama, it's important to keep track of causes and effects. As you read, remember that one effect can be the result of more than one cause. Below, in the center of the word web is one effect— everyone on Maple Street is frightened. In each outer circle, write one cause that leads to this effect. The first one has been done for you.

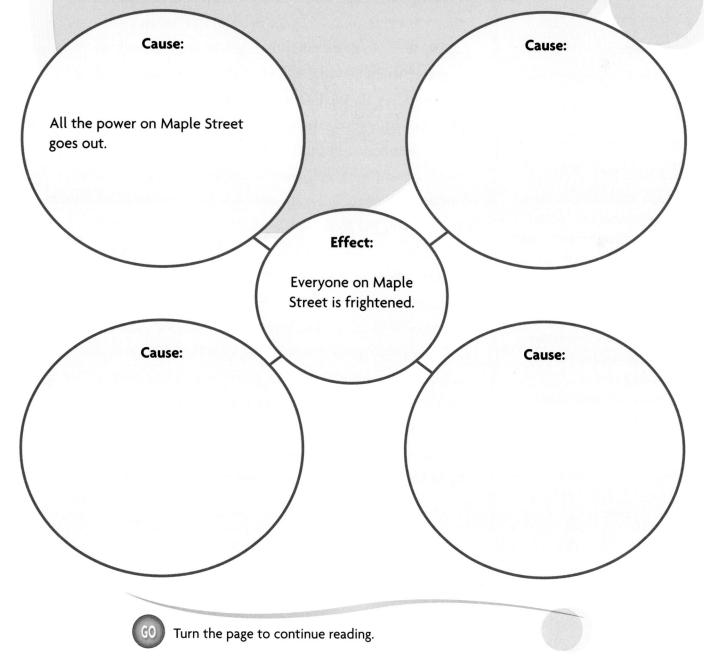

Cause:

All the power on Maple Street goes out.

Cause:

Effect:

Everyone on Maple Street is frightened.

Cause:

Cause:

GO Turn the page to continue reading.

Connect to the Text

Reread the boxed text. Think about a time when you were scared because you saw something in the dark and weren't sure what it was. How did you react?

_____

_____

_____

_____

Reading Skill

Cause and Effect Reread the highlighted text. What causes Charlie to fire the gun? Check each correct response.

☐ He is afraid of monsters from outer space.

☐ He wants to hear what the gunshot will sound like.

☐ He sees a dark figure coming near.

☐ He accidentally shoots during a struggle.

[Another woman lets out a wail and the people fall back in a group, staring toward the darkness and the approaching figure.]

We see a medium group shot of the people as they stand in the shadows watching. DON MARTIN joins them, carrying a shotgun. He holds it up.]

DON.   We may need this.

STEVE.   A shotgun? [He pulls it out of DON's hand.] Good Lord—will anybody think a thought around here? Will you people wise up? What good would a shotgun do against—

[Now CHARLIE pulls the gun from STEVE's hand.]

CHARLIE.   No more talk, Steve. You're going to talk us into a grave! You'd let whatever's out there walk right over us, wouldn't yuh? Well, some of us won't!

[He swings the gun around to point it toward the sidewalk. The dark figure continues to walk toward them.

The group stands there, fearful, **apprehensive,** mothers clutching children, men standing in front of wives. CHARLIE slowly raises the gun. As the figure gets closer and closer he suddenly pulls the trigger. The sound of it explodes in the stillness. There is a long angle shot looking down at the figure, who suddenly lets out a small cry, stumbles forward onto his knees and then falls forward on his face. DON, CHARLIE, and STEVE race forward over to him. STEVE is there first and turns the man over. Now the crowd gathers around them.]

STEVE.   [Slowly looks up.] It's Pete Van Horn.

DON.   [In a hushed voice.] Pete Van Horn! He was just gonna go over to the next block to see if the power was on—

WOMAN.   You killed him, Charlie. You shot him dead!

Word Power

apprehensive (ap ́ ri hen ́ siv) _adj._ anxious or fearful that something bad will happen

CHARLIE. [*Looks around at the circle of faces, his eyes frightened, his face contorted.*] But... but I didn't know who he was. I certainly didn't know who he was. He comes walkin' out of the darkness—how am I supposed to know who he was? [*He grabs STEVE.*] Steve—you know why I shot! How was I supposed to know he wasn't a monster or something? [*He grabs DON now.*] We're all scared of the same thing, I was just tryin' to... tryin' to protect my home, that's all! Look, all of you, that's all I was tryin' to do. [*He looks down wildly at the body.*] I didn't know it was somebody we knew! I didn't know—

[*There's a sudden hush and then an intake of breath. We see a medium shot of the living room window of CHARLIE's house. The window is not lit, but suddenly the house lights come on behind it.*]

WOMAN. [*In a very hushed voice.*] Charlie... Charlie... the lights just went on in your house. Why did the lights just go on?

DON. What about it, Charlie? How come you're the only one with lights now?

GOODMAN. That's what I'd like to know.

[*A pause as they all stare toward CHARLIE.*]

Imagine you saw a shadowy figure like this one approaching. How would you react?

Reading Skill
Respond Reread the highlighted text. How do you feel about Charlie's reaction to shooting his neighbor?

151

English Coach

Here, the word *gag* means "practical joke." Write two other words that mean "practical joke."

_____

_____

Comprehension Check

Reread the boxed text. What does the crowd do after Charlie runs toward his house?

_____

_____

_____

_____

GOODMAN. You were so quick to kill, Charlie and you were so quick to tell us who we had to be careful of. Well, maybe you had to kill. Maybe Peter there was trying to tell us something. Maybe he'd found out something and came back to tell us who there was amongst us we should watch out for—

[*CHARLIE backs away from the group, his eyes wide with fright.*]

CHARLIE. No...no...it's nothing of the sort! I don't know why the lights are on, I swear I don't. Somebody's pulling a gag or something.

[*He bumps against STEVE, who grabs him and whirls him around.*]

STEVE. A gag? A gag? Charlie, there's a dead man on the sidewalk and you killed him. Does this thing look like a gag to you?

[*CHARLIE breaks away and screams as he runs toward his house.*]

CHARLIE. No! No! Please!

[*A man breaks away from the crowd to chase CHARLIE. We see a long angle shot looking down as the man tackles CHARLIE and lands on top of him. The other people start to run toward them. CHARLIE is up on his feet, breaks away from the other man's grasp, lands a couple of desperate punches that push the man aside. Then he forces his way, fighting, through the crowd to once again break free, jumps up on his front porch. A rock thrown from the group smashes a window alongside of him, the broken glass flying past him. A couple of pieces cut him. He stands there perspiring, rumpled, blood running down from a cut on the cheek. His wife breaks away from the group to throw herself into his arms. He buries his face against her. We can see the crowd **converging** on the porch now.*]

Word Power

converging (kən vurj´ ing) *v.* coming together at a place or point

152

VOICES.

It must have been him.

He's the one.

We got to get Charlie.

[*Another rock lands on the porch. Now CHARLIE pushes his wife behind him, facing the group.*]

CHARLIE.   Look, look I swear to you . . . it isn't me . . . but I do know who it is . . . I swear to you, I do know who it is. I know who the monster is here. I know who it is that doesn't belong. I swear to you I know.

GOODMAN.   [*Shouting.*] What are you waiting for?

WOMAN.   [*Shouting.*] Come on, Charlie, come on.

MAN ONE.   [*Shouting.*] Who is it, Charlie, tell us!

DON.   [*Pushing his way to the front of the crowd.*] All right, Charlie, let's hear it!

[*CHARLIE's eyes dart around wildly.*]

CHARLIE.   It's . . . it's . . .

MAN TWO.   [*Screaming.*] Go ahead, Charlie, tell us.

CHARLIE.   It's . . . it's the kid. It's Tommy. He's the one.

[*There's a gasp from the crowd as we cut to a shot of SALLY holding her son TOMMY. The boy at first doesn't understand and then, realizing the eyes are all on him, buries his face against his mother.*]

SALLY.   [*Backs away.*] That's crazy! That's crazy! He's a little boy.

WOMAN.   But he knew! He was the only one who knew! He told us all about it. Well, how did he know? How could he have known?

[*The various people take this up and repeat the question aloud.*]

VOICES.

How could he know?

Who told him?

Make the kid answer.

DON.   It was Charlie who killed old man Van Horn.

My Workspace

Comprehension Check

Reread the boxed text. What happens after Steve tells everyone to stop?

_____

_____

_____

_____

_____

Reading Skill

Cause and Effect Reread the highlighted text. At this point in the play, the neighbors are all accusing one another. Read the events below. On the line next to each event, write the name of the character who becomes a suspect because of this event.

_____ tells a story about space monsters.

_____ looks at the stars at night.

_____ has a radio set up in his basement.

_____ shoots Pete Van Horn.

WOMAN. But it was the kid here who knew what was going to happen all the time. He was the one who knew!

[*We see a close-up of STEVE.*]

STEVE. Are you all gone crazy? [*Pause as he looks about.*] Stop. [*A fist crashes at STEVE's face, staggering him back out of the frame of the picture. There are several close camera shots suggesting the coming of violence. A hand fires a rifle. A fist clenches. A hand grabs the hammer from VAN HORN's body, etc. Meanwhile, we hear the following lines.*]

DON. Charlie has to be the one—Where's my rifle—

WOMAN. Les Goodman's the one. His car started! Let's wreck it.

MRS. GOODMAN. What about Steve's radio—He's the one that called them—

MR. GOODMAN. Smash the radio. Get me a hammer. Get me something.

STEVE. Stop—Stop—

CHARLIE. Where's that kid—Let's get him.

MAN ONE. Get Steve—Get Charlie—They're working together.

[*The crowd starts to converge around the mother, who grabs the child and starts to run with him. The crowd starts to follow, at first walking fast, and then running after him. We see a full shot of the street as suddenly CHARLIE's lights go off and the lights in another house go on. They stay on for a moment, then from across the street other lights go on and then off again.*]

MAN ONE. [*Shouting.*] It isn't the kid . . . it's Bob Weaver's house.

WOMAN. It isn't Bob Weaver's house, it's Don Martin's place.

CHARLIE. I tell you it's the kid.

DON. It's Charlie. He's the one.

[*We move into a series of close-ups of various people as they shout, accuse, scream, interspersing these shots with shots of houses as the lights go on and off, and then slowly in the middle of this nightmarish morass of sight and sound the camera starts to pull away, until once again we've reached the opening shot looking at the Maple Street sign from high above. The camera continues to move away until we dissolve to a shot looking toward the metal side of a space craft, which sits shrouded in darkness. An open door throws out a beam of light from the illuminated interior. Two figures silhouetted against the bright lights appear. We get only a vague feeling of form, but nothing more **explicit** than that.*]

FIGURE ONE.   Understand the procedure now? Just stop a few of their machines and radios and telephones and lawn mowers…Throw them into darkness for a few hours, and then you just sit back and watch the pattern.

FIGURE TWO.   And this pattern is always the same?

Literary Element

Science Fiction Reread the highlighted text. How do the stage directions and dialogue show that this is science fiction?

_____

_____

_____

_____

_____

_____

_____

Look at the town in this picture. Does it seem very peaceful? Can you imagine the people who live in this town acting the way the people on Maple Street act? Why or why not?

_____

Word Power

explicit (eks plis′ it) *adj.* very clear

155

Comprehension Check

Reread the boxed text. Who does Figure One say is the most dangerous enemy of the people on Maple Street? Underline the answer in the text.

Reading Skill

Respond Reread the highlighted text. The narrator explains that fear and mistrust can lead people to harm each other. How do you feel about this statement? Why?

_____

_____

_____

_____

_____

_____

FIGURE ONE.   With few variations. They pick the most dangerous enemy they can find . . . and it's themselves. And all we need do is sit back . . . and watch.

FIGURE TWO.   Then I take it this place . . . this Maple Street . . . is not unique.

FIGURE ONE.   [*Shaking his head.*] By no means. Their world is full of Maple Streets. And we'll go from one to the other and let them destroy themselves. One to the other . . . one to the other . . . one to the other—

[*Now the camera pans up for a shot of the starry sky and over this we hear the NARRATOR'S VOICE.*]

NARRATOR'S VOICE.   The tools of conquest do not necessarily come with bombs and explosions and fallout. There are weapons that are simply thoughts, attitudes, **prejudices**—to be found only in the minds of men. For the record, prejudices can kill and suspicion can destroy and a thoughtless frightened search for a scapegoat has a fallout all its own for the children . . . and the children yet unborn. [*A pause.*] And the pity of it is . . . that these things cannot be confined to . . . The Twilight Zone!

Word Power

prejudices (prej´ ə dis iz) *n.* critical opinions that are formed unfairly

Respond to Literature

THE MONSTERS ARE DUE ON MAPLE STREET

A Comprehension Check

Answer the following questions in the spaces provided.

1. Why does Charlie shoot Pete Van Horn? _____

_____

_____

2. Whom does Charlie accuse of being a space monster when the neighbors suspect him of being responsible for everything? _____

_____

B Reading Skills

Answer the following questions in the spaces provided.

1. **Cause and Effect** What effect does Tommy's story about space monsters have on his neighbors? _____

_____

2. **Cause and Effect** We don't find out until the very end of the story what causes the power failure on Maple Street. What is the actual cause?

_____

_____

3. **Respond** How would you feel if you were one of the people being accused of being the space monster? Why? _____

_____

C Word Power

Complete each sentence below, using one of the words in the box.

> legitimate   defiantly   scapegoat   apprehensive
>
> converging   explicit   prejudices

1. The storm made Rasmus _____ about driving in the steep mountains.

2. Before the concert started, the fans were _____ on the stage.

3. If you want someone to do something right, you have to give _____ instructions.

4. Haruki's mother told him that forming _____ against people was not fair.

5. Cecilie had a _____ reason for missing Luke's birthday party.

6. The soldier raised his fist _____ and refused to surrender to the enemy.

7. The king looked for a _____ to blame for his country's many problems.

D Literary Element: Science Fiction

Read the following passages from the ending of "The Monsters Are Due on Maple Street." As you read, think about the elements of science fiction. Then answer the questions that follow.

[*The camera continues to move away until we dissolve to a shot looking toward the metal side of a space craft, which sits shrouded in darkness.*[1] *An open door throws out a beam of light from the illuminated interior.*[2] *Two figures silhouetted against the bright lights appear.*[3] *We get only a vague feeling of form, but nothing more explicit than that.*[4]]

NARRATOR'S VOICE.   The tools of conquest do not necessarily come with bombs and explosions and fallout.[5] There are weapons that are simply thoughts, attitudes, prejudices—to be found only in the minds of men.[6]

1. Science fiction often explores non-human beings and worlds beyond our own. How do sentences 1–4 show that this play is science fiction?

   _____

   _____

2. Science fiction also often features characters who have to deal with things we are all familiar with. How do sentences 5–6 show this part of science fiction? _____

   _____

   _____

   _____

E The Monster's Space Log

Imagine that you are one of the "figures" in the space craft, watching from above as Maple Street goes into chaos. Write a space log entry in which you describe what happened below on Earth. At the end, add the name of your own street!

Space Log: Maple Street, Planet Earth

After our craft first passed over, and the power went out, the boy creature called Tommy told a story about _____

_____

When we made the car of the man creature Les Goodman start by itself, the people creatures suspected the man creature Goodman of being

_____

The people creatures saw a dark shape coming toward them. They panicked. The man creature Charlie was so scared that he _____

_____

It turned out to only be the man creature Van Horn.

After that, it was all over. We watched from our space craft as the people

creatures _____

_____

It is amazing how easy it is to control the people creatures of Earth. We don't need bombs. We simply _____

_____

After that, they will destroy themselves.

Now we will set our sights on the people creatures of

the street _____

Assessment

Fill in the circle next to each correct answer.

1. What is the first strange thing that happens on Maple Street?
   - ○ A. Les Goodman's car starts.
   - ○ B. The neighbors sit on their porches.
   - ○ C. Tommy buys ice cream, and it melts.
   - ○ D. There is a flash of light and a loud roar.

2. What causes Charlie to shoot Pete Van Horn?
   - ○ A. Pete accuses Charlie of being a space monster.
   - ○ B. Charlie and Pete are fighting over the gun.
   - ○ C. It's dark, and Charlie thinks Pete may be a space monster.
   - ○ D. Pete is the real space monster, and he attacks Charlie.

3. What happens to Charlie after he shoots Pete Van Horn?
   - ○ A. The neighbors suspect Charlie of being a space monster.
   - ○ B. Charlie tells everyone that he is really the space monster.
   - ○ C. Charlie runs away and hides.
   - ○ D. Charlie escapes in Goodman's car.

4. Which of the following stage directions from the play shows that it is science fiction?
   - ○ A. *long shot looking down the street*
   - ○ B. *medium shot of the Goodman entry hall at night*
   - ○ C. *shot looking toward the metal side of a space craft*
   - ○ D. *medium group shot of the people as they stand in the shadows*

5. Which of the following words means "anxious or fearful"?
   - ○ A. defiantly
   - ○ B. apprehensive
   - ○ C. scapegoat
   - ○ D. legitimate

Myth and Folktale

What's a Myth? What's a Folktale?

Before written language, there were stories called folklore. Different cultures used different types of folklore to tell stories of heroes, humor, and tragedy. These stories usually have a message about life. Myths and folktales are two kinds of folklore.

A **myth** is a traditional story about gods and goddesses or how things came to be. Myths usually reflect a culture's religious or other deeply held beliefs.

A **folktale** is a story that has been passed down through generations by word of mouth. Folktales often reflect what is important to the people who tell them. Folktale characters can be animals or people who have unusual powers or experiences.

Hercules is a character from a myth. Paul Bunyan is a folktale hero. What other characters and creatures from myths and folktales can you think of? Write your responses below.

_____

_____

Why Read Myths and Folktales?

People today read these kinds of tales to enjoy a good story! But these stories can also tell you about the cultures they came from. You can learn how the people in a culture viewed the world and what was important to them. Reading these stories and sharing them makes the oldest stories in the world feel new.

How Do I Read Myths and Folktales?

Focus on key **literary elements** and **reading skills** to get the most out of reading the myth and folktales in this unit. Here are two key literary elements and two key reading skills that you will practice in this unit.

Key Literary Elements

• Tone

The **tone** of a piece of writing expresses to readers the author's feelings toward his or her subject, ideas, theme, or characters. A written piece may express seriousness, humor, sadness, excitement, or any number of other feelings. To find the tone, look at the writer's choice of words, the kinds of details used, and the images created.

• Fantasy

Fantasy explores unreal worlds. It can also explore the real world with unreal elements, like ghosts, magic, or people with superhuman qualities. However, in fantasy, the emotions of characters and the conflicts they face are often like those of ordinary people. Readers can recognize themselves in the personal struggles and adventures of the characters.

Key Reading Skills

• Visualize

When you **visualize**, you picture in your mind what you are reading. As you read, use the details and exact words to help you create mental pictures. Visualize the characters and events in your mind. For example, if the main character says the teacher towered over him or her, you would picture a student standing in front of a very tall teacher. Use your own experiences to help you understand as well as imagine the scene.

• Sequence

The order in which thoughts or actions are arranged is called the **sequence**. Many stories tell events in the order in which the events happen. As you read, look for words like *first*, *then*, *meanwhile*, *eventually*, and *later*. These words can help you figure out when things happen.

Get Ready to Read!

PROMETHEUS

Meet Bernard Evslin

Bernard Evslin was born in 1922. When he was a young author, he wrote plays and movies. In the 1960s, his writing goals changed. He began retelling ancient tales for young readers. Even though the tales were very old, Evslin rewrote them in ways that were familiar to readers. He made the tales interesting for young people. Evslin died in 1993. "Prometheus" was first published in 1966.

What You Know

Think about the saying "Knowledge is power." What does it mean? Do you agree or disagree with this saying? Why?

Reason to Read

Read this myth to find out what happens when two powerful figures do not agree about knowledge and people's right to that knowledge.

Background Info

The story of Prometheus is a myth that was first told in ancient Greece thousands of years ago. In those days, the people of Greece thought that gods and goddesses lived on Olympus, a real mountain in Greece. They believed that these gods and goddesses ruled people's lives. The Greeks used myths to explain beliefs, customs, forces of nature, or how things first came to be. In this myth, the giant Prometheus and Zeus, the ruler of the gods, have a disagreement that affects all men and women.

Word Power

ignorance (ig′nər əns) *n.* lack of knowledge or education; p. 166
We often eat the wrong foods out of *ignorance*.

enlighten (en līt′ən) *v.* to teach; show the truth; p. 166
My report will *enlighten* the history class.

destiny (des′tə nē) *n.* something that will happen to a person or people in the future; fate; p. 167
It is this baseball team's *destiny* to become champions.

unpredictability (un′pri dik′tə bil′ə tē) *n.* quality of being unable to be counted on or expected; p. 167
The *unpredictability* of spring weather makes the mountain roads dangerous.

vengeance (ven′jəns) *n.* an act of getting even; p. 169
After losing the battle, the king promised *vengeance*.

torment (tôr′ment) *n.* extreme pain; p. 170
She was in *torment* after being stung by a wasp.

Answer the following questions, using one of the new words above.
Write your answers in the spaces provided.

1. Which word goes with "getting even with someone"? _____

2. Which word goes with "what will happen to you in the future"? _____

3. Which word goes with "great pain or suffering"? _____

4. Which word goes with "lack of knowledge"? _____

5. Which word goes with "what cannot be expected"? _____

6. Which word goes with "showing someone the truth"? _____

Adapted from

PROMETHEUS

Retold by Bernard Evslin

. . . .

Background Info

According to Greek myths, the Titans belonged to a race of giants who once ruled the world. They were overthrown by Zeus and the other gods.

English Coach

A *decree* is the order of a powerful ruler. Zeus is a god who gives a decree. What other kinds of rulers might give decrees?

_____

_____

_____

Prometheus was a young Titan, no great admirer of Zeus. Although he knew the great lord of the sky hated questions, he did not hesitate to meet him face to face when there was something he wanted to know.

One morning he came to Zeus and said, "O Thunderer, I do not understand your design. You have caused the race of man to appear on earth, but you keep him in **ignorance** and darkness."

"Perhaps you had better leave the race of man to me," said Zeus. "What you call ignorance is innocence. What you call darkness is my decree. Man is happy now. And he is made so that he will remain happy unless someone persuades him that he is unhappy. Let us not speak of this again."

But Prometheus said, "Look at him. Look below. He crouches in caves. He is at the mercy of beast and weather. He eats his meat raw. If you mean something by this, **enlighten** me with your wisdom. Tell me why you refuse to give man the gift of fire."

Word Power

ignorance (ig´nər əns) *n.* lack of knowledge or education
enlighten (en līt´ən) *v.* to teach; show the truth

Zeus answered, "Do you not know, Prometheus, that every gift brings a penalty? This is the way the Fates weave **destiny.** Man does not have fire, true, nor the crafts which fire teaches. On the other hand, he does not know disease, warfare, old age, or that inward pest called worry. He is happy, I say, happy without fire. And so he shall remain."

"Happy as beasts are happy," said Prometheus. "What use is it to make a separate race called man and endow him with little fur, some wit, and a curious charm of **unpredictability**? If he must live like this, why separate him from the beasts at all?"

"He has another quality," said Zeus, "the capacity for worship. A skill for admiring our power, being puzzled by our riddles and amazed by our caprice. That is why he was made."

"Would not fire, and the graces he can put on with fire, make him more interesting?"

"More interesting, perhaps, but infinitely more dangerous. For there is this in man too: a pride that can easily swell to giant size. Improve his lot, and he will forget that which makes him pleasing—his sense of worship, his humbleness. He will grow big and poisoned with pride and fancy himself a god, and before we know it, we shall see him storming Olympus. Enough, Prometheus! I have been patient with you, but do not try me too far. Go now and trouble me no more with your speculations."

Prometheus was not satisfied. All that night he lay awake making plans. Then he left his couch at dawn and, standing tiptoe on Olympus, stretched his arm to where the first faint flames of the sun were flickering. In his hand he held a reed filled with a dry fiber; he thrust it into the sunrise until a spark smoldered. Then he put the reed in his tunic and came down from the mountain.

Word Power

destiny (des´tə nē) *n.* something that will happen to a person or people in the future; fate

unpredictability (un´pri dik´tə bil´ə tē) *n.* quality of being unable to be counted on or expected

English Coach

Caprice means a sudden change of mind for no reason. Which word means the same thing as *caprice*? Check the correct response.

☐ assured
☐ firm
☐ whim

Reading Skill

Sequence Reread the highlighted paragraph. Number the actions of Prometheus in the order in which he does them.

___ uses a reed to get fire from the sunrise

___ goes to Mount Olympus

___ makes plans

___ carries a burning reed down the mountain

167

At first men were frightened by the gift. It was so hot, so quick; it bit sharply when you touched it. They thanked Prometheus and asked him to take it away. But he took the leg of a newly killed deer and held it over the fire. And when the meat began to sear and sputter, filling the cave with its rich smells, the people felt themselves melting with hunger. They flung themselves on the meat and devoured it greedily, burning their tongues.

"This that I have brought you is called 'fire,'" Prometheus said. "It is an ill-natured spirit, a little brother of the sun. If you handle it carefully, it can change your whole life. It is very greedy; you must feed it twigs, but only until it becomes a proper size. Then you must stop, or it will eat everything in sight—and you too. If it escapes, use this magic: water. It fears the water spirit, and if you touch it with water, it will fly away until you need it again."

He left the fire burning in the first cave, with children staring at it wide-eyed, and then went to every cave in the land.

Then one day Zeus looked down from the mountain and was amazed. Everything had changed. Man had come out of his cave. Zeus saw huts, farmhouses, villages, walled towns, even a castle. He saw men cooking their food, carrying torches to light their way at night. He saw forges blazing, men making ploughs, swords, spears. They were making ships and raising white wings of sails and daring to use the fury of the winds for their journeys. They were wearing helmets, riding out in chariots to do battle, like the gods themselves.

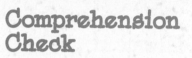
Zeus was full of rage. He seized his largest thunderbolt. "So they want fire," he said to himself. "I'll give them fire—more than they can use. I'll turn their miserable little ball of earth into ashes." But then another thought came to him, and he lowered his arm. "No," he said to himself, "I shall have **vengeance**—and entertainment too. Let them destroy themselves with their new skills. This will make a long, twisted game, interesting to watch. I'll attend to them later. My first business is with Prometheus."

Comprehension Check

Reread the boxed sentences. What does Zeus do when he gets angry?

_____

_____

_____

Think about how you visualize Zeus. Does the Zeus in this picture look like the Zeus you have been imagining? Why or why not?

Word Power

vengeance (ven´jəns) *n.* an act of getting even

169

Literary Element

Tone Reread the highlighted paragraph. Think about the tone as you read. What two words would you use to describe the tone of this paragraph?

_____

_____

Did You Know?
In Greek art, Prometheus is often pictured in his moment of punishment, being attacked by birds.

· ·

He called his giant guards and had them capture Prometheus, drag him off to the Caucasus, and there bind him to a mountain peak with great chains specially made by Hephaestus—chains which even a Titan in agony could not break. And when the friend of man was bound to the mountain, Zeus sent two vultures to hover about him forever, tearing at his belly and eating his liver.

Men knew a terrible thing was happening on the mountain, but they did not know what. But the wind shrieked like a giant in **torment** and sometimes like fierce birds.

Many centuries he lay there—until another hero was born brave enough to defy the gods. He climbed to the peak in the Caucasus and struck the chains from Prometheus and killed the vultures. His name was Heracles.

Prometheus Giving Fire to Man. 1st century A.D. Mosaic tile. Museo delle Terme, Rome.

The ancient Greeks considered the gift of fire an important event. They celebrated the Prometheus myth in their stories and in their art. Can you think of any modern "gift" that has had such an influence?

_____

Word Power

torment (tôr´ment) _n._ extreme pain

PROMETHEUS

A Comprehension Check

Answer the following questions in the spaces provided.

1. What gift does Prometheus want Zeus to give to people? _____

   _____

2. How does Zeus punish Prometheus? _____

   _____

   _____

B Reading Skills

Answer the following questions in the spaces provided.

1. **Visualize** Read this phrase describing how Prometheus uses a reed to get fire: "he thrust it into the sunrise until a spark smoldered." How does this phrase help you picture Prometheus's size and his movements?

   _____

   _____

   _____

2. **Sequence** What does Prometheus do after Zeus refuses to give fire to people?

   _____

   _____

C Word Power

Complete each sentence below, using one of the words in the box.

ignorance	enlighten	destiny
unpredictability	vengeance	torment

1. Fire can burn you and cause terrible _____ .

2. The _____ of the waves can make swimming in the ocean dangerous.

3. It is important to learn things so you don't make decisions out of _____ .

4. Just because someone hurts you does not mean you should seek _____ .

5. A newspaper's job is to inform and _____ readers.

6. It is Anthony's _____ to become known around the world.

Respond to Literature

D Literary Element: Tone

Read the passages below from "Prometheus." In the first passage, Prometheus has just given fire to people. In the second passage, Zeus realizes that Prometheus has given fire to people, and great changes have happened in the world. As you read, think about the tone. Then answer the questions that follow.

"This that I have brought you is called 'fire,'" Prometheus said.[1] "It is an ill-natured spirit, a little brother of the sun.[2] If you handle it carefully, it can change your whole life.[3] It is very greedy; you must feed it twigs, but only until it becomes a proper size.[4] Then you must stop, or it will eat everything in sight—and you too."[5]

Zeus was full of rage.[6] He seized his largest thunderbolt.[7] "So they want fire," he said to himself.[8] "I'll give them fire—more than they can use.[9] I'll turn their miserable little ball of earth into ashes."[10]

1. In sentences 1–5, do you think the tone is serious or funny? Use examples from the passage to explain your answer. _____

_____

_____

2. In sentences 6–10, what do you think the tone is? What does the tone of this passage tell you about Zeus? _____

_____

_____

_____

E A Speech to the Gods

Imagine that you are Zeus. You are writing a speech that you will give to the other gods. You want to tell them about your talk with Prometheus and how angry you are at what he has done.

NOT LONG AGO, PROMETHEUS CAME TO ME—
ZEUS, RULER OF EVERYTHING—AND ASKED
ME TO GIVE FIRE TO MAN! I TOLD HIM MAN
SHOULD NOT HAVE FIRE BECAUSE

_____

_____

NOT LONG AFTER, I—THE GREAT GOD ZEUS—
LOOKED DOWN FROM THE MOUNTAIN. I SAW

THAT _____

_____

IMAGINE MY ANGER! I—POWERFUL ZEUS—
THEN PUNISHED PROMETHEUS BECAUSE

_____

_____

HOWEVER, I—MIGHTY ZEUS—WILL NOT PUNISH

MAN. I BELIEVE MAN WILL _____

_____

_____

SO LET THIS BE A LESSON FROM ME, ZEUS THE
THUNDERER!

Assessment

Fill in the circle next to each correct answer.

1. Who is Prometheus?
   - ○ A. a Titan
   - ○ B. a human being
   - ○ C. a god
   - ○ D. a goddess

2. What event happens right after Zeus and Prometheus discuss giving fire to people?
   - ○ A. Heracles saves Prometheus.
   - ○ B. Prometheus gives fire to people.
   - ○ C. Zeus has Prometheus chained to a rock.
   - ○ D. Fire eats everything, including people.

3. Which phrase about Prometheus from the story **best** helps you visualize him?
   - ○ A. friend of man
   - ○ B. was not satisfied
   - ○ C. no great admirer of Zeus
   - ○ D. standing tiptoe on Olympus

4. Which words **best** describe the tone of the story?
   - ○ A. light and funny
   - ○ B. important and serious
   - ○ C. confusing and boring
   - ○ D. sad and miserable

5. Which of the following words means "an act of getting even"?
   - ○ A. ignorance
   - ○ B. enlighten
   - ○ C. vengeance
   - ○ D. destiny

Aunty Misery

Meet Judith Ortiz Cofer

Judith Ortiz Cofer was born in Puerto Rico in 1952. Her first language was Spanish. She learned English only after her family moved to the United States. Cofer's writing reflects the split between her two childhood homes: the island of Puerto Rico and the United States. Cofer says she uses her writing to learn more about her family and herself. "Aunty Misery" was first published in 1993.

What You Know

Do you think most people would like to live forever? Would you like to live forever? What do you think would happen if people actually did live forever?

Reason to Read

Read to enjoy this folktale about a woman who finds a way to live forever.

Background Info

In many stories, death is described as a person—a creepy fellow who shows up to take people away when it is their time to die. All kinds of scary or gloomy images have been used to describe the character Death. From ancient times until today, writers have explored the idea of trying to cheat death. However, most tales end up showing that death is a fact of life that no one can escape nor should want to escape.

Word Power

permission (pər mish´ ən) *n.* an act of allowing someone to do something; p. 178
The three students had *permission* to be late for class that day.

sorcerer (sôr´ sər ər) *n.* a person who practices magic; p. 178
In the fairy tale, the *sorcerer* put a spell on the young princess.

trustworthy (trust´ wur´ <u>th</u>ē) *adj.* able to be trusted or depended on; p. 179
Our large dog proved to be *trustworthy* with the small children.

tomb (to͞om) *n.* a grave or a building in which a dead body is placed; p. 179
The famous queen was buried in a *tomb* filled with gold.

druggists (drug´ ists) *n.* people who prepare and sell medicine; p. 180
Two *druggists* supplied medicine to the animal hospital.

**Answer the following questions that contain the new words above.
Write your answers in the spaces provided.**

1. When people visit a *tomb*, are they visiting someone who is alive or someone who
   is dead? _____

2. If you think that a boy is *trustworthy*, would you lend him your bike or not lend it
   to him?_____

3. If you get something from *druggists*, are you feeling well or feeling ill?

   _____

4. If you have *permission* to swim at the beach, does it mean that you can go into the
   water or that you cannot go into the water? _____

5. Would you expect a *sorcerer* to cast a spell or cast a fishing line? _____

   _____

Adapted from

Aunty Misery

Judith Ortiz Cofer

Reading Skill

Sequence Reread the paragraph highlighted in green. Number the actions in the order in which they occur.

___ The stranger offers to grant a wish.
___ Aunty Misery prepares an extra bed.
___ The stranger asks to spend the night.

Literary Element

Fantasy Reread the sentences highlighted in blue. Fantasy stories sometimes explore a world that seems very real, but has unreal elements. What hints in these sentences tell you that the story is a fantasy?

_____

_____

_____

_____

This is a story about an old, a very old woman who lived alone in her little hut with no other company than a beautiful pear tree that grew at her door. She spent all her time taking care of this tree. The neighborhood children drove the old woman crazy by stealing her fruit. They would climb her tree and shake its easily broken branches. Then they would run away with armloads of golden pears, yelling insults at *la Tía Miseria*, Aunty Misery, as they called her.

One day, a traveler stopped at the old woman's hut and asked her for **permission** to spend the night there. Aunty Misery saw that he had an honest face and asked the traveler to come in. She fed him and made a bed for him in front of her fireplace. In the morning the stranger told her that he wanted to show his thanks for her welcome by granting her one wish.

"There is only one thing that I desire," said Aunty Misery.

"Ask, and it shall be yours," replied the stranger, who was a **sorcerer** in disguise.

"I wish that anyone who climbs up my pear tree should not be able to come back down until I permit it."

"Your wish is granted," said the stranger, touching the pear tree as he left Aunty Misery's house.

Word Power

permission (pər mish′ ən) *n.* an act of allowing someone to do something
sorcerer (sôr′ sər ər) *n.* a person who practices magic

When the children came back to tease the old woman and to steal her fruit, she stood at her window watching them. Several of them climbed up the trunk of the pear tree and immediately got stuck to it as if with glue. She let them cry and beg her for a long time before she gave the tree permission to let them go—but only if they promised never again to steal her fruit, or bother her.

Time passed and both Aunty Misery and her tree grew bent and twisted with age. One day another traveler stopped at her door. This one did not look **trustworthy** to her. Before letting him into her home the old woman asked him what he was doing in her village. He answered her in a voice that was dry and rough, as if he had swallowed a desert. "I am Death, and I have come to take you with me."

Thinking fast Aunty Misery said, "All right, but before I go I would like to pluck some pears from my beloved tree to remember how much pleasure it brought me in this life. But I am a very old woman and cannot climb to the tallest branches where the best fruit is. Will you be so kind as to do it for me?"

With a heavy sigh like wind through a **tomb,** Señor Death climbed the pear tree. Immediately he became stuck to it as if with glue. And no matter how much he cursed and threatened, Aunty Misery would not allow the tree to let Death go.

Is this how you picture the character Death? Do you think Aunty Misery is right not to trust this visitor? Why or why not?

_____

Reading Skill

Visualize Reread the highlighted sentence. Think about the way the author describes how Aunty Misery and her tree look. Then draw a picture of Aunty Misery and her tree in the box below.

Your sketch

Comprehension Check

Reread the boxed text. How does Death get stuck in the pear tree?

_____

_____

_____

_____

_____

Word Power

trustworthy (trust´ wur´ <u>th</u>ē) *adj.* able to be trusted or depended on

tomb (to͞om) *n.* a grave or a building in which a dead body is placed

Many years passed and there were no deaths in the world. The people who make their living from death began to complain loudly. The doctors claimed no one bothered to come in for checkups or treatments anymore, because they did not fear dying. The **druggists'** business suffered too because medicines are bought to prevent or put off dying. Priests and undertakers were unhappy also, for similar reasons. There were also many old folks tired of life who wanted to pass on to the next world to rest from miseries of this one.

La Tía Miseria was blamed by these people for their troubles, of course. Not wishing to be unfair, the old woman made a deal with her prisoner, Death. If he promised not ever to come for her again, she would give him his freedom. He agreed. And that is why there are two things you can always count on running into in this world: Misery and Death: *La miseria y la muerte.*

Dona Rosita Morillo, 1944. Frida Kahlo. Oil on canvas mounted on Masonite, 30½ x 28½ in. Fundación Dolores Olmedo, Mexico City, D.F., Mexico.

Does the woman in this painting look like how you picture Aunty Misery? Why or why not?

Word Power

druggists (drug´ ists) *n.* people who prepare and sell medicine

Respond to Literature

Aunty Misery

A Comprehension Check

Answer the following questions in the spaces provided.

1. Why does the first stranger offer to grant one wish for Aunty Misery?

   _____

   _____

2. How does Aunty Misery trick Death? _____

   _____

   _____

B Reading Skills

Answer the following questions in the spaces provided.

1. **Visualize** Read these lines describing how children taunted Aunty Misery: "They would climb her tree and shake its easily broken branches. Then they would run away with armloads of golden pears, yelling insults at *la Tía Miseria*, Aunty Misery, as they called her." What details help you picture

   the scene? _____

   _____

2. **Sequence** Think about when Death comes to Aunty Misery's house. Name one event that happens **before** Death comes, and name one event that

   happens **after** Death comes. _____

   _____

   _____

   _____

C Word Power

Complete each sentence below, using one of the words in the box.

| permission | sorcerer | trustworthy |
| tomb | druggists | |

1. The children asked their parents for _____ to go on the field trip.

2. People go to _____ to get their medicine.

3. After getting caught stealing, the boy thought his parents would never consider him _____ again.

4. Every morning the old woman placed fresh flowers near her husband's _____.

5. The _____ waved his wand to cast the spell.

Circle the word that best completes each sentence.

6. I hope the (**druggists**, **trustworthy**) gave us the correct pills.

7. My mother gave me (**permission**, **tomb**) to go to the concert.

8. On the dark, stormy night, the sight of the old stone (**druggists**, **tomb**) frightened us!

9. Spot was the most (**trustworthy**, **sorcerer**) guard dog the family ever had.

10. The king worried that the (**permission**, **sorcerer**) would use evil magic against him.

D Literary Element: Fantasy

Read the passage below from "Aunty Misery." Think about what makes a story a fantasy as you read the passage. Then answer the questions that follow.

La Tía Miseria was blamed by these people for their troubles, of course. Not wishing to be unfair, the old woman made a deal with her prisoner, Death. If he promised not ever to come for her again, she would give him his freedom. He agreed. And that is why there are two things you can always count on running into in this world: Misery and Death: *La miseria y la muerte.*

1. What details in the passage tell you that this story is a fantasy?

_____

_____

_____

2. In a fantasy, characters often have the same emotions as ordinary people. What does Aunty Misery want that is similar to the wishes of many ordinary people? _____

_____

_____

E A Letter from Death

Imagine that you are Death from the tale "Aunty Misery." Aunty Misery has trapped you in the tree. Write a persuasive letter to Aunty Misery, asking her to set you free.

Dear Aunty Misery,

Do you remember how the children used to _____

_____

That is, until that sorcerer offered to grant you a wish. You are very

clever. You wished that _____

_____

However, when I came to you, you tricked me by _____

_____

It is a bad idea to keep me stuck in this pear tree, because _____

_____

Many people are upset because _____

_____

_____

Let us make a deal. If you let me go, I promise _____

_____

Sincerely,

Death

Assessment

Fill in the circle next to each correct answer.

1. How does Aunty Misery treat the first traveler?
   - ○ A. She insults him.
   - ○ B. She welcomes him into her home.
   - ○ C. She tries to trick him into climbing the tree.
   - ○ D. She gives him food and sends him away.

2. Which phrase from the story **best** helps you picture what Aunty Misery looks like?
   - ○ A. grew bent and twisted with age
   - ○ B. let them cry and beg her for a long time
   - ○ C. asked him what he was doing in her village
   - ○ D. made a deal with her prisoner

3. Which of the following could only happen in a fantasy?
   - ○ A. Children steal pears.
   - ○ B. People complain loudly.
   - ○ C. An old woman meets a stranger.
   - ○ D. A sorcerer grants a wish.

4. Which action does Aunty Misery do last?
   - ○ A. She gives the traveler permission to stay.
   - ○ B. She sets Death free.
   - ○ C. She tricks Death into climbing the tree.
   - ○ D. She makes a wish.

5. Which of the following words means "honest"?
   - ○ A. tomb
   - ○ B. permission
   - ○ C. trustworthy
   - ○ D. druggists

We Are All One

Meet Laurence Yep

Laurence Yep was born in San Franciso in 1948. Before he became an award-winning writer, Yep was exposed to different cultures. He grew up as a Chinese American in an African American neighborhood in San Francisco. He went to school first in Chinatown, and then in a white neighborhood. He has said, "In a sense I have no one culture . . . in my writing, I can create my own." "We Are All One" was first published in 1973.

What You Know

Do you think animal life is as important as human life? Would you give food and shelter to an animal or an insect? Why or why not?

Reason to Read

Read this folktale to find out how a person's good deeds toward the natural world are rewarded.

Background Info

This tale takes place in an imaginary, long-ago time in China. Many folktales from China involve magic and have lessons about life. Sometimes a magical creature helps the hero of the story overcome an enemy or finish a task. When Chinese immigrants moved to the United States, they brought these magical tales with them. "We Are All One" is Laurence Yep's retelling of one of these Chinese folktales.

Word Power

herb (urb) *n.* a plant used in cooking or medicine; p. 188
I use a special *herb* in my tea when I have a cold.

larvae (lär′ vē) *n.* early forms of insects before they change into another form; p. 189
The *larvae* crawled all over the plant, looking for leaves to eat.

lacquer (lak′ ər) *n.* a smooth, glossy coating; p. 189
I put some *lacquer* on my pottery project to make it shine.

omen (ō′ mən) *n.* a sign or warning about something that will happen in the future; p. 190
We were planning a picnic, but the dark clouds seemed like a bad *omen*.

dissolve (di zolv′) *v.* to break down and mix into a liquid; p. 192
You can *dissolve* a sugar cube in a cup of hot tea.

**Answer the following questions, using one of the new words above.
Write your answers in the spaces provided.**

1. Which word goes with "caterpillars that turn into butterflies"? _____

2. Which word goes with "mix something with water until it seems to disappear"?

    _____

3. Which word goes with "something you grow in a garden"? _____

4. Which word goes with "a shiny surface"? _____

5. Which word goes with "something that might tell you about the future"?

    _____

Adapted from
We Are All One

Laurence Yep

Background Info

Since few people could read long ago, people called criers would shout out news and announcements. A peddler is someone who sells things by traveling from place to place.

Literary Element

Fantasy Reread the highlighted text. In a fantasy, there are both unreal elements and examples of things ordinary people have to deal with every day. In the text, underline the unreal element that tells you this is a fantasy. Then circle something that is an example of something ordinary people have to deal with.

Long ago there was a rich man with a disease in his eyes. For many years, the pain was so great that he could not sleep at night. He saw every doctor he could, but none of them could help him.

"What good is all my money?" he groaned. Finally, he became so desperate that he sent criers through the city offering a reward to anyone who could cure him.

Now in that city lived an old candy peddler. He would walk around with his baskets of candy, but he was so kind-hearted that he gave away as much as he sold, so he was always poor.

When the old peddler heard the news, he remembered something his mother had said. She had once told him about a magical **herb** that was good for the eyes. So he packed up his baskets and went back to the single tiny room in which his family lived.

When he told his plan to his wife, she scolded him, "If you go off on this crazy hunt, how are we supposed to eat?"

Word Power
herb (urb) *n.* a plant used in cooking or medicine

Usually the peddler gave in to his wife, but this time he was stubborn. "There are two baskets of candy," he said. "I'll be back before they're gone."

The next morning, as soon as the soldiers opened the gates of the city, he was the first one to leave. He did not stop until he was deep inside the woods. As a boy, he had often roamed there. He had liked to pretend that the shadowy forest was a green sea and he was a fish slipping through the cool waters.

As he examined the ground, he noticed ants scurrying about. On their backs were **larvae** like white grains of rice. A rock had fallen into a stream, so the water was now spilling into the ants' nest.

"We're all one," the kind-hearted peddler said. So he waded into the shallow stream and put the rock on the bank. Then with a sharp stick, he dug a shallow ditch that sent the rest of the water back into the stream.

Without another thought about his good deed, he began to search through the forest. He looked everywhere. As the day went on, he grew sleepy. "Ho-hum. I got up too early. I'll take just a short nap," he decided. He lay down in the shade of an old tree, where he fell right asleep.

In his dreams, the old peddler found himself standing in the middle of a great city. Tall buildings rose high overhead. He couldn't see the sky even when he tilted back his head. A group of soldiers marched up to him with a loud clatter of their black **lacquer** armor. "Our queen wishes to see you," the captain said.

The frightened peddler could only obey and let the fierce soldiers lead him into a shining palace. There, a woman with a high crown sat upon a tall throne. Trembling, the old peddler fell to his knees and touched his forehead against the floor.

Word Power

larvae (lär′ vē) *n.* early forms of insects before they change into another form

lacquer (lak′ ər) *n.* a smooth, glossy coating

Comprehension Check

Why are the ants scurrying about?

_____

_____

_____

Reading Skill

Visualize Reread the highlighted paragraphs. Think about how the details help you picture this scene. In the box below, draw the city.

Your Sketch

English Coach

Sometimes when the suffix -ly is added to a word, the new word describes the way in which something is done. Here, when the queen says something *regretfully*, it means she says it "with regret." What word would you use to describe doing something in a *wild* manner?

Comprehension Check

Reread the boxed paragraph. How does the peddler get lost in the woods?

_____

_____

_____

_____

_____

_____

But the queen ordered him to stand. "Like the great Emperor Yü of long ago, you tamed the great flood. We are all one now. You have only to ask, and I or any of my people will come to your aid."

The old peddler cleared his throat. "I am looking for a certain herb. It will cure any disease of the eyes."

The queen shook her head regretfully. "I have never heard of that herb. But you will surely find it if you keep looking for it."

And then the old peddler woke. Sitting up, he saw that in his wanderings he had come back to the ants' nest. It was there he had taken his nap. His dream city had been the ants' nest itself.

"This is a good **omen,**" he said to himself, and he began searching even harder. He was so determined to find the herb that he did not notice how time had passed. He was surprised when he saw how the light was fading. He looked all around then. There was no sight of his city—only strange hills. He realized then that he had searched so far he had gotten lost.

Night was coming fast and with it the cold. He rubbed his arms and hunted for shelter. In the twilight, he thought he could see the green tiles of a roof.

River Scene. 18th century, China. Free Library, Philadelphia, PA.

How does this painting help you picture where this story takes place?

Word Power

omen (ō´ mən) *n.* a sign or warning about something that will happen in the future

He stumbled through the growing darkness until he reached a ruined temple. Weeds grew through cracks in the stones and most of the roof itself had fallen in. Still, the ruins would provide some protection.

As he started inside, he saw a centipede with bright orange skin and red tufts of fur along its back. Yellow dots covered its sides like a dozen tiny eyes. It was also rushing into the temple as fast as it could, but there was a bird swooping down toward it.

The old peddler waved his arms and shouted, scaring the bird away. Then he put down his palm in front of the insect. "We are all one, you and I." The many feet tickled his skin as the centipede climbed onto his hand.

Inside the temple, he gathered dried leaves and found old sticks of wood and soon he had a fire going. The peddler even picked some fresh leaves for the centipede from a bush near the temple doorway. "I may have to go hungry, but you don't have to, friend."

Stretching out beside the fire, the old peddler pillowed his head on his arms. He was so tired that he soon fell asleep, but even in his sleep he dreamed he was still searching in the woods. Suddenly he thought he heard footsteps near his head. He woke instantly and looked about, but he saw only the brightly colored centipede.

"Was it you, friend?" The old peddler chuckled and, lying down, he closed his eyes again. "I must be getting nervous."

Did You Know?

A centipede is a long, flat insect with many pairs of legs. The prefix *centi-* means either "hundred" or "hundredth part of," and *pede* comes from the Latin word for "foot."

. . . .

Reading Skill

Sequence Reread the highlighted paragraphs. Number the peddler's actions in the order in which he does them.

___ starts a fire
___ gets food for the centipede
___ scares away the bird

"We are one, you and I," a voice said faintly—as if from a long distance. "If you go south, you will find a pine tree with two trunks. By its roots, you will find a magic bead. A cousin of mine spat on it years ago. **Dissolve** that bead in wine and tell the rich man to drink it if he wants to heal his eyes."

The old peddler trembled when he heard the voice, because he realized that the centipede was magical. He wanted to run from the temple, but he couldn't even get up. It was as if he were glued to the floor.

But then the old peddler reasoned with himself: If the centipede had wanted to hurt me, it could have, long ago. Instead, it seems to want to help me.

So the old peddler stayed where he was, but he did not dare open his eyes. When the first sunlight fell through the roof, he raised one eyelid cautiously. There was no sign of the centipede. He sat up and looked around, but the magical centipede was gone.

He followed the centipede's instructions when he left the temple. Traveling south, he kept a sharp eye out for the pine tree with two trunks. He walked until late in the afternoon, but all he saw were normal pine trees.

Wearily he sat down and sighed. Even if he found the pine tree, he couldn't be sure that he would find the bead. Someone else might even have discovered it a long time ago.

But something made him look a little longer. Just when he was thinking about turning back, he saw the odd tree. Somehow his tired legs managed to carry him over to the tree, and he got down on his knees. But the ground was covered with fallen pine needles and his old eyes were too weak to see whether the bead was among them. The old peddler could have wept with frustration, and then he remembered the ants.

___

Word Power

dissolve (di zolv´) *v.* to break down and mix into a liquid

He began to call, "Ants, ants, we are all one."

Almost immediately, thousands of ants came boiling out of nowhere. Delighted, the old man told them, "I'm looking for a bead. It might be very tiny."

Then, careful not to crush any of his little helpers, the old man sat down to wait. In no time, the ants reappeared with a tiny bead. With trembling fingers, the old man took the bead from them and examined it. It was colored orange and looked as if it had yellow eyes on the sides.

There was nothing very special about the bead, but the old peddler treated it like a fine jewel. Putting the bead into his pouch, the old peddler bowed his head. "I thank you and I thank your queen," the old man said. After the ants disappeared among the pine needles, he made his way out of the woods.

The next day, he reached the house of the rich man. However, he was so poor and ragged that the gatekeeper only laughed at him. "How could an old beggar like you help my master?"

The old peddler tried to argue. "Beggar or rich man, we are all one."

But it so happened that the rich man was passing by the gates. He went over to the old peddler. "I said anyone could see me. But it'll mean a stick across your back if you're wasting my time."

The old peddler took out the pouch. "Dissolve this bead in some wine and drink it down." Then, turning the pouch upside down, he shook the tiny bead into the palm of his hand and gave it to the rich man.

The rich man immediately called for a cup of wine. Dropping the bead into the wine, he waited a moment and then drank it down. Instantly the pain vanished. Shortly after that, his eyes healed.

The rich man was so happy and grateful that he doubled the reward. And the kindly old peddler and his family lived comfortably for the rest of their lives.

Reading Skill

Visualize Reread the sentence highlighted in green. Picture the bead. Does the bead look like something else in the story? What does the bead look like? (Hint: Think about the different animals the peddler has helped!)

_____

_____

_____

Literary Element

Fantasy Reread the paragraph highlighted in blue. Underline the two clues that tell you that the bead has magical powers.

We Are All One

A Comprehension Check

Answer the following questions in the spaces provided.

1. Why does the peddler decide to leave the city and go to the woods?

   _____

   _____

2. How does the centipede help the peddler? _____

   _____

B Reading Skills

Answer the following questions in the spaces provided.

1. **Visualize** Read these lines about the peddler's dream visit to the ant city: "Tall buildings rose high overhead. He couldn't see the sky even when he tilted back his head." How do the details help you picture the city?

   _____

   _____

   _____

2. **Sequence** What is the **first** thing the peddler does to show kindness to other creatures? _____

   _____

3. **Sequence** What important event happens immediately **after** the peddler finds the ruined temple? _____

   _____

C Word Power

Complete each sentence below, using one of the words in the box.

herb	larvae	lacquer
omen	dissolve	

1. Helen found _____ underneath the log.

2. Pedro had trouble swallowing the pill, so he decided to _____ it in a glass of fruit juice.

3. Some people think finding a four-leaf clover is a good _____.

4. After painting the table, Ali coated it with _____.

5. Manoj thought the chopped fresh _____ gave the salad a delicious flavor.

Circle the word that best completes each sentence.

6. Elena added a picture of a dried (**herb, omen**) to her book of plants.

7. The potter covered the vase with a layer of (**larvae, lacquer**).

8. The beetles brought bits of food to the (**dissolve, larvae**) in their nest.

9. The sugar will (**dissolve, lacquer**) quickly in the hot water.

10. Some people believe that a rainbow is an (**omen, herb**) of good luck.

D Literary Element: Fantasy

Read the two passages below from "We Are All One." In the first passage, the peddler tells his plan to his wife. In the second passage, the peddler is having trouble finding the bead. As you read, think about what details show fantasy and what details show ordinary life.

So he packed up his baskets and went back to the single tiny room in which his family lived.[1]

When he told his plan to his wife, she scolded him, "If you go off on this crazy hunt, how are we supposed to eat?"[2]

He began to call, "Ants, ants, we are all one."[3]

Almost immediately, thousands of ants came boiling out of nowhere.[4] Delighted, the old man told them, "I'm looking for a bead.[5] It might be very tiny."[6]

Then, careful not to crush any of his little helpers, the old man sat down to wait.[7] In no time, the ants reappeared with a tiny bead.[8]

1. How do sentences 1–2 show that even though this story is a fantasy, people still face ordinary problems?

_____

_____

_____

2. In sentences 3–8, what happens that is magical? _____

_____

_____

_____

E The Peddler's Postcard

Pretend you are the peddler, on a journey through the woods. While you are traveling, you send a postcard to your family back home. Write to tell them about your adventures.

My Dear Family,

In the woods, some strange things have been happening. After I
helped a nest of ants, I dreamed that _____

_____

At an old temple, I met a _____

I was told where to find _____

_____

I got help finding it from _____

The rich man was cured, and he _____

Now our family can _____

But the most important thing to remember is what I've been
saying all along: _____

Your Loving Peddler

_____

To:
My Family

At:
My Home

Assessment

Fill in the circle next to each correct answer.

1. When does the peddler dream about the tall city?
   ○ A. after he helps the ants near the stream
   ○ B. before he hears about the rich man's reward
   ○ C. after he meets the centipede at the temple
   ○ D. before he remembers the story of the magic herb

2. How does the peddler save the centipede?
   ○ A. He builds a nest for it.
   ○ B. He scares the bird away.
   ○ C. He gives it to the rich man.
   ○ D. He keeps water from filling its nest.

3. Which line from the story **best** describes what the magic bead looks like?
   ○ A. nothing very special about the bead
   ○ B. the old peddler treated it like a fine jewel
   ○ C. colored orange and looked as if it had yellow eyes
   ○ D. the old man took the bead from them and examined it

4. Which of the following events shows that this story is a fantasy?
   ○ A. The peddler has a dream about the ants.
   ○ B. The rich man gives the peddler a big reward.
   ○ C. The peddler is kind to every animal he meets.
   ○ D. The centipede tells the peddler where to find the bead.

5. Which of the following words means "a sign" or "a warning"?
   ○ A. lacquer
   ○ B. larvae
   ○ C. dissolve
   ○ D. omen

Wrap-up

Compare and Contrast

Both "Aunty Misery" and "We Are All One" are filled with elements of **fantasy.** Think about the strange and fantastic events in each story.

Complete the chart below. In the left column, explain how the elements of fantasy in the two stories are alike. In the right column, explain how the elements of fantasy are different in the tales. An example has been done for you in each column.

Alike	Different
• People deal with normal, everyday things.	• There are no talking animals in "Aunty Misery"; "We Are All One" has talking animals.

UNIT 5

Nonfiction

What's Nonfiction?

Pick up a newspaper or magazine, or check out many Web sites, and you will find writing that is nonfiction.

Nonfiction is the name for writing that is about real people and real events. This kind of writing concentrates on facts. There are many kinds of nonfiction. Biography, autobiography, memoir, and essay are popular types of this kind of writing.

A **biography** is the story of a person's life written by someone other than that person. An **autobiography** is the story of a person's life written by that person. A **memoir** is a story of the narrator's personal experience. An **essay** is a short piece of nonfiction about a single topic.

Nonfiction can deal with many topics. What nonfiction subjects would you like to read about? It can be a biography of someone you admire, or maybe an essay about a different country or a famous historical event. Write your responses below.

_____

_____

Why Read Nonfiction?

Read nonfiction to learn about new places, new people, and new ideas. By reading nonfiction and learning so many new things, you can better understand the world around you. Nonfiction can even help you understand yourself better.

How Do I Read Nonfiction?

Focus on key **literary elements** and **reading skills** to get the most out of reading the nonfiction in this unit. Here are two key literary elements and two key reading skills that you will practice in this unit.

Key Literary Elements

• Description

Description is writing that includes many details about a person, animal, object, place, or event. Description helps readers picture what they are reading about. Use all your senses to imagine what the writer is describing.

• Point of View

Point of view is the viewpoint from which a piece of writing is told. The person who tells the events in a story is the narrator.

When a story is told by a narrator who is referred to as *I* or *me*, that story is told from the first-person point of view. The reader sees everything that happens through the narrator's eyes. A first-person narrator can describe only what he or she sees, hears, knows, or feels. The feelings of other characters can only be revealed through their actions and dialogue.

When someone outside the story is the narrator, that story is told from the third-person point of view. A third-person narrator can tell the thoughts and actions of all the characters.

Key Reading Skills

• Author's Purpose

All writers have a **purpose** or goal when they write something. An author may want to entertain readers, describe or explain something to readers, or persuade readers to believe something. As you read, ask yourself: What is the author trying to do here? Why is the author telling this story?

• Main Idea and Details

Skillful readers know how to look for the **main idea,** the most important point, in a passage. The main idea can usually be found in the first or last sentence of a paragraph. Other sentences support, or tell something about, the main idea. These are called the **details.** As you read, ask yourself: What is this paragraph about? What details help show what this paragraph is about?

WE WILL REMAIN AT PEACE WITH YOUR PEOPLE FOREVER

Meet Cochise, Chiricahua Apache Chief

Chief Cochise was born in the early 1800s. He was the leader of the Chiricahua (chir´ i kä´ wə) Apache (ə pach´ ē) tribe, Native Americans who lived in the southwestern United States. For years he led his people in the fight for their land against Mexican and American enemies. After reaching an agreement with the U.S. government, Cochise moved to a reservation in Arizona, where he died in 1874. This speech was given in 1872.

What You Know

Think about a time when you had to stand up for your rights. Why did you think the situation was unfair? What did you say or do to try to change it?

Reason to Read

Read this speech to learn how a great Native American leader stood up for the rights of his people.

Background Info

In the 1800s, there were many problems between Native Americans and white settlers in the western part of the United States. As the settlers moved west, they often took over Native American hunting grounds and used natural resources that the Native American tribes relied upon. The tribes fought to protect the land they had lived upon for many years. When the U.S. Army got involved, the fighting increased, and many lives were lost. In the 1860s, President Ulysses S. Grant attempted to stop the wars by creating reservations for Native Americans. These reservations were areas of land set aside for Native American tribes. Tribes often had to move very far from their original land to live on a reservation. Most of the land set aside for reservations was not very good for growing crops or hunting, so life was very difficult for the tribes in their new land.

Word Power

feeble (fē′ bəl) *adj.* weak; p. 204
The little kitten was *feeble* and could barely walk when we found it.

perish (per′ ish) *v.* to die; disappear completely; p. 205
Some endangered animals may *perish* if we do not protect their environment.

conquered (kong′ kərd) *adj.* defeated; p. 206
The *conquered* knights bowed to the new king.

vanish (van′ ish) *v.* to disappear; p. 206
The fog will *vanish* when the sun comes out.

remnant (rem′ nənt) *n.* something that is left over; p. 206
After I made the coat, I had a small *remnant* of cloth that I used to sew a hat.

**Answer the following questions that contain the new words above.
Write your answers in the spaces provided.**

1. If something were to *vanish,* would it appear or disappear? _____

2. Would a *conquered* team be the winner or the loser in a contest? _____

3. If Carlos is *feeble,* is he strong or weak? _____

4. If you have a *remnant* of ribbon, do you have a lot or a little? _____

5. If your dreams of becoming famous *perish,* do your dreams come true or do
   they die? _____

WE WILL REMAIN AT PEACE WITH YOUR PEOPLE FOREVER

Cochise, Chiricahua Apache Chief

Literary Element

Description Reread the text highlighted in blue. The author is describing how his people grew from few to many. Underline the description that best helps you picture what he is saying.

English Coach

Here, *drive* means "to use force to make someone or something move." Think of another meaning of *drive* and use it in a sentence.

_____

_____

_____

This for a very long time has been the home of my people. . . . We came to these mountains about us; no one lived here, and so we took them for our home and country. Here we grew from the first **feeble** band to be a great people and covered the whole country as the clouds cover the mountains. Many people came to our country. First the Spanish, with their horses and their iron shirts, their long knives and guns, great wonders to my simple people. We fought some, but they never tried to drive us from our homes in these mountains. After many years the Spanish soldiers were driven away and the Mexican ruled the land. With these, little wars came, but we were now a strong people, and we did not fear them.

Word Power
feeble (fē´ bəl) *adj.* weak

At last in my youth came the white man, under your people.... I have fought long and as best I could against you. I have destroyed many of your people, but where I have destroyed one white man many have come in his place; where an Indian has been killed, there has been none to come in his place, so that the great people that welcomed you with acts of kindness to this land are now but a feeble band that fly before your soldiers as the deer before the hunter, and must all **perish** if this war continues.

On the left is a picture of the kind of Spanish soldier Cochise's people had to fight. On the right is an example of a U.S. soldier Cochise and his people fought against. Do these pictures help you understand why so many of Cochise's people were dying in the battles? Why or why not?

_____

Reading Skill

Main Idea and Details Reread the highlighted text. Which of the following sentences **best** states the main idea that these details support? Check the correct response.

☐ Cochise's people cannot win because there are more white people.

☐ Cochise's people killed many white people during the wars.

☐ The population of Cochise's people is quickly growing.

Word Power

perish (per´ ish) *v.* to die; disappear completely

Reading Skill

Author's Purpose Reread the highlighted text. What is Cochise's main purpose in giving this speech? Put a check next to the **best** response.

- ☐ to tell white people to leave the land
- ☐ to praise white people
- ☐ to end the war and save his people

Comprehension Check

Reread the boxed paragraph. What does Cochise promise to do?

_____

_____

_____

_____

_____

_____

I have come to you, not from love for you or for your great father in Washington, or from any regard for his or your wishes, but as a **conquered** chief, to try to save the few people that still remain to me. I am the last of my family, a family that for very many years have been the leaders of this people; and on me depends their future, whether they shall totally **vanish** from the land or that a small **remnant** remain for a few years to see the sun rise over these mountains, their home.

I here pledge my word, a word that has never been broken, that if your great father will set aside a part of my own country, where I and my little band can live, we will remain at peace with your people forever. . . . I have spoken.

Did You Know?

The phrase "great father in Washington" refers to Ulysses S. Grant, the U.S. president at the time of this speech. Grant had been the commander of the Union army during the last years of the Civil War.

. . . .

This picture shows land in the southwestern United States. Do you think it would be easy or difficult to live on this land? Why?

_____

Word Power

conquered (kong′ kərd) *adj.* defeated

vanish (van′ ish) *v.* to disappear

remnant (rem′ nənt) *n.* something that is left over

Respond to Literature

WE WILL REMAIN AT PEACE WITH YOUR PEOPLE FOREVER

A Comprehension Check

Answer the following questions in the spaces provided.

1. What happened to Cochise's people after the white man came to their land? _____

   _____

2. What does Cochise promise to the white people in return for part of the land for his people? _____

   _____

B Reading Skills

Answer the following questions in the spaces provided.

1. **Author's Purpose** What is Cochise's purpose in speaking to the white men?

   _____

   _____

2. **Main Idea and Details** Cochise mentions the different enemies his people have faced and the wars they have fought. How do these details support the main idea that there are not many of his people left?

   _____

   _____

   _____

C Word Power

Complete each sentence below, using one of the words in the box.

feeble	perish	conquered
vanish	remnant	

1. The general met with the leader of the _____ soldiers to accept their surrender.

2. When I got the flu, I felt too _____ to do anything but sleep.

3. The only _____ of our picnic was a slice of watermelon.

4. When the magician waved his wand, his assistant seemed to _____ into thin air!

5. If not watered properly, the plants will _____.

Circle the word that best completes each sentence.

6. Did the deer (**vanish, remnant**) into the woods when you honked your horn?

7. Only a small (**remnant, feeble**) of the group finished the long, hard hike.

8. Our hopes and dreams will (**perish, conquered**) if we don't win the game.

9. Bente did not believe Matt's (**feeble, perish**) excuse for being late.

10. They shook hands with the (**vanish, conquered**) team after they won the spelling bee.

D Literary Element: Description

Read the passages below from "We Will Remain at Peace with Your People Forever." As you read, think about the descriptions Cochise uses. Then answer the questions that follow.

Many people came to our country.[1] First the Spanish, with their horses and their iron shirts, their long knives and guns, great wonders to my simple people.[2]

At last in my youth came the white man, under your people. . . .[3] I have fought long and as best I could against you.[4] I have destroyed many of your people, but where I have destroyed one white man many have come in his place; where an Indian has been killed, there has been none to come in his place, so that the great people that welcomed you with acts of kindness to this land are now but a feeble band that fly before your soldiers as the deer before the hunter, and must all perish if this war continues.[5]

1. In sentences 1–2, Cochise uses details to describe the Spanish soldiers. What details help you picture the soldiers? How do the details help you imagine what they sound like? _____

    _____

    _____

2. In sentences 3–5, Cochise talks about how fighting the white people has hurt his own people. How does the description of the deer and the hunter help you imagine the relationship between Cochise's people and the

    white soldiers? _____

    _____

    _____

E Today's News: A Speech for His People

Pretend you are a reporter for a Southwest newspaper in 1872. You have just seen Cochise give his famous speech. Write to tell your readers about the event.

Today, the Apache leader, Chief Cochise, gave a speech to an audience of _____

In his speech, he told of the many invaders his people faced. First came _____

Later, the Apaches had wars with _____

Now, after fighting with the white people, the Apache leader does not want to fight anymore because _____

_____

_____

He has promised to _____

_____

In return, the Apaches are asking _____

_____

_____

The great chief hopes that this will be the best thing for his people.

Article written by _____

Staff Reporter

Assessment

Fill in the circle next to each correct answer.

1. Who ruled the land of Cochise's people after the Spanish soldiers were driven away?
   - ○ A. the Europeans
   - ○ B. the Mexicans
   - ○ C. the Apaches
   - ○ D. the Americans

2. Which detail from the speech **best** supports the main idea that the Apache tribe grew large?
   - ○ A. covered the whole country as the clouds cover the mountains
   - ○ B. great wonders to my simple people
   - ○ C. where an Indian has been killed, there has been none to come in his place
   - ○ D. a small remnant remain for a few years to see the sun rise over these mountains

3. What comparison does Cochise use in his description of his people against the white soldiers?
   - ○ A. His people are like deer; the whites are like Spanish soldiers.
   - ○ B. His people are like iron shirts; the whites are like knives and guns.
   - ○ C. The whites are like deer; his people are like hunters.
   - ○ D. His people are like deer; the whites are like hunters.

4. Which sentence **best** explains Cochise's purpose in speaking?
   - ○ A. He wants to persuade his people to fight harder.
   - ○ B. He wants to entertain future people with a good story.
   - ○ C. He wants to make peace and save his people.
   - ○ D. He wants to inform the Mexican people about a new war.

5. Which of the following words means "weak"?
   - ○ A. remnant
   - ○ B. feeble
   - ○ C. vanish
   - ○ D. perish

Get Ready to Read!

Barrio Boy

Meet Ernesto Galarza

Ernesto Galarza was born in 1905. Galarza spent most of his life fighting for the rights of farmworkers. He used his writing to show the difficulties of their lives. Galarza died in 1984. This selection is from his autobiography *Barrio Boy*, which was first published in 1971.

What You Know

The first day of school is an important time. How did you feel the first time you walked into your school? What do you remember about the building, the teachers, and your new classmates?

Reason to Read

Read this autobiography to learn how the author, as a young boy, feels as he starts at a new school and learns a new language.

Background Info

Starting at a new school can be an exciting but challenging time. It is especially challenging if you do not speak the language at your new school. This story takes place at Lincoln School in Sacramento, California. It tells about when the author has just moved from Mexico to California. Galarza remembers what it was like to be a new student who could not understand the language. He says the story will be familiar to many people who moved from Mexico to the United States in the early part of the twentieth century.

Word Power

wholeheartedly (hōl´ här´ tid lē) *adv.* completely; sincerely; with enthusiasm; p. 215
Mark *wholeheartedly* supported his friend's decision to buy a new bike.

maneuvered (mə no͞o´ vərd) *v.* moved skillfully; p. 215
The red car *maneuvered* around a slower car.

menace (men´ is) *n.* a danger; p. 215
Mosquitoes can be a *menace* in the summer.

obnoxious (ob nok´ shəs) *adj.* annoying; not nice; p. 216
When my sister broke my CD, I thought she was *obnoxious*.

persistently (pər sis´ tənt lē) *adv.* many times; over and over; p. 217
The small child *persistently* asked his mother for some candy.

Answer the following questions that contain the new words above. Write your answers in the spaces provided.

1. If you *wholeheartedly* agree with someone, do you agree with them completely or just a little bit?_____

2. If you *maneuvered* through a crowd, did you walk around people or stand still?

   _____

3. If someone were driving like a *menace*, would they be driving too fast or driving safely? _____

4. Which action would be considered *obnoxious*: saying something nice or saying something mean? _____

5. If you wanted to practice soccer *persistently*, would you practice once a day or once a month? _____

Adapted from

Barrio Boy

Cabeza de Nino, 1921–1929. Diego Rivera. Dibujo a la sanguina, 38 x 27.5 cm.

Ernesto Galarza

Enrolling in School

The two of us walked south on Fifth Street one morning to the corner of Q Street and turned right. Half of the block was taken up by the Lincoln School. The school was a wooden building with three floors. It had two wings that gave it the shape of a double-T connected by a hall in the middle. The building was new, painted yellow, with a shingled roof that was not like the red tile of the school in Mazatlán. I noticed other differences, and none of them made me feel any better.

We walked up the wide staircase hand in hand and through the door, which closed by itself. Something screwed to the top of the door shut it behind us without a sound.

Up to this point the adventure of enrolling me in the school had been carefully rehearsed. Mrs. Dodson had told us how to find it, and we had circled it several times on our walks. Friends in the *barrio* explained that the director was called a principal, and that it was a lady and not a man. They said that there was always a person at the school who could speak Spanish.

Exactly as we had been told, there was a sign on the door in both Spanish and English: "Principal." We crossed the hall and entered the office of Miss Nettie Hopley.

214

Miss Hopley was at a roll-top desk to one side, sitting in a swivel chair that moved on wheels. There was a sofa against the opposite wall, flanked by two windows and a door that opened on a small balcony. Chairs were set around a table, and framed pictures hung on the walls of a man with long white hair and another with a sad face and a black beard.

The principal half turned in the chair to look at us over the pinch glasses resting on the top of her nose. To do this she had to duck her head slightly as if she were about to step through a low doorway.

Did You Know?
Pinch glasses are eyeglasses that clip to the nose.

What Miss Hopley said to us we did not know, but we saw in her eyes a warm welcome, and when she took off her glasses and straightened up she smiled, **wholeheartedly,** like Mrs. Dodson. We were, of course, saying nothing, only catching the friendliness of her voice and the sparkle in her eyes while she said words we did not understand. She signaled us to the table. Almost tiptoeing across the office, I **maneuvered** myself to keep my mother between me and the *gringo* lady. In a matter of seconds I had to decide whether she was a possible friend or a **menace.** We sat down.

Then Miss Hopley did something that at first seemed exciting and a little bit scary. She stood up. Had she been standing when we entered, she would have seemed tall. But rising from her chair she soared. And what she carried up and up with her was a powerful body, firm shoulders, a straight sharp nose, full cheeks, thin lips that moved like steel springs, and a high forehead topped by hair gathered in a bun. Miss Hopley was not a giant in body, but when she stood up she seemed a match for giants. I decided I liked her.

Word Power

wholeheartedly (hōl´ här´ tid lē) *adv.* completely; sincerely; with enthusiasm

maneuvered (mə nōō´ vərd) *v.* moved skillfully

menace (men´ is) *n.* a danger

Comprehension Check

Reread the boxed text. Why don't Ernesto and his mother know what Miss Hopley says?
- [ ] It is loud in the room.
- [ ] Miss Hopley speaks softly.
- [ ] They do not understand English.

Reading Skill

Main Idea and Details
Reread the highlighted sentence and the rest of the paragraph. The main idea here is that Miss Hopley seems very large and powerful to the narrator. What details from the paragraph support this idea?

_____

_____

_____

_____

Literary Element

Description Reread the highlighted paragraph. Underline the descriptive words or phrases that help you picture the boy who comes into the room.

She walked, with long steps, to a door in the far corner of the office, opened it and called a name. A boy of about ten years appeared in the doorway. He sat down at one end of the table. He was brown like us, a kid with shiny black hair combed straight back, neat, cool, and faintly **obnoxious.**

Miss Hopley joined us with a large book and some papers in her hand. She, too, sat down, and the questions and answers began by way of our interpreter. My name was Ernesto. My mother's name was Henriqueta. My birth certificate was in San Blas. Here was my last report card from the school in Mazatlán, and so forth. Miss Hopley put things down in the book, and my mother signed a card.

As long as the questions continued, my mother could stay and I was secure. Now that they were over, Miss Hopley saw her to the door, dismissed our interpreter, and then took me by the hand and walked down the hall to Miss Ryan's first grade.

This class picture was taken in the early 1900s. That is around the time Ernesto Galarza attended Lincoln School. What can you learn about the school and its students from studying the picture?

Word Power

obnoxious (ob nok´ shəs) *adj.* annoying; not nice

216

First Grade

Miss Ryan took me to a seat at the front of the room, into which I shrank—the better to watch her. She was, to skinny, somewhat tiny me, of a massive height when she patrolled the class. And when I least expected it, there she was, crouching by my desk, her blond happy face level with mine, her voice patiently helping me with the very complicated English language.

During the next few weeks Miss Ryan overcame my fears of tall, energetic teachers as she bent over my desk to help me with a word in the book. Step by step, she loosened me and my classmates from the safe anchorage of the desks for practicing out loud at the blackboard and for visits to her desk. There were many times when she burst into happy announcements to the whole class. "Ito can read a sentence," and small Japanese Ito, very shy, slowly read aloud while the class listened in wonder: "Come, Skipper, come. Come and run." The Korean, Portuguese, Italian, and Polish first-graders had similar moments of glory, no less shining than mine the day I conquered *butterfly,* which I had been **persistently** pronouncing in standard Spanish as "boo-ter-flee." "Children," Miss Ryan called for attention. "Ernesto has learned how to pronounce *butterfly*!" And I proved it with a perfect imitation of Miss Ryan. From that celebrated success, I was soon able to match Ito's progress as a sentence reader with "Come, butterfly, come fly with me."

Like Ito and several other first graders who did not know English, I received private lessons from Miss Ryan in the closet, a narrow hall off the classroom with a door at each end.

Word Power
persistently (pər sis′ tənt lē) *adv.* many times; over and over

Connect to the Text
Reread the paragraph boxed in purple. At first, Ernesto thinks Miss Ryan is big, and he is scared of her. After she is nice to him, he is no longer scared. Think of a time when you felt scared of a person but changed your mind when he or she did something nice.

_____

_____

_____

_____

_____

Comprehension Check
Reread the sentence boxed in green. Why does Ernesto get private lessons from his teacher?

_____

_____

_____

_____

Comprehension Check

Reread the boxed text. Why do Ernesto and the other students work so hard for Miss Ryan? Check the correct responses.

- [ ] They believe they love her.
- [ ] They want to show off to other students.
- [ ] They know she works hard for them.

Reading Skill

Main Idea and Details

Reread the highlighted paragraph. The author gives details about students at Lincoln School being from Japan, Italy, Portugal, and other countries. What main idea do these details support?

_____

_____

_____

_____

_____

Next to one of these doors Miss Ryan placed a large chair for herself and a small one for me. Keeping an eye on the class through the open door, she read with me about sheep in the meadow and a frightened chicken going to see the king, coaching me out of my trouble with words like *pasture, bow-wow-wow, hay,* and *pretty,* which to my Mexican ear and eye had so many unnecessary sounds and letters. She made me watch her lips and then close my eyes as she repeated words I found hard to read. When we came to know each other better, I tried interrupting to tell Miss Ryan how we said it in Spanish. It didn't work. She only said "oh" and went on with *pasture, bow-wow-wow,* and *pretty.* It was as if in that closet we were both discovering together the secrets of the English language and grieving together over the tragedies of Bo-Peep. The main reason I was graduated with honors from the first grade was that I had fallen in love with Miss Ryan. Her happy, no-nonsense character made us either afraid not to love her or love her so we would not be afraid, I am not sure which. It was not only that we sensed she was with it, but also that she was with us.

Becoming a Proud American

Like the first grade, the rest of the Lincoln School was a sample of the lower part of town where many races made their home. My pals in the second grade were Kazushi, whose parents spoke only Japanese; Matti, a skinny Italian boy; and Manuel, a fat Portuguese who would never get into a fight but wrestled you to the ground and just sat on you. Our group of nationalities included Koreans, Yugoslavs, Poles, Irish, and home-grown Americans.

Miss Hopley and her teachers never let us forget why we were at Lincoln: for those who were from somewhere else, to become good Americans; for those who were so born, to accept the rest of us. Off the school grounds we traded the same insults we heard from our elders. On the playground we were sure to be marched up to the principal's office for using bad words for different nationalities. The school was not so much a melting pot as a griddle where Miss Hopley and her helpers warmed knowledge into us and roasted racial hatreds out of us.

English Coach

The word *playground* is a compound word. Write another compound word that uses *play*. Then write another compound word that uses *ground*.

_____

_____

_____

Playtime. Diana Ong (b. 1940). Computer graphics, 5 x 4 mm chrome.

Look at the children in this painting. In what ways might they be similar to the students at Lincoln School?

_____

Reading Skill

Author's Purpose Reread the highlighted sentence and the rest of the paragraph. What do you think the author's purpose is for describing how all the students told stories about their own cultures? Check the correct response.

☐ to show that all the students are homesick

☐ to show that they liked making up stories of things that never happened

☐ to show they are becoming American but are still proud of their cultures

At Lincoln, making us into Americans did not mean scrubbing away what made us originally foreign. The teachers called us as our parents did, or as close as they could pronounce our names in Spanish or Japanese. No one was punished for speaking in his native tongue on the playground. Matti told the class about his mother's down quilt, which she had made in Italy with the fine feathers of a thousand geese. Encarnación acted out how boys learned to fish in the Philippines. I surprised the third grade with the story of my travels on a stagecoach, which nobody else in the class had seen except in the museum at Sutter's Fort. After a visit to the Crocker Art Gallery and its collection of heroic paintings of the golden age of California, someone showed a silk scroll with a Chinese painting. Miss Hopley herself had a way of expressing wonder over these matters before a class, her eyes wide open until they popped slightly. It was easy for me to feel that becoming a proud American, as she said we should, did not mean feeling ashamed of being a Mexican.

Respond to Literature

Barrio Boy

A Comprehension Check

Answer the following questions in the spaces provided.

1. Where are Ernesto and his mother going as they walk down Fifth Street at the beginning of the story? _____

   _____

2. Why does Ernesto get private lessons from Miss Ryan? _____

   _____

   _____

B Reading Skills

Answer the following questions in the spaces provided.

1. **Main Idea and Details** Ernesto first describes Miss Ryan as having "a massive height." Then he describes her "crouching by my desk, her blond happy face level with mine." What main idea do these details support?

   _____

   _____

   _____

2. **Author's Purpose** The author writes, "At Lincoln, making us into Americans did not mean scrubbing away what made us originally foreign." What do you think the author is trying to explain with this sentence?

   _____

   _____

   _____

C Word Power

Complete each sentence below, using one of the words in the box.

wholeheartedly	maneuvered	menace
obnoxious	persistently	

1. I think it is _____ to burp during dinner.

2. Matches are a _____ to young children.

3. The players _____ agreed with their coach when he told them that they could win the big game.

4. I quickly _____ my grocery cart around a broken jar of applesauce.

5. It rained _____ last week, so we couldn't play outside very much.

Circle the word that best completes each sentence.

6. Alice's parents **(menace, wholeheartedly)** supported her decision to learn to play guitar.

7. The **(maneuvered, obnoxious)** boys shouted mean things at the baseball players.

8. The student **(persistently, obnoxious)** asked the teacher for a hall pass.

9. Rakesh **(wholeheartedly, maneuvered)** his bicycle through the trash on the street.

10. Mean dogs can be a **(menace, persistently)** to people in the park.

D Literary Element: Description

Read the passages below from "Barrio Boy." As you read, think about what words and phrases are most descriptive. Then answer the questions that follow.

What Miss Hopley said to us we did not know, but we saw in her eyes a warm welcome, and when she took off her glasses and straightened up she smiled, wholeheartedly, like Mrs. Dodson.[1] We were, of course, saying nothing, only catching the friendliness of her voice and the sparkle in her eyes while she said words we did not understand.[2]

She walked, with long steps, to a door in the far corner of the office, opened it and called a name.[3] A boy of about ten years appeared in the doorway.[4] He sat down at one end of the table.[5] He was brown like us, a kid with shiny black hair combed straight back, neat, cool, and faintly obnoxious.[6]

1. In sentences 1–2, how does the way the author describes Miss Hopley show that she is making him and his mother feel welcome?

   _____

   _____

   _____

2. Which phrases in sentences 3–6 help you **see** the scene?

   _____

   _____

   _____

E A Photo and a Letter

Imagine you are Ernesto in the story. You want to send a photo of yourself and your new teacher, Miss Ryan, to your friends at your old school. Draw the picture you would send in the box below. Then write a letter that tells your friends what they are seeing and how you feel about your new school.

Dear _____,

Here is a picture of me with my new teacher, Miss Ryan. As you can see, she is

_____

_____

When I first got to the school, I felt _____

_____

_____

My new friends are from many places, but they are like me because _____

_____

_____

I miss you and hope you are well.

Your friend,
Ernesto

Assessment

Fill in the circle next to each correct answer.

1. Who is the first person Ernesto meets at his new school?
   - ○ A. the principal
   - ○ B. a teacher
   - ○ C. a student
   - ○ D. the janitor

2. Which of the following phrases from the story is a description that helps you picture the principal, Miss Hopley?
   - ○ A. the director was called a principal
   - ○ B. entered the office of Miss Nettie Hopley
   - ○ C. when she took off her glasses and straightened up, she smiled
   - ○ D. I had to decide whether she was a possible friend or a menace

3. The narrator tells about students on the playground getting "marched up to the principal's office" for calling someone a bad name. Which main idea does this detail support?
   - ○ A. Students are told not to talk loudly when they play.
   - ○ B. Students are taught to accept and respect each other.
   - ○ C. Students are allowed to speak only English at school.
   - ○ D. Students are supposed to be studying instead of playing.

4. Which of the following phrases best states what might be Ernesto Galarza's purpose for writing *Barrio Boy*?
   - ○ A. to persuade people to speak only Spanish
   - ○ B. to explain why his family moved from Mexico
   - ○ C. to describe how he got used to life in a new country
   - ○ D. to entertain people with funny stories about his family

5. Which action makes a dog a *menace*?
   - ○ A. begging for treats
   - ○ B. wagging its tail
   - ○ C. fetching a stick
   - ○ D. growling at a person

THE
HORSE SNAKE

Meet
Huynh Quang Nhuong

Huynh Quang Nhuong (hwin
kwän nōōn) was born in 1946 in
Vietnam. When he was a child,
he wanted to be a teacher in his
village one day. After attending
Saigon University, Huynh was
drafted into the South
Vietnamese army. He was
seriously wounded in the
Vietnam War. Huynh now lives
in the United States, in Missouri.
"The Horse Snake" is from his
autobiography, *The Land I Lost*,
which was first published in 1982.

What You Know

Think about what you already know about snakes. How do they
look and feel? How do they move? What sounds do they make?
How do they catch food and eat it?

Reason to Read

Read this autobiography to find out what a horse snake is and
how it affects life in a village in Vietnam.

Background Info

Sometimes when people live in an area close to nature, they must
live near wild and dangerous animals. As they go about their daily
lives, they learn to look out for danger. This story is set in
Vietnam, in a small village near the jungle. Many different wild
animals live in the jungles of Vietnam. Some of the most feared
animals here are tigers, wild hogs, crocodiles, and horse snakes.
Villagers often work together to guard and defend each other
against threats from the jungle.

Word Power

hamlet (ham´ lit) *n.* a small village in the country; p. 229
We stayed in a charming *hamlet* on our trip through the countryside.

presumed (pri zoomd´) *v.* supposed; assumed to be true; p. 229
I *presumed* that the new student was lost because she was looking at a map.

terrorized (ter´ ə rīzd´) *v.* filled with fear; controlled by using fear or force; p. 229
The play was about a dragon that *terrorized* the people in a castle.

hammock (ham´ ək) *n.* a swinging bed made of netting or cloth, hung from supports at each end; p. 233
We have a comfortable *hammock* hung between two trees in our backyard.

unconscious (un kon´ shəs) *adj.* not able to see, feel, or think; p. 234
The rider was knocked *unconscious* after he fell off his horse.

rejoiced (ri joisd´) *v.* expressed great happiness; p. 234
I *rejoiced* when I won an award for my science project.

**Answer the following questions, using one of the new words above.
Write your answers in the spaces provided.**

1. Which word goes with "a place that's smaller than a city"? _____

2. Which word goes with "not awake or aware"? _____

3. Which word goes with "a comfortable place to take a nap"? _____

4. Which word goes with "shouted with joy"? _____

5. Which word goes with "made very afraid"? _____

6. Which word goes with "assumed that something was true"? _____

Adapted from

THE HORSE SNAKE

Huynh Quang Nhuong

Reading Skill

Main Idea and Details Reread the highlighted paragraph. Which of the following statements **best** tells the main idea of this passage? Check the correct response.

- [ ] The horse snake is the most dangerous snake in the jungle.
- [ ] No one could agree on the correct name for the snake.
- [ ] Horses are the fastest animals in the jungle.

Despite all his courage there was one creature in the jungle that Tank always tried to avoid—the snake. And there was one kind of snake that was more dangerous than other snakes—the horse snake. In some areas people called it the bamboo snake because it was as long as a full-grown bamboo tree. In other regions, the people called it the thunder or lightning snake, because it attacked so fast and with such power that its victim had neither time to escape nor strength to fight it. In our area, we called it the horse snake because it could move as fast as a horse.

One night a scared friend of our family's banged on our door and asked us to let him in. On his way home from a wedding, he had heard the hiss of a horse snake. We became very worried; not only for us and our friend, but also for the cattle and other animals we raised.

It was too late to wake all our neighbors and go to search for the snake. But my father told my cousin to blow three times on his horn, the signal that a dangerous wild beast was loose in the **hamlet.** A few seconds later we heard three long sounds of a horn at the far end of the hamlet answering our warning. We **presumed** that the whole hamlet was now on guard.

I stayed up that night, listening to all the sounds outside, while my father and my cousin sharpened their hunting knives.

The next day early in the morning all the able-bodied men of the hamlet gathered in front of our house and divided into groups of four to go and look for the snake. My father and my cousin grabbed their lunch and joined a searching party.

They found an old horse in the rice field. The snake had squeezed it to death. Its chest was smashed, and all its ribs broken. But the snake had disappeared.

Everybody agreed that it was the work of one of the giant horse snakes which had **terrorized** our area as far back as anyone could remember. The horse snake usually eats small game, such as turkeys, monkeys, chickens, and ducks, but for unknown reasons sometimes it will attack people and cattle. A fully grown horse snake can reach the size of a king python. But, unlike pythons, horse snakes have a very poisonous bite. Because of their bone-breaking squeeze and deadly bite they are one of the most dangerous creatures.

Did You Know?

A python grows as long as thirty feet. Although it is not poisonous, a python coils its long, powerful body around a victim to smother it.

· ·

Literary Element

Point of View Reread the paragraphs highlighted in blue. Underline the pronouns that tell you that this story is told from the first-person point of view.

Reading Skill

Author's Purpose Reread the text highlighted in green. The author provides a lot of information about the horse snake. Do you think his purpose here is to entertain, inform, or persuade? Why?

_____

_____

_____

_____

_____

_____

_____

Word Power

hamlet (ham′ lit) *n.* a small village in the country

presumed (pri zoomd′) *v.* supposed; assumed to be true

terrorized (ter′ ə rīzd′) *v.* filled with fear; controlled by using fear or force

229

My Workspace

Literary Element

Point of View Reread the text highlighted in blue. The author has now moved from the main story to an "inner story." What point of view is this inner story told from? How do you know?

_____

_____

_____

_____

_____

_____

English Coach

The word *nowhere* is a compound word meaning "no place." Write the compound word that means "some other place." Write the compound word that means "every place."

_____

_____

The men searched all day, but at nightfall they gave up and went home. My father and my cousin looked very tired when they returned. My grandmother told them to go right to bed after their dinner and that she would wake them up if she or my mother heard any unusual sounds.

The men went to bed and the women prepared to stay up all night. My mother sewed torn clothing and my grandmother read a novel she had just borrowed from a friend. And for the second night in a row, they allowed my little sister and me to stay awake and listen with them for as long as we could. But hours later, seeing the worry on our faces, my grandmother put aside her novel and told us a story:

Once upon a time a happy family lived in a small village on the shore of the South China Sea. They respected the laws of the land and loved their neighbors very much. The father and his oldest son were woodcutters. The father was quite old, but he still could carry home a heavy load of wood.

One day on his way home from the jungle he was happier than usual. He and his son had discovered a wild chicken nest containing twelve eggs. Now he would have something special to give to his grandchildren when he came home.

The father looked at his son, and he had no doubt that when he became even older still his son would take good care of him and his wife.

As he was thinking this he saw his son suddenly throw the load of wood at a charging horse snake that had come out of nowhere. The heavy load of wood crashed into the snake's head and stunned it. That gave them enough time to draw their sharp woodcutting knives. But instead of attacking the horse snake from the front, the father shouted to his son to run behind the big bush of grass nearby while he, who was a little too old to run fast, jumped into the front end of the bush.

Each time the snake passed by him the old man hit it with his knife. He struck the snake many times. Finally it became weak and slowed down; so he came out of his hiding place and attacked the snake's tail, while his son attacked the snake's head. The snake fought back, but finally it gave up.

When the snake was dead, they grabbed its tail and proudly dragged it to the edge of their village. Everyone rushed out to see their prize. They all argued over who would have the honor of carrying the snake to their house for them.

The old woodcutter and his son had to tell the story of how they had killed the snake at least ten times, but the people never tired of hearing it, again and again. They all agreed that the old woodcutter and his son were not only brave but clever as well. Then and there the villagers decided that when their chief, also a brave and clever man, died, the old woodcutter was the only one who deserved the honor of replacing him.

When my grandmother finished the story, my little sister and I became a bit more cheerful. People could defeat this dangerous snake after all. The silent darkness outside became less scary. Nevertheless, we were still too scared to sleep in our room, so my mother made a bed in the sitting room, close to her and our grandmother.

When we woke up the next morning, life in the hamlet had almost returned to normal. The snake had not struck again that night, and the farmers, in groups of three or four, slowly went back to their fields. Then, late in the afternoon, cries for help were heard in the western part of the hamlet. My cousin and my father grabbed their knives and rushed off to help.

Comprehension Check

Reread the text boxed in green. Why does the grandmother's tale make the narrator feel cheerful and less scared? Underline the answer in the passage.

Connect to the Text

Reread the text boxed in purple. Think about a time when you were scared or upset. What happened to make you feel that things were better and back to normal?

_____

_____

_____

_____

_____

Connect to the Text

Look at the picture. Does this scene remind you of Huynh's village? Have you ever been near a place where animals run free? How did that make you feel?

_____

_____

_____

_____

_____

Shadow. Pham Duc Cuong. Private collection.

It was Minh, a farmer, who was crying for help. Minh, like most farmers in the area, stored the fish he had caught in the rice field at the end of the rainy season in a small pond. That day Minh's wife had wanted a good fish for dinner. When Minh went to the fish pond he heard what sounded like someone trying to steal his fish by using a bucket to empty water from the pond. Minh was very angry and rushed over to catch the thief, but when he reached the pond, what he saw scared him so bad that he fell over backward, speechless. Then he crawled away as fast as he could and yelled loudly for help.

The thief he saw was not a person but a huge horse snake, perhaps the same one that had squeezed the old horse to death two nights before. The snake had hooked its head to the branch of one tree and its tail to another and was splashing the water out of the pond by swinging its body back and forth, like a **hammock.** Then, when the shallow pond was dry, it planned to swallow all the fish.

All the villagers rushed to the scene to help Minh, and our village chief quickly organized an attack. He ordered all the men to stand around the pond. Then two strong young men approached the snake, one at its tail and the other at its head. As they crept closer and closer, the snake assumed a striking position, its head above the pond, and its tail swaying from side to side. It was ready to strike in either direction. As the two young men moved in closer, the snake watched them. Each man tried to draw the attention of the snake, while a third man crept to its side. Suddenly he struck the snake with his long knife.

English Coach
The suffix *-less* means "without." So speechless means "without speech" or "unable to speak." Write two other words that have the suffix *-less*.

_____

_____

Reading Skill
Main Idea and Details Reread the sentence highlighted in green and the rest of the page. The author gives many details about what the men do when they find the snake. What main idea do these details support? Check the correct response.

- ☐ Whenever the snake is near, all the men panic.
- ☐ The men can fight the snake by working together.
- ☐ There is only one man who can kill the snake.

Word Power

hammock (ham ′ ək) *n.* a swinging bed made of netting or cloth, hung from supports at each end

The surprised snake shot out of the pond like an arrow and knocked the young man **unconscious** as it rushed by. It broke through the circle of men and went into an open rice field. But it received two more wounds on its way out.

The village chief ordered all the women and children to form a long line between the open rice field and the jungle and to yell as loudly as they could, hoping to scare the snake so that it would not go into the jungle. It would be easier for the men to fight the wounded snake in an open field than to follow it there.

But now there was a new problem. The snake started heading toward the river. Normally a horse snake could beat any man in a race, but since this one was badly wounded, our chief was able to cut off its escape by sending half his men running to the river. Blocked off from the river and jungle, the snake decided to stay and fight.

The hunting party surrounded the snake again, and this time four of the best men attacked the snake from four different directions. The snake fought bravely, but it died. During the struggle some of the men were hurt. Luckily none of them were bitten by the snake.

We **rejoiced** that the danger was over. But we knew it would only be a matter of time until we would once again have to face our most dangerous natural enemy—the horse snake.

Comprehension Check

Reread the boxed text. Why does the village chief want to stop the snake from going into the jungle?

_____

_____

_____

_____

_____

Word Power

unconscious (un kon′ shəs) *adj.* not able to see, feel, or think

rejoiced (ri joisd′) *v.* expressed great happiness

234

THE HORSE SNAKE

A Comprehension Check

Answer the following questions in the spaces provided.

1. Why do the people in the author's village call the dangerous snake the "horse snake"? _____

   _____

2. How does the grandmother try to make the children feel less afraid?

   _____

   _____

B Reading Skills

Answer the following questions in the spaces provided.

1. **Author's Purpose** At the end of the story, the author writes, "We knew it would only be a matter of time until we would once again have to face our most dangerous natural enemy—the horse snake." What is the author trying to explain in this passage? _____

   _____

   _____

2. **Main Idea and Details** When the author describes the horse snake, he says it is as long as a tree, it attacks quickly and powerfully, and it moves as fast as a horse. What main idea do these details support?

   _____

   _____

   _____

C Word Power

Complete each sentence below, using one of the words in the box.

| hamlet | presumed | terrorized |
| hammock | unconscious | rejoiced |

1. I _____ that Mrs. Blanco had a bad cold because she was coughing and sneezing.

2. The boy was _____ after falling out of the tree.

3. In the summer, I like to lazily swing back and forth in my _____.

4. The people who live in the _____ know their neighbors very well.

5. Our family _____ when the tornado did not touch our home.

6. The mean dog _____ all the other dogs in my neighborhood.

D Literary Element: Point of View

Read the passage below from "The Horse Snake." As you read, think about the point of view in each paragraph. Then answer the questions that follow.

My mother sewed torn clothing and my grandmother read a novel she had just borrowed from a friend.[1] And for the second night in a row, they allowed my little sister and me to stay awake and listen with them for as long as we could.[2] But hours later, seeing the worry on our faces, my grandmother put aside her novel and told us a story:[3]

Once upon a time a happy family lived in a small village on the shore of the South China Sea.[4] They respected the laws of the land and loved their neighbors very much.[5] The father and his oldest son were woodcutters.[6] The father was quite old, but he still could carry home a heavy load of wood.[7]

1. In sentences 1–3, is the story being told from the first-person or third-person point of view? How do you know?

   _____

   _____

   _____

2. In sentences 4–7, what point of view is the story being told from? How do you know?

   _____

   _____

   _____

E Warning: Beware of Horse Snakes!

Pretend you are young Huynh. You decide to post flyers in a nearby village, warning the villagers of the dangerous snake. Write to tell about your experience and give advice.

ATTENTION VILLAGERS!

The people of my hamlet and I want to warn you about
a dangerous animal called _____

We call it this because _____

_____

It can kill animals or people in these two ways:

_____

_____

Just recently, we had one loose in our village. When the men
first went to look for it, all they found was _____

_____

We finally found the snake. Our whole town worked to kill
it by _____

_____

_____

If you see one in your area, you should _____

_____

_____

_____

Assessment

Fill in the circle next to each correct answer.

1. Why does the farmer Minh yell for help?
   - ○ A. He can't find the horse snake anywhere.
   - ○ B. He sees the horse snake near his pond.
   - ○ C. His wife needs help cooking the fish for dinner.
   - ○ D. He sees a thief running through the field.

2. Which of the following sentences from the story **best** supports the main idea that the horse snake is a serious threat to people?
   - ○ A. The snake fought back, but finally it gave up.
   - ○ B. The snake had not struck again that night.
   - ○ C. The snake had hooked its head to the branch of one tree and its tail to another and was splashing the water.
   - ○ D. Because of their bone-breaking squeeze and deadly bite they are one of the most dangerous creatures.

3. Which sentence from the story is **not** an example of the first-person point of view?
   - ○ A. I stayed up that night.
   - ○ B. We became very worried.
   - ○ C. My little sister and I became a bit more cheerful.
   - ○ D. The father and his oldest son were woodcutters.

4. Which choice **best** states the author's purpose in writing the story?
   - ○ A. to entertain and persuade
   - ○ B. to persuade and inform
   - ○ C. to inform and entertain
   - ○ D. to entertain and argue

5. Which of the following words means "expressed great happiness"?
   - ○ A. rejoiced
   - ○ B. terrorized
   - ○ C. presumed
   - ○ D. unconscious

Get Ready to Read!

Names/Nombres

Meet Julia Alvarez

Julia Alvarez was born in New York City. When she was a baby, Alvarez moved with her family to the Dominican Republic, a small country in the Caribbean Sea. She lived there until she was ten, then her family returned to New York City. Julia Alvarez began writing poems and stories in her American English classes when she was a young girl. "Names/Nombres" was first published in 1985.

What You Know

A nickname is an extra name, something that people call you in addition to your real name. Do your friends or family have nicknames for you? Do you have nicknames for them? Why do you think people use nicknames?

Reason to Read

Read this autobiography to see how young Julia Alvarez feels about the English and Spanish names that people call her as she grows up in the United States.

Background Info

The word *nombres* (nōm′brās) means "names" in Spanish. In the story's title, *Names* refers to the English names people call Julia Alvarez. *Nombres* refers to the Spanish names people call her. Sometimes when people move to the United States from different countries, they change their names or the way their names are pronounced. This makes their names more familiar to the people in their new country, and easier for them to say. Changing their names can also make immigrants feel more like a part of their new country.

Word Power

foreign (fôr′ən) *adj.* having to do with a different place or country; unfamiliar or different; p. 243
Hot dogs are a *foreign* food to her because she never ate them in her country.

hesitated (hez′ə tā′tid) *v.* paused or stopped; p. 244
I *hesitated* when my mother asked who broke the lamp.

vaguely (vāg′lē) *adv.* in a way that is not clear, exact, or definite; p. 245
My friend only *vaguely* remembered the words to the song.

generations (jen′ə rā′shənz) *n.* groups of people, in a family or in a society, who were born around the same time; p. 245
We have different experiences growing up than people in our parents' and grandparents' *generations*.

extended (iks ten′did) *adj.* bigger, larger; p. 246
When his aunts, uncles, and cousins arrived, he was amazed at the size of his *extended* family.

portable (pôr′ tə bəl) *adj.* able to be carried easily; p. 247
Bente took a *portable* DVD player with her on the plane.

**Answer the following questions, using one of the new words above.
Write your answers in the spaces provided.**

1. Which word goes with "when someone says something that is
   not clear"? _____

2. Which word goes with "food and customs of another country"? _____

3. Which word goes with "new buildings added to make a
   school larger"? _____

4. Which word goes with "thought before you spoke"? _____

5. Which word goes with "something you can easily carry in
   your hands"? _____

6. Which word goes with "grandparents and grandchildren"? _____

Adapted from

Names/Nombres

Julia Alvarez

Literary Element

Point of View Reread the highlighted sentences. Which words tell you that this story is told from the first-person point of view?

_____

_____

_____

Connect to the Text

Reread the boxed sentences. Has anyone ever mispronounced your name or called you by the wrong name? How did that make you feel?

_____

_____

_____

When we arrived in New York City, our names changed almost immediately. At Immigration, the officer asked my father, *Mister Elbures*, if he had anything to declare. My father shook his head, "No," and we were waved through. I was too afraid we wouldn't be let in if I corrected the man's pronunciation. But I said our name to myself, opening my mouth wide for the organ blast of the *a*, rattling my tongue for the drumroll of the *r*, *All-vah-rrr-es!* How could anyone get *Elbures* out of that orchestra of sound?

At the hotel my mother was *Missus Alburest*. I was *little girl,* as in, "Hey, little girl, stop riding the elevator up and down. It's *not* a toy!"

When we moved into our new apartment building, the manager called my father *Mister Alberase*. The neighbors who became mother's friends pronounced her name *Jew-lee-ah* instead of *Hoo-lee-ah*. I, who was named after her, was known as *Hoo-lee-tah* at home. But at school, I was *Judy* or *Judith*, and once an English teacher mistook me for *Juliet*.

It took awhile to get used to my new names. I wondered if I shouldn't correct my teachers and new friends. But my mother argued that it didn't matter. "You know what your friend Shakespeare said, '*A rose by any other name would smell as sweet.*'" My family had gotten into the habit of calling any author my "friend" because I had begun to write poems and stories in English class.

By the time I was in high school, I was a popular kid. It showed in my name. Friends called me *Jules* or *Hey Jude*. Once a group of troublemaking friends my mother wouldn't let me hang out with called me Alcatraz. I was *Hoo-lee-tah* only to Mami and Papi and uncles and aunts who came over to eat a meat stew called *sancocho* on Sunday afternoons. They were old-fashioned people. I would just as soon have had them go back to where they came from and leave me to pursue whatever mischief I wanted to in America. *JUDY ALCATRAZ:* the name on the Wanted Poster would read. Who would ever trace her to me?

My older sister had the hardest time getting an American name for herself because Mauricia did not translate into English. Although she had the most **foreign**-sounding name, she and I were the Americans in the family. We had been born in New York City when our parents had first tried immigration. Then they went back "home," too homesick to stay. My mother often told the story of how she had almost changed my sister's name in the hospital.

After the delivery, Mami and some other new mothers were fussing over their new baby sons and daughters and exchanging names and weights and delivery stories. My mother was embarrassed among the Sallys and Janes and Georges and Johns to reveal the rich, noisy name of *Mauricia*. When her turn came to brag, she gave her baby's name as *Maureen*.

"Why'd ya give her an Irish name with so many pretty Spanish names to choose from?" one of the women asked her.

My mother blushed and admitted her baby's real name to the group. She apologized by saying that her mother-in-law had recently died and her husband had insisted that the first daughter be named after his mother, *Mauran*. My mother thought it the ugliest name she had ever heard. She talked my father into what she believed was an improvement. It was a combination of *Mauran* and her own mother's name *Felicia*.

Word Power

foreign (fôr´ən) *adj.* having to do with a different place or country; unfamiliar or different

Background Info

Alcatraz is an island in San Francisco Bay. It once was the home of a prison for the worst criminals.

Literary Element

Point of View Reread the highlighted text. This event happens before the narrator is born. In first-person point of view, the narrator can only tell about what she sees, hears, or knows. How is she able to tell this story about her older sister's birth? How can she know how her mother feels at this event?

_____

_____

_____

_____

_____

Portrait of Virginia, 1929. Frida Kahlo. Fundacion Dolores Olmedo, Mexico City, D.F., Mexico.

Think about the young Julia Alvarez in the story. Does this painting remind you of the narrator? Why or why not?

"Her name is *Mao-ree-chee-ah,*" my mother said to the group.

"Why that's a beautiful name," the new mothers cried.

"*Moor-ee-sha, Moor-ee-sha,*" they said softly into the pink blanket.

Moor-ee-sha it was when we returned to the States eleven years later. Sometimes, American tongues found even that tough to say. They called her *Maria* or *Marsha* or *Maudy* from her nickname *Maury.* I pitied her. What an awful name to have to carry across borders!

My little sister, Ana, had the easiest time of all. She was plain *Anne.* Only her name was plain. She turned out to be the pale, blond "American beauty" in the family. The only Hispanic-seeming thing about her was the nickname her boyfriends sometimes gave her, *Anita.*

Later, during her college years in the late '60s, there was a push to pronounce Third World names correctly. I remember calling her long distance at her group house and a roommate answering.

"Can I speak to Ana?" I asked, pronouncing her name the American way.

"Ana?" The man's voice **hesitated.** "Oh! you mean *Ah-nah!*"

Word Power

hesitated (hez´ə tā´tid) *v.* paused or stopped

Background Info

'60s means the 1960s, a time of great change in the United States. Many people began to think more openly about immigrants during that time. Third World names are those of people who were born in poorer, less developed countries in places like Latin America, Africa, and Asia.

Our first few years in the States, though, being a member of a minority group was not yet "in." Those were the blond, blue-eyed, bobby socks years of junior high and high school before the '60s brought in peasant blouses, hoop earrings, *serapes*. My wish to be known by my correct Dominican name faded. I just wanted to be Judy and blend in with the Sallys and Janes in my class. But my accent and coloring gave me away. "So where are you from, Judy?"

"New York," I told my classmates. After all, I had been born blocks away at Columbia Presbyterian Hospital.

"I mean, *originally*."

"From the Caribbean," I answered **vaguely.** If I gave the exact name, no one was quite sure what continent our island was on.

"Really? I've been to Bermuda. We went last April for spring vacation. I got the worst sunburn! So, are you from Portoriko?"

"No," I shook my head. "From the Dominican Republic."

"Where's that?"

"South of Bermuda."

They were just being curious, but I burned with shame whenever they singled me out as a "foreigner," a rare, strangely attractive friend.

"Say your name in Spanish, oh please say it!" I had made mouths drop one day by rattling off my full name. According to Dominican custom, it included my middle names and my mother's and father's family names for four **generations** back.

Word Power

vaguely (vāg′lē) *adv.* in a way that is not clear, exact, or definite
generations (jen′ə rā′shənz) *n.* groups of people, in a family or in a society, who were born around the same time

245

Reading Skill
Main Idea and Details Reread the sentence highlighted in green and the rest of the paragraph. The main idea of this paragraph is about how the author feels about her extended family. Underline the details that support this idea. Hint: Look for words and phrases that describe her family.

English Coach

Here, *nuclear* means "a central group." Earlier on this page, the author talks about members of her *extended* family. If an extended family includes aunts, uncles, and cousins, who is part of a *nuclear family*, or central family?

_____

_____

_____

"Julia Altagracia María Teresa Alvarez Tavares Perello Espaillat Julia Pérez Rochet González," I pronounced it slowly. It was a name as confused with sounds as a Middle Eastern bazaar or market day in a South American village.

I suffered most whenever my **extended** family attended school occasions. For my graduation, they all came, the whole noisy, foreign-looking lot. There were old, fat aunts in their dark mourning dresses and hair nets, uncles with full, droopy mustaches and baby-blue or salmon-colored suits and white pointy shoes and fedora hats, many little cousins who snuck in without tickets. They sat in the first row in order to better understand the Americans' fast-spoken English. But how could they listen when they were constantly speaking among themselves in flowery phrases, highly decorated consonants, rich, rhyming vowels. Their loud voices carried . . . .

How could I introduce them to my friends? These relatives had such complicated names and there were so many of them, and their relationships to myself were so tangled. There was my Tía Josefina, who was not really an aunt but a much older cousin. And her daughter, Aída Margarita, who was adopted, *una hija de crianza*. My uncle of affection, Tío José, brought my *madrina* Tía Amelia and her *comadre* Tía Pilar. My friends rarely had more than their nuclear family to introduce.

After the graduation ceremony my family waited outside in the parking lot while my friends and I signed yearbooks with nicknames which recalled our high school good times: "Beans" and "Pepperoni" and "Alcatraz."

We hugged and cried and promised to keep in touch.

Our good-byes went on too long. I heard my father's voice calling out across the parking lot, "*Hoo-lee-tah! Vámonos!*"

Word Power
extended (iks ten´ did) *adj.* bigger, larger

Back home, my *tíos* and *tías* and *primas*, Mami and Papi, and *mis hermanas* had a party for me with *sancocho* and a store bought cake that had *Happy Graduation, Julie*, written on it. There were many gifts. That was a plus to a large family! I got several wallets and a suitcase with my initials and a graduation charm from my godmother and money from my uncles. The biggest gift was a **portable** typewriter from my parents for writing my stories and poems.

Someday, the family predicted, my name would be well-known throughout the United States. I laughed to myself, wondering which one I would go by.

The Musicians, 1979. Fernando Botero. Oil on canvas, 83¾ x 74¾ in. Private collection.

Which scene from the story would you like to see painted in the style of this painting?

Word Power

portable (pôr´ tə bəl) *adj.* able to be carried easily

Background Info

Tíos (tē´ ōs) and *tías* (tē´ äs) mean "uncles" and "aunts." *Primas* (prē´ mäs) means "cousins." *Mis hermanas* (mēs är mä´ näs) means "my sisters."

Reading Skill

Author's Purpose Reread the highlighted sentences. The author says that if she becomes famous, she wonders which name she will go by. What does this tell you about the author's message?

_____

_____

_____

_____

Names/Nombres

A Comprehension Check

Answer the following questions in the spaces provided.

1. How does the Alvarez family's name change when they first arrive at Immigration? _____

    _____

2. What country does Julia's family come from originally? Where is it located?

    _____

B Reading Skills

Answer the following questions in the spaces provided.

1. **Author's Purpose** The author uses English and Spanish in the title. What does this tell you about the author's purpose? _____

    _____

    _____

2. **Main Idea and Details** The author says her family speaks in "flowery phrases, highly decorated consonants, rich, rhyming vowels." How do you think the author truly feels about her original language? How do the details support this idea? _____

    _____

    _____

C Word Power

Complete each sentence below, using one of the words in the box.

foreign	hesitated	vaguely
generations	extended	portable

1. My sister answered _____ when I asked where she was going.

2. Tadahito brought his _____ computer with him so he could check baseball scores.

3. Eating with chopsticks is a _____ custom to me.

4. My father gave me a book that had been passed down through many _____ in our family.

5. The holiday on Monday gives us an _____ weekend.

6. Mother _____ before allowing me to sleep at my friend's house.

D Literary Element: Point of View

Read the passages below from "Names/Nombres." Then answer the questions that follow.

My wish to be known by my correct Dominican name faded.[1] I just wanted to be Judy and blend in with the Sallys and Janes in my class.[2] But my accent and coloring gave me away.[3]

My mother often told the story of how she had almost changed my sister's name in the hospital.[4]

After the delivery, Mami and some other new mothers were fussing over their new baby sons and daughters and exchanging names and weights and delivery stories.[5] My mother was embarrassed among the Sallys and Janes and Georges and Johns to reveal the rich, noisy name of *Mauricia*.[6] When her turn came to brag, she gave her baby's name as *Maureen*.[7]

1. Read sentences 1–3. How do you know this is a first-person narrator? What words help you figure out who the narrator is? _____

   _____

   _____

2. In sentences 5–7, the narrator tells about an event that happened before she was born. A first-person narrator can only tell what he or she sees, hears, or knows. What detail from the text explains how the narrator is able to tell this story about her older sister's birth? _____

   _____

   _____

E A Letter to My Friends

Imagine you are Julia. You are writing a letter to your friends in the Dominican Republic. Tell them about your high school graduation.

Dear Friends/Amigas,

Today I graduated from high school. Everyone from my family came, including _____

_____

I love them all very much, but I didn't introduce them to my friends because _____

_____

_____

It seems like so long ago since I moved here. You remember me as Julia. However, I have had many other names over the years, like _____

_____

I have learned to like all my names because _____

_____

_____

I hope you visit soon!

Julia

Assessment

Fill in the circle next to each correct answer.

1. A story told in the first person uses the pronoun *I*. In this story, who is the *I*?
   - ○ A. Julia
   - ○ B. Julia's mother
   - ○ C. Julia's sister
   - ○ D. the Immigration officer

2. When the author talks about the way her family's name is pronounced, she says "organ blast of the *a*" and "drumroll of the *r*." What main idea is supported by these details?
   - ○ A. She cannot understand her own family's name.
   - ○ B. Her family's name sounds musical and beautiful.
   - ○ C. Everyone in her family wants a nickname.
   - ○ D. Spanish names are plain.

3. Where was Julia born?
   - ○ A. Bermuda
   - ○ B. California
   - ○ C. New York
   - ○ D. Puerto Rico

4. Which of the following might be Julia Alvarez's purpose for writing "Names/Nombres"?
   - ○ A. to teach kids how to make up nicknames
   - ○ B. to persuade kids not to have only one name
   - ○ C. to describe how her mother feels about her name
   - ○ D. to explain how she feels about her different names

5. Which of the following words means "paused"?
   - ○ A. vaguely
   - ○ B. extended
   - ○ C. hesitated
   - ○ D. generations

Wrap-up

Compare and Contrast

Point of view is an important literary element in the "The Horse Snake" and "Names/Nombres." Both selections are examples of autobiography. That means they are told from the first-person point of view. Since the narrators in both stories talk about their personal experiences, we see events through their eyes.

Use the Venn diagram below to write how "The Horse Snake" and "Names/Nombres" are alike and different in the ways they are told. In the outer parts of the circles, write about how the ways in which the stories are told are different. In the overlapping part, write how the stories are told in similar ways. An example has been done for you in each section.

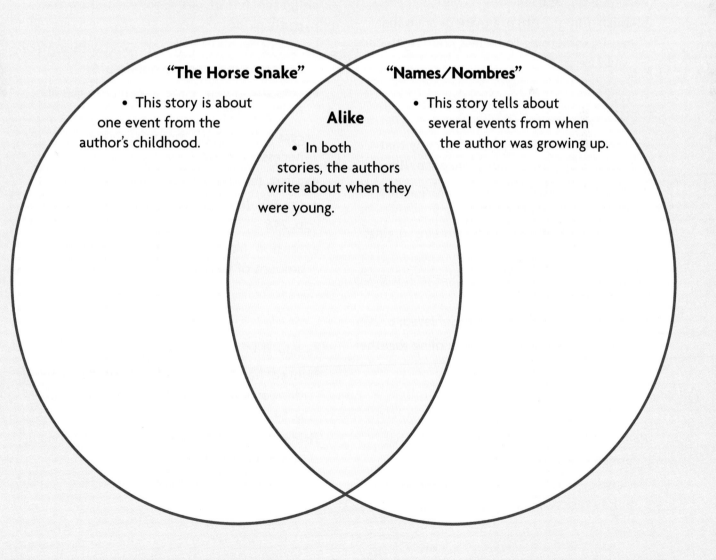

"The Horse Snake"

- This story is about one event from the author's childhood.

Alike

- In both stories, the authors write about when they were young.

"Names/Nombres"

- This story tells about several events from when the author was growing up.

Glossary

A

accompanied (ə kum´ pə nēd) *v.* went along with; p. 28

allergic (ə lur´ jik) *adj.* having a condition that causes reactions like sneezing or sensitive skin after contact with certain things; p. 102

apprehensive (ap´ ri hen´ siv) *adj.* anxious or fearful that something bad will happen; p. 150

assured (ə shoord´) *v.* promised; made a person sure of something; p. 29

B

barrage (bə räzh´) *n.* a heavy attack; p. 45

barren (bar´ ən) *adj.* empty; bare; p. 92

blemish (blem´ ish) *n.* a mark or stain that causes something to be less pleasing than it could be; p. 17

C

casually (kazh´ oo ə lē) *adv.* in a way that happens by chance; not planned; p. 118

characteristic (kar´ ik tə ris´ tik) *n.* a special quality of a person or thing; p. 5

compelling (kəm pel´ ing) *v.* forcing; urging; p. 6

congenial (kən jēn´ yəl) *adj.* pleasant; friendly and agreeable; p. 6

conquered (kong´ kərd) *adj.* defeated; p. 206

converging (kən vurj´ ing) *v.* coming together at a place or point; p. 152

D

decisively (di sī´ siv lē) *adv.* in a way that brings a clear decision; p. 26

defiantly (di fī´ ənt lē) *adv.* in a way that boldly resists; p. 147

desperation (des´ pə rā´ shən) *n.* a hopeless feeling; p. 74

destiny (des´ tə nē) *n.* something that will happen to a person or people in the future; fate; p. 167

dissolve (di zolv´) *v.* to break down and mix into a liquid; p. 192

druggists (drug´ ists) *n.* people who prepare and sell medicine; p. 180

dutifully (doo´ ti fəl ē) *adv.* doing something you are supposed to do; p. 28

E

embraced (em brāsd´) *v.* hugged; p. 56

enlighten (en līt´ən) *v.* to teach; show the truth; p. 166

escorted (es kor´ tid) *v.* traveled with someone to show support or to honor; p. 51

eventually (i ven´ choo ə lē) *adv.* in the end; finally; p. 129

excess (ek´ ses) *adj.* more than usual or necessary; p. 126

explicit (eks plis´ it) *adj.* very clear; p. 155

extended (iks ten´ did) *adj.* bigger, larger; p. 246

extension (iks ten´ shən) *n.* an additional amount of time; p. 116

F

feeble (fē´ bəl) *adj.* weak; p. 204

feinted (fān´ tid) *v.* made a tricky move to draw attention away from the real attack; p. 54

firing (fīr´ ing) *n.* starting up a fire; lighting up something; p. 117

flat (flat) *n.* an apartment; p. 116

Glossary

foreign (fôr´ən) *adj.* having to do with a different place or country; unfamiliar or different; p. 243

frail (frāl) *adj.* weak; thin; easily broken; p. 89

frantically (fran´ tik lē) *adv.* in a fast, nervous, and anxious manner; p. 105

frustrated (frus´ trāt əd) *adj.* unhappy because something is not working as hoped or expected; p. 73

G

generations (jen´ə rā´shənz) *n.* groups of people, in a family or in a society, who were born around the same time; p. 245

glimpse (glimps) *n.* a brief look at something; p. 106

H

hamlet (ham´ lit) *n.* a small village in the country; p. 229

hammock (ham´ ək) *n.* a swinging bed made of netting or cloth, hung from supports at each end; p. 233

hardy (här´ dē) *adj.* strong and sturdy; able to hold up under bad conditions; p. 132

herb (urb) *n.* a plant used in cooking or medicine; p. 188

hesitated (hez´ ə tā´ tid) *v.* paused or stopped; p. 244

I

ignorance (ig´ nər əns) *n.* lack of knowledge or education; p. 166

illuminated (i lōō´ mə nāt´ id) *v.* lit up; p. 128

inclining (in klīn´ ing) *v.* bending or slanting; leaning; p. 18

intently (in tent´ lē) *adv.* in a firmly focused way; with concentration; p. 130

L

lacquer (lak´ ər) *n.* a smooth, glossy coating; p. 189

lapsed (lapsd) *v.* gradually fell or slipped into a different condition; p. 17

larvae (lär´ vē) *n.* early forms of insects before they change into another form; p. 189

legitimate (li jit´ ə mit) *adj.* that which follows the rules; lawful; p. 145

lurking (lurk´ ing) *v.* waiting in a hidden place, usually for a sneaky purpose; p. 105

M

maneuvered (mə nōō´ vərd) *v.* moved skillfully; p. 215

menace (men´ is) *n.* a danger; p. 215

mute (mūt) *adj.* silent; p. 55

O

objection (əb jek´ shən) *n.* a feeling of dislike; a protest; p. 29

obnoxious (ob nok´ shəs) *adj.* annoying; not nice; p. 216

obstinate (ob´ stə nit) *adj.* stubborn; not willing to give in; p. 116

omen (ō´ mən) *n.* a sign or warning about something that will happen in the future; p. 190

Glossary

P

perish (per´ ish) *v.* to die; disappear completely; p. 205

permission (pər mish´ ən) *n.* an act of allowing someone to do something; p. 178

permit (pər mit´) *v.* to allow; p. 88

persistently (pər sis´ tənt lē) *adv.* many times; over and over; p. 217

piston (pis´ tən) *n.* part of an engine that goes up and down very fast; p. 53

portable (pôr´ tə bəl) *adj.* able to be carried easily; p. 247

prejudices (prej´ ə dis iz) *n.* critical opinions that are formed unfairly; p. 156

presentable (pri zen´ tə bəl) *adj.* looking nice, clean, or neat; p. 91

presumed (pri zo͞omd´) *v.* supposed; assumed to be true; p. 229

psyching (sī´ king) *v.* getting into the right state of mind; p. 47

R

rejoiced (ri joisd´) *v.* expressed great happiness; p. 234

remnant (rem´ nənt) *n.* something that is left over; p. 206

resolutions (rez´ ə lo͞o´ shənz) *n.* things that have been decided or determined; p. 28

retrieved (ri trēvd´) *v.* brought back; p. 73

S

sabotage (sab´ ə tazh´) *v.* to harm something in order to get it to fail; p. 103

scapegoat (skāp´ gōt´) *n.* a person who is blamed for the mistakes of others; p. 148

scatterbrained (skat´ ər brānd´) *adj.* unable to pay attention; forgets things; p. 100

sentinel (sent´ ən əl) *n.* a person or animal that stands guard and keeps watch; p. 102

slung (slung) *adj.* hung or thrown loosely; p. 88

sorcerer (sôr´ sər ər) *n.* a person who practices magic; p. 178

strictly (strikt´ lē) *adv.* following a rule in an exact way; p. 35

swaggered (swag´ ərd) *v.* walked in a bold, superior way; p. 65

T

tantalizing (tant´ əl īz´ ing) *adj.* teasingly out of reach; p. 15

taut (tôt) *adj.* stretched tight; p. 127

terrorized (ter´ ə rīzd´) *v.* filled with fear; controlled by using fear or force; p. 229

tomb (to͞om) *n.* a grave or a building in which a dead body is placed; p. 179

torment (tôr´ment) *n.* extreme pain; p. 170

trudging (truj´ ing) *v.* walking heavily or slowly; p. 74

trustworthy (trust´ wur´ t͟hē) *adj.* able to be trusted or depended on; p. 179

U

unconscious (un kon´ shəs) *adj.* not able to see, feel, or think; p. 234

unpredictability (un´ pri dik´ tə bil´ə tē) *n.* quality of being unable to be counted on or expected; p. 167

Glossary

V

vaguely (vāg´lē) *adv.* in a way that is not clear, exact, or definite; p. 245

vanish (van´ish) *v.* to disappear; p. 206

vengeance (ven´jəns) *n.* an act of getting even; p. 169

W

wadded (wod´əd) *adj.* something made into the shape of a ball; p. 71

wholeheartedly (hōl´här´tid lē) *adv.* completely; sincerely; with enthusiasm; p. 215

winced (winst) *v.* pulled back slightly in pain or fear; p. 68

_____

_____

_____

_____

_____

_____

_____

_____

_____

_____

_____

_____

_____

_____

_____

_____

_____

_____

_____

_____

_____

My Personal Dictionary

My Personal Dictionary

My Personal Dictionary

My Personal Dictionary

ACKNOWLEDGMENTS

LITERATURE

UNIT 1

"The Landlady" from *Kiss, Kiss* by Roald Dahl. Copyright © 1959 by Roald Dahl. Reprinted by permission of David Higham Associates.

Adapted from "Lob's Girl" from *A Whisper in the Night* by Joan Aiken. Delacorte Press. Copyright © 1984 by Joan Aiken Enterprises, Ltd. Adaptation copyright © 2005 by Elizabeth Delano Charlass and John Sebastian Brown. Reprinted by permission of Brandt & Hochman Literary Agents, Inc.

Adaptation of "Amigo Brothers" by Piri Thomas. Adapted and reprinted by permission of the author.

"Broken Chain," from *Baseball in April and Other Stories.* Copyright © 1990 by Gary Soto, reprinted by permission of Harcourt, Inc.

UNIT 2

"Thank You M'am" from *Short Stories* by Langston Hughes. Copyright © 1996 by Ramona Bass and Arnold Rampersad. Reprinted by permission of Hill and Wang, a division of Farrar, Straus and Giroux, LLC, and Harold Ober Associates.

Adaptation of "Duffy's Jacket" from *Oddly Enough: Stories* by Bruce Coville, copyright © 1989 by Bruce Coville. Adapted and reprinted by permission of Bruce Coville and the Ashley Grayson Literary Agency.

"Home" by Gwendolyn Brooks. Reprinted by consent of Brooks Permissions.

Adaptation of "A Crush" from *A Couple of Kooks and Other Stories About Love* by Cynthia Rylant. Published by Orchard Books/Scholastic Inc. Copyright © 1990 by Cynthia Rylant. Adapted and reprinted by permission.

UNIT 3

From *The Monsters Are Due on Maple Street* by Rod Serling. Copyright © 1960 by Rod Serling, renewed © 1988 by Carolyn Serling, Jodi Serling and Anne Serling. Reprinted by permission of The Rod Serling Trust.

UNIT 4

Adaptation of "Prometheus" from *Heroes, Gods and Monsters of Greek Myths* by Bernard Evslin et. al. Copyright © 1967 by Scholastic Inc. Adapted and reprinted by permission.

Adaptation of "Aunty Misery" by Judith Ortiz Cofer, reprinted by permission of the author. www.english.uga.edu/~jcofer

Adapted from "We Are All One" by Laurence Yep. Copyright © 1989 by Laurence Yep. Used by permission of HarperCollins Publishers.

UNIT 5

Adapted from *Barrio Boy* by Ernesto Galarza. Copyright © 1971 by the University of Notre Dame Press: Notre Dame, Indiana. Adapted and reprinted by permission of the publisher.

Adapted from "The Horse Snake" from *The Land I Lost* by Huynh Quang Nhuong. Copyright © 1982 by Huynh Quang Nhuong. Used by permission of HarperCollins Publishers.

Adaptation of "Names/Nombres" Copyright © 1985 by Julia Alvarez. First published in *Nuestro,* March 1985. Adapted and reprinted by permission of Susan Bergholz Literary Services, New York. All rights reserved.